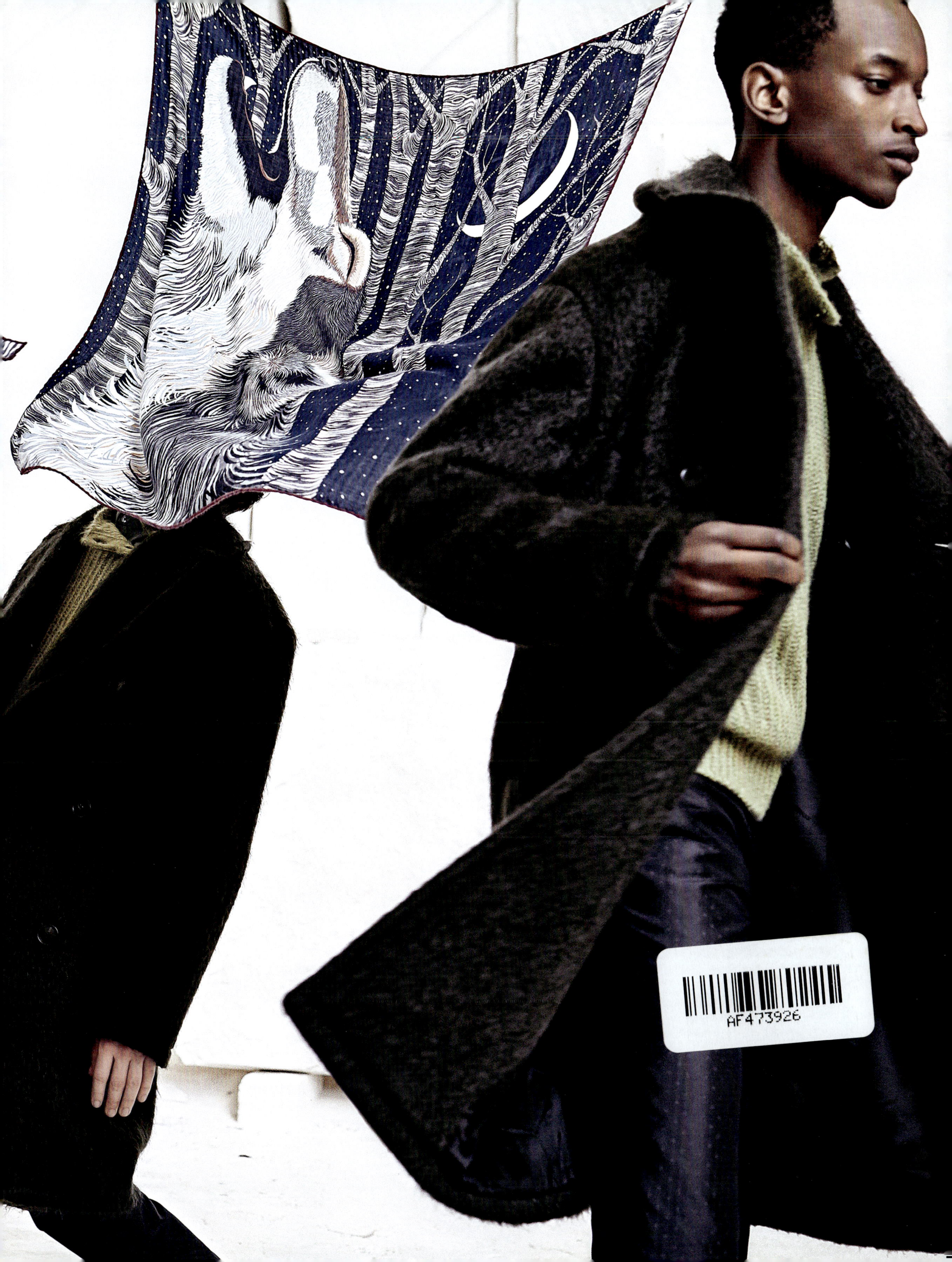
AF473926

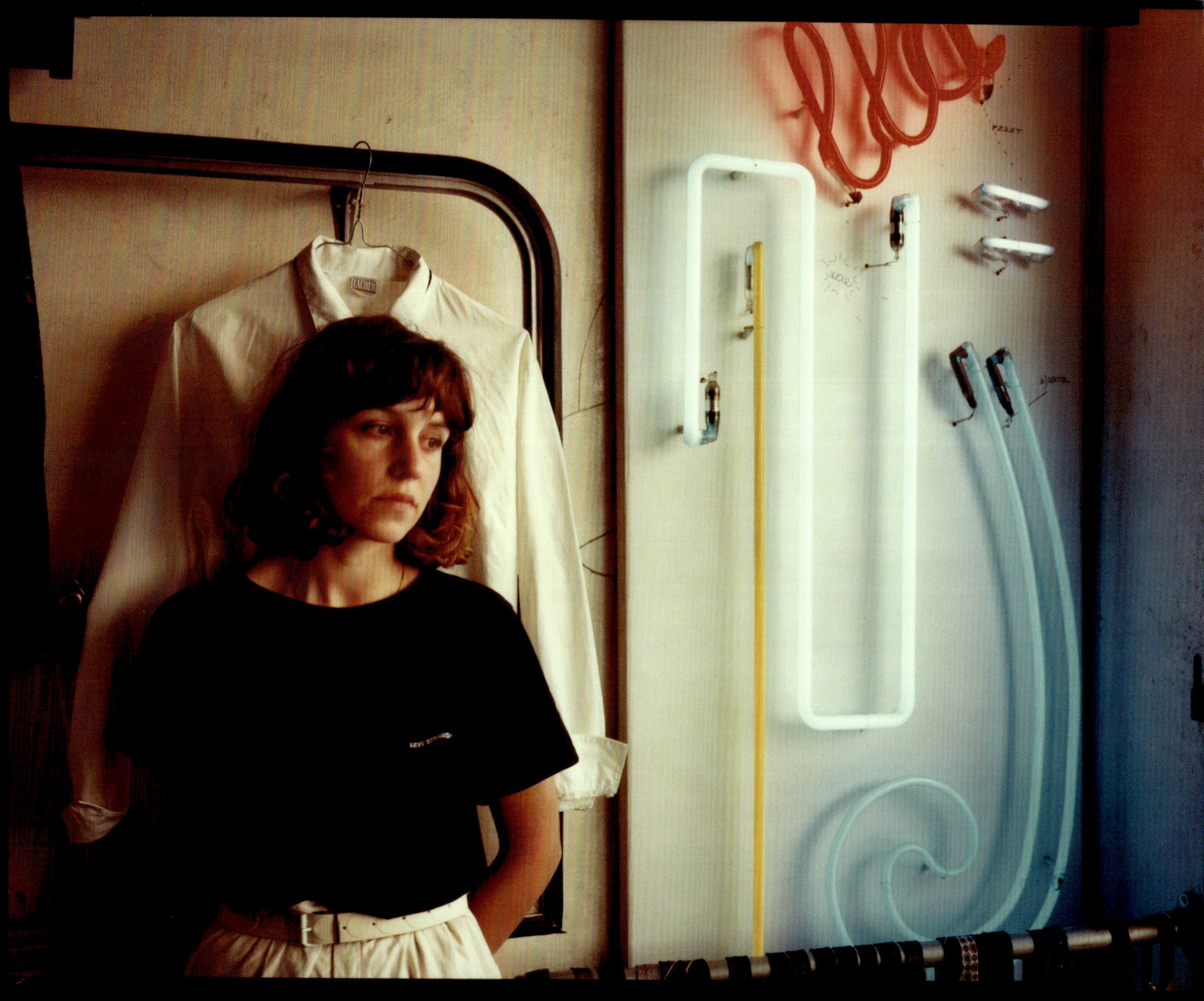

GUIDO
GUIDI

PER STRADA

Photographs along the Via Emilia
1983–1993

MACK

Fall 2018

Front

Back

Words

Pictures

Opposite:
Star Montana, *Marina, East Los Angeles*, 2016
Courtesy the artist

Front cover:
Photographer unknown, Gata and Tootsie from Boyle Heights and East LA, Newberry's Department Store, Downtown LA, 1971
Courtesy Michelle Padilla

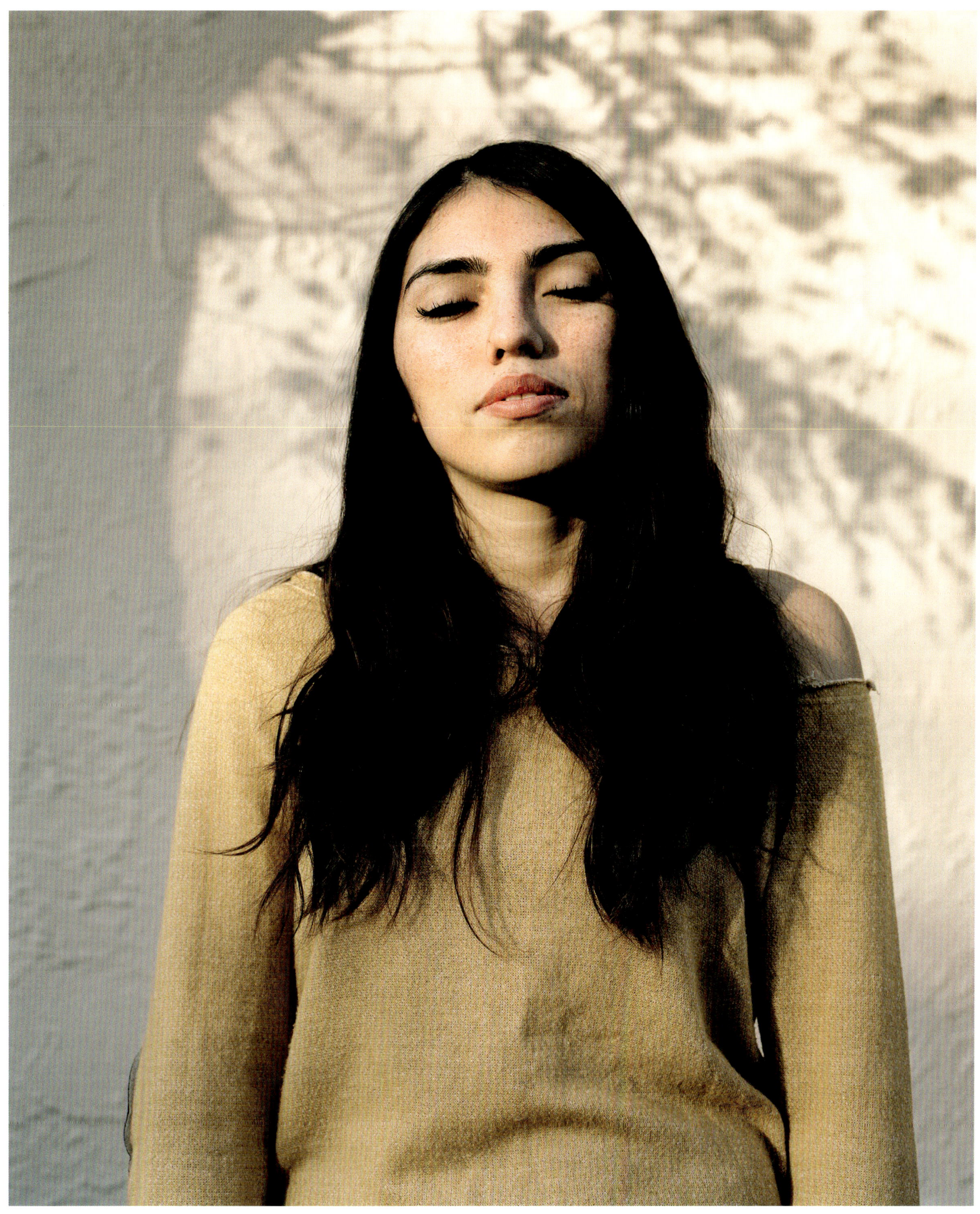

aperture

The Magazine of Photography and Ideas

Aperture, a not-for-profit foundation, connects the photo community and its audiences with the most inspiring work, the sharpest ideas, and with each other—in print, in person, and online.

Aperture (ISSN 0003-6420) is published quarterly, in spring, summer, fall, and winter, at 547 West 27th Street, 4th Floor, New York, N.Y. 10001. In the United States, a one-year subscription (four issues) is $75; a two-year subscription (eight issues) is $124. In Canada, a one-year subscription is $95. All other international subscriptions are $105 per year. Visit aperture.org to subscribe. Single copies may be purchased at $24.95 for most issues. Subscribe to the *Aperture Digital Archive* at aperture.org/archive. Periodicals postage paid at New York and additional offices. Postmaster: Send address changes to *Aperture*, P.O. Box 3000, Denville, N.J. 07834. Address queries regarding subscriptions, renewals, or gifts to: *Aperture* Subscription Service, 866-457-4603 (U.S. and Canada), or email custsvc_aperture@fulcoinc.com.

Newsstand distribution in the U.S. is handled by Curtis Circulation Company, 201-634-7400. For international distribution, contact Central Books, centralbooks.com. Other inquiries, email orders@aperture.org or call 212-505-5555.

Help maintain Aperture's publishing, education, and community activities by joining our general member program. Membership starts at $75 annually and includes invitations to special events, exclusive discounts on Aperture publications, and opportunities to meet artists and engage with leaders in the photography community. Aperture Foundation welcomes support at all levels of giving, and all gifts are tax-deductible to the fullest extent of the law. For more information about supporting Aperture, please visit aperture.org/join or contact the Development Department at membership@aperture.org.

Library of Congress Catalog Card No: 58-30845.

ISBN 978-1-59711-435-6

Printed in Turkey by Ofset Yapimevi

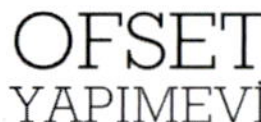

Lead funding for the "Los Angeles" issue of *Aperture* magazine is provided by the Henry Luce Foundation. Further generous support for *Aperture* magazine is provided in part by The Andy Warhol Foundation for the Visual Arts, the New York State Council on the Arts with the support of Governor Andrew M. Cuomo and the New York State Legislature, and the New York City Department of Cultural Affairs in partnership with the City Council.

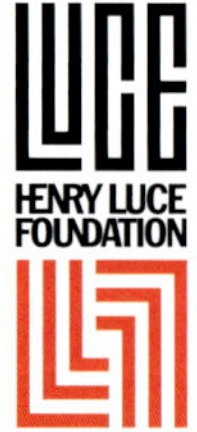

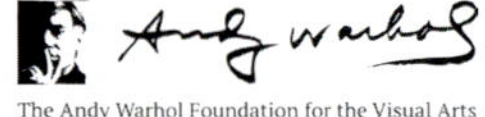

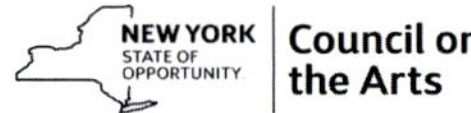

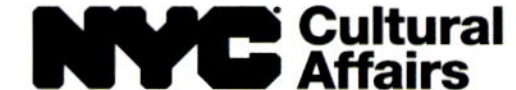

Editor
Michael Famighetti
Managing Editor
Brendan Embser
Assistant Editor
Annika Klein
Copy Editors
Olivia Casa, Donna Ghelerter
Senior Production Manager
True Sims
Production Managers
Nelson Chan, Bryan Krueger
Work Scholars
Lauren Harper, Izzy Leung

Art Direction, Design & Typefaces
A2/SW/HK, London

Publisher
Dana Triwush
magazine@aperture.org

Director of Brand Partnerships
Isabelle McTwigan
212-946-7118
imctwigan@aperture.org

Advertising
Elizabeth Morina
917-691-2608
emorina@aperture.org

Executive Director, Aperture Foundation
Chris Boot

Minor White, Editor (1952–1974)

Michael E. Hoffman, Publisher and Executive Director (1964–2001)

aperture.org

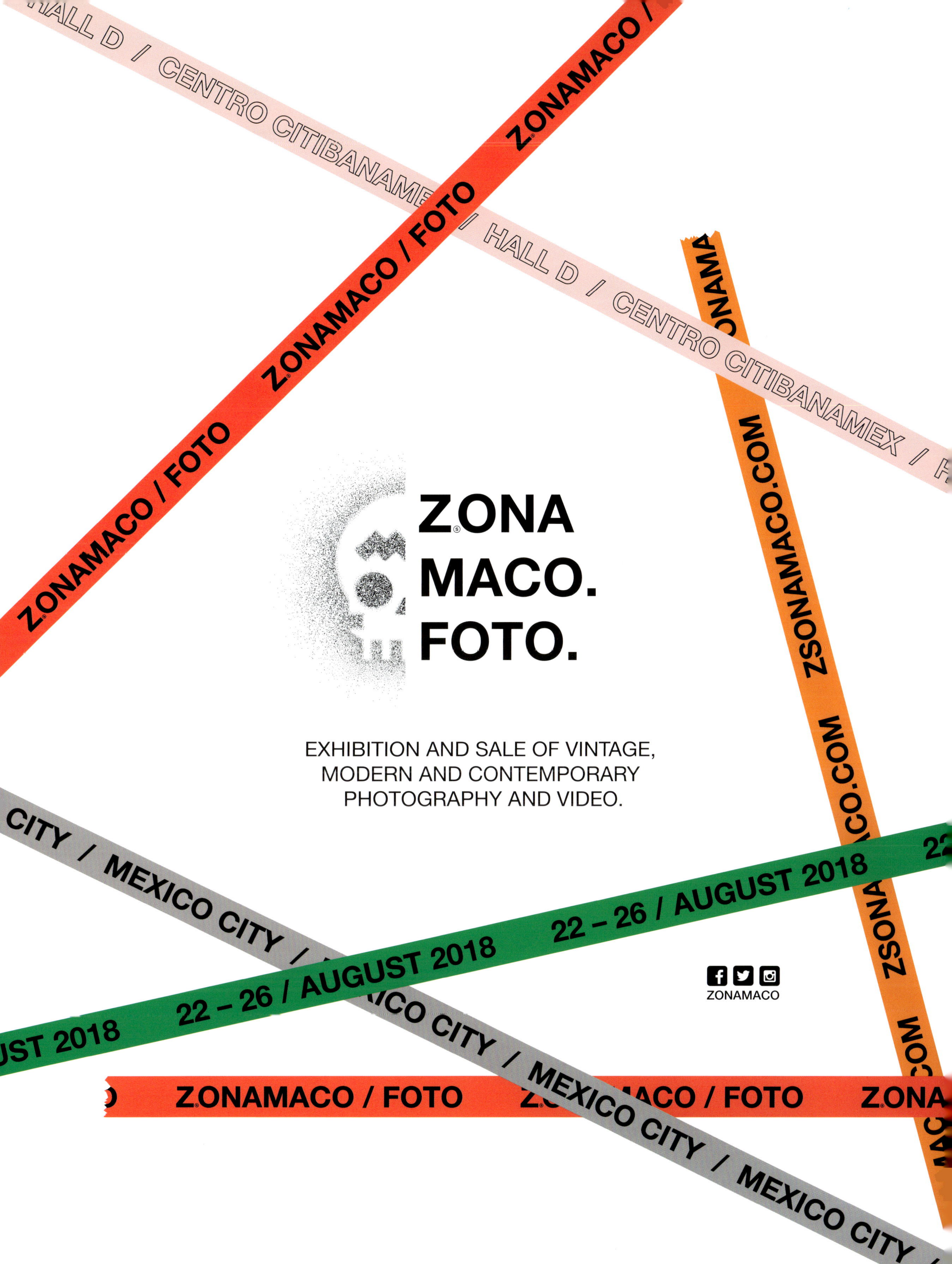
ZONA
MACO.
FOTO.
EXHIBITION AND SALE OF VINTAGE, MODERN AND CONTEMPORARY PHOTOGRAPHY AND VIDEO.
ZONAMACO / FOTO
HALL D / CENTRO CITIBANAMEX
ZSONAMACO.COM
MEXICO CITY
22 – 26 / AUGUST 2018
ZONAMACO

Agenda
Exhibitions to See

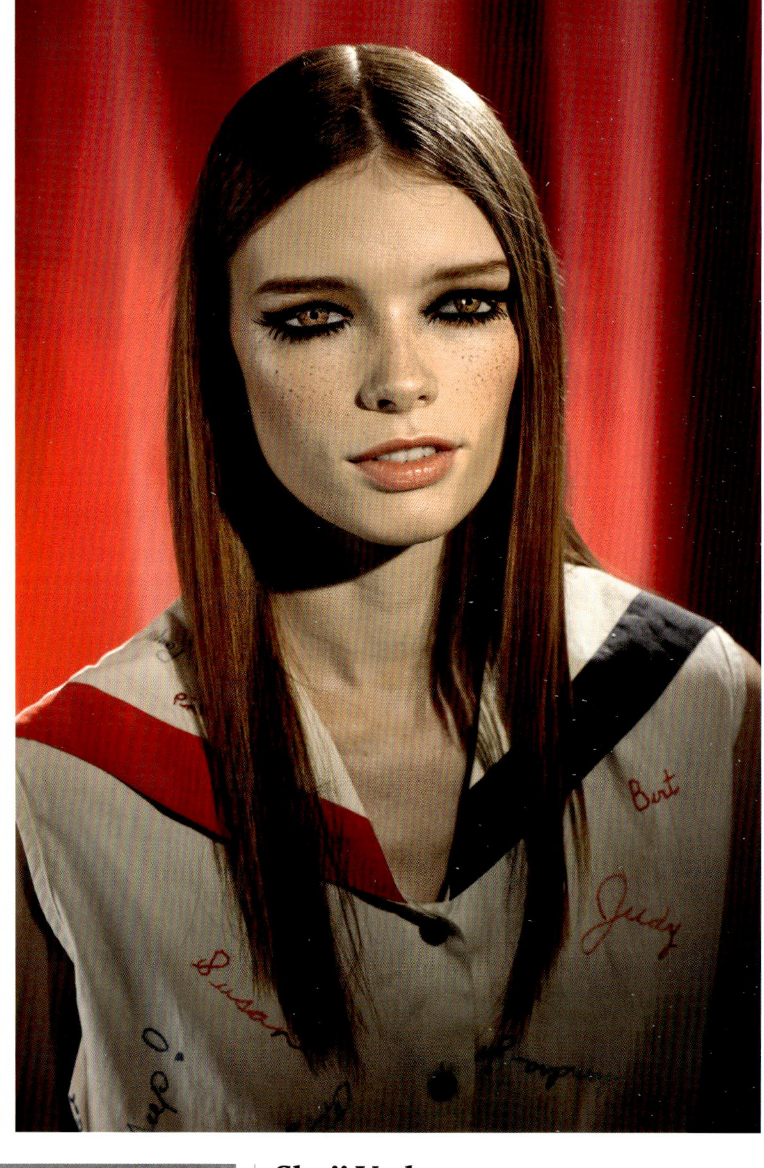

Laurie Simmons

For the past forty years, Laurie Simmons has provocatively explored notions of gender roles, identity, and self-image through beguiling photographs of dolls, giant props, and cosplayers portrayed in fictionalized settings. "Laurie's images acknowledge something we all do to a certain degree—dramatize portions of our actual lives through a combination of memory, nostalgia, and romanticizing of the past," says Andrea Karnes, curator of *Laurie Simmons: Big Camera/Little Camera* at the Modern Art Museum of Fort Worth, a major survey of Simmons's photographs, films, and sculptures. Her work animates deep-set psychological tensions, leading the viewer to question how we envision desire and the ways we choose to see and project ourselves.

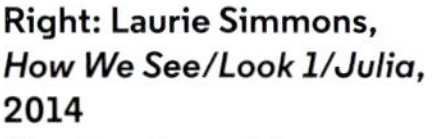

Right: Laurie Simmons, *How We See/Look 1/Julia*, 2014
Courtesy the artist

***Laurie Simmons: Big Camera/Little Camera* at the Modern Art Museum of Fort Worth, October 14, 2018–January 27, 2019**

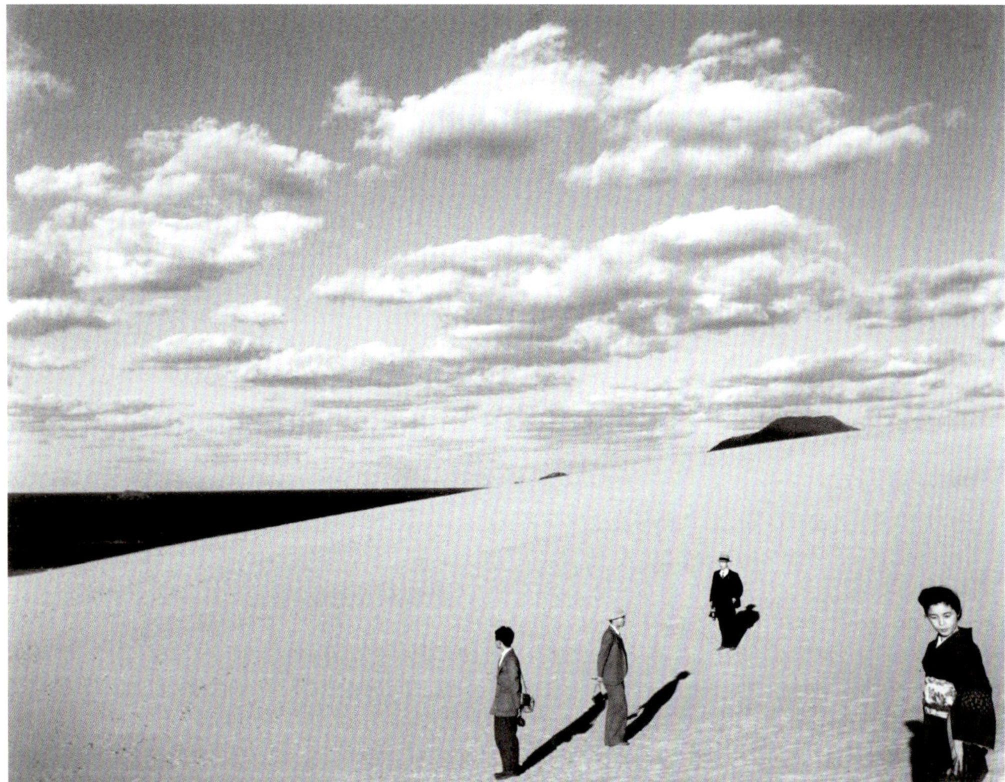

Above: Shoji Ueda, *Scenery of the dune with my wife*, 1950
© and courtesy Shoji Ueda Office and Three Shadows Photography Art Centre, Beijing

Shoji Ueda

Under the influence of the Western avant-garde, Japanese photographer Shoji Ueda created decades of filmic, dreamlike works, often posing subjects on the sand dunes near his home. Following his wife's death in 1983, Ueda ceased photographing until later that year, when he agreed to make a picture for the catalog of fashion designer Takeo Kikuchi's work. Ueda's forays into fashion work, at the age of seventy, returned him to photography and his beloved dunes. "His style of mise-en-scène made his photography instantly compatible with the fashion world," says Masako Sato, curator of a retrospective of 150 of Ueda's early and late images, at Three Shadows Photography Art Centre, Beijing, which "embody his playful mind and the experimental spirit that he maintained throughout his life."

***Shoji Ueda Retrospective* at Three Shadows Photography Art Centre, Beijing, September 23–November 25, 2018**

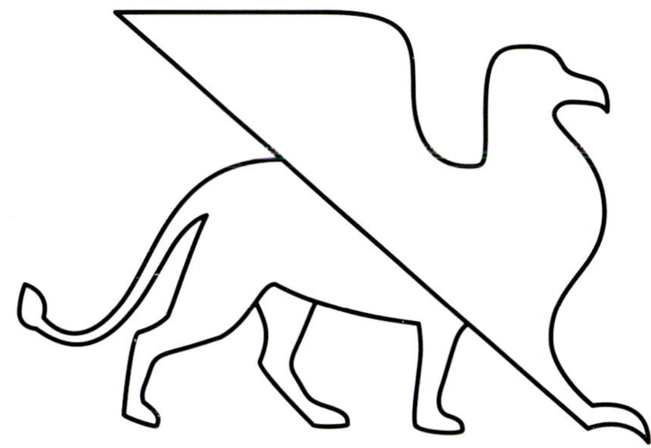

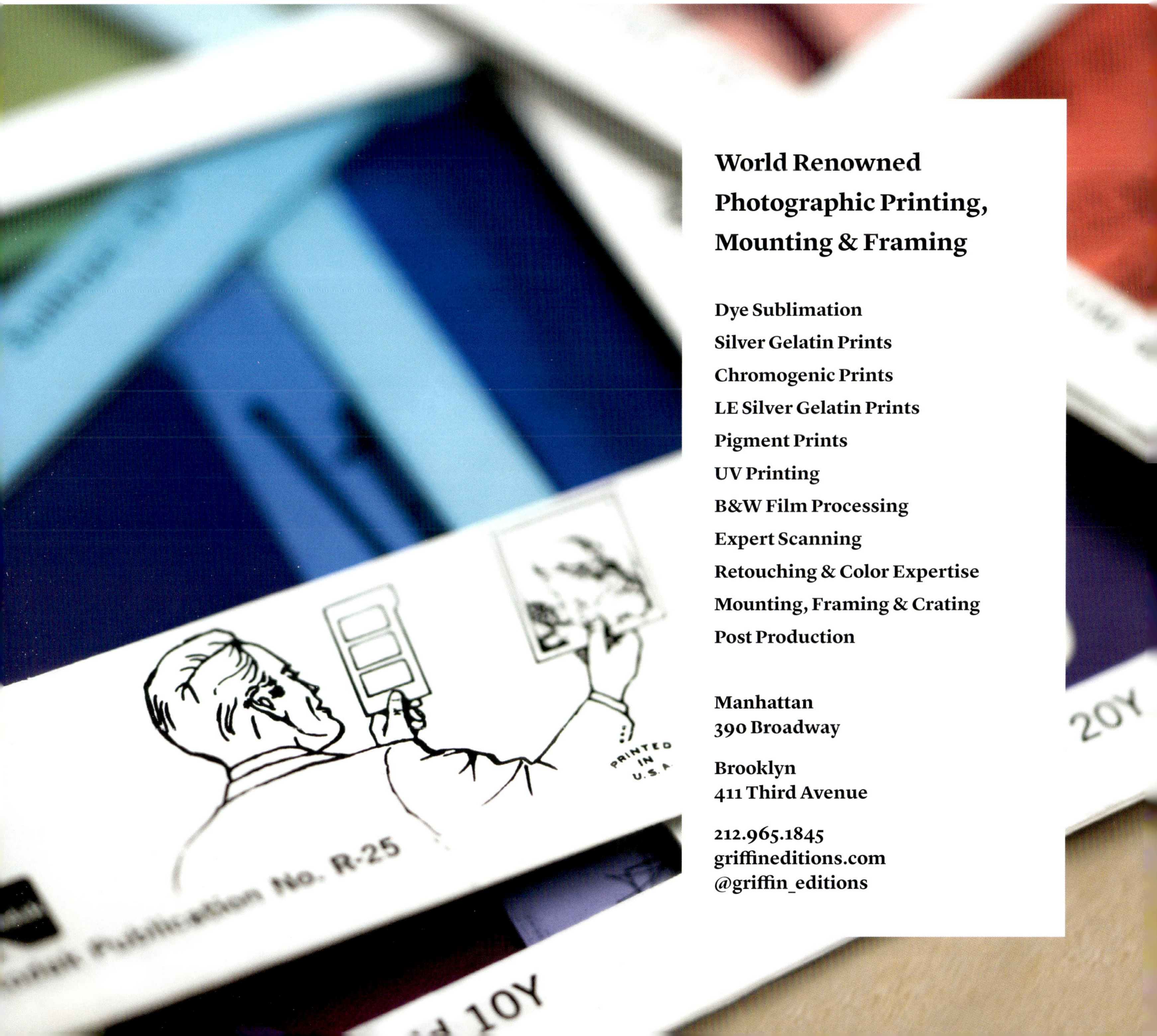

Gordon Parks

In 1944, Gordon Parks traveled in the United States and Canada while making pictures for Standard Oil—an extensive and scarcely seen body of work. Parks remains best known for his iconic civil rights photographs and images for *Vogue*, *Ebony*, *Essence*, and *Life*, but *Gordon Parks: The New Tide, Early Work 1940–1950* compellingly considers this little-explored decade of his career. In 1942, Parks's fellowship with the Farm Security Administration led to his portrait of janitorial worker Ella Watson, *Washington, D.C. Government Charwoman (American Gothic)*, inspired by Grant Wood's famous painting. "During the 1940s," the exhibition's consulting curator Philip Brookman says, "Parks became well known for his innovative role in determining how African Americans were seen and understood in the black and mainstream media."

Gordon Parks: The New Tide, Early Work 1940–1950 **at the National Gallery of Art, Washington, D.C., November 4, 2018–February 18, 2019**

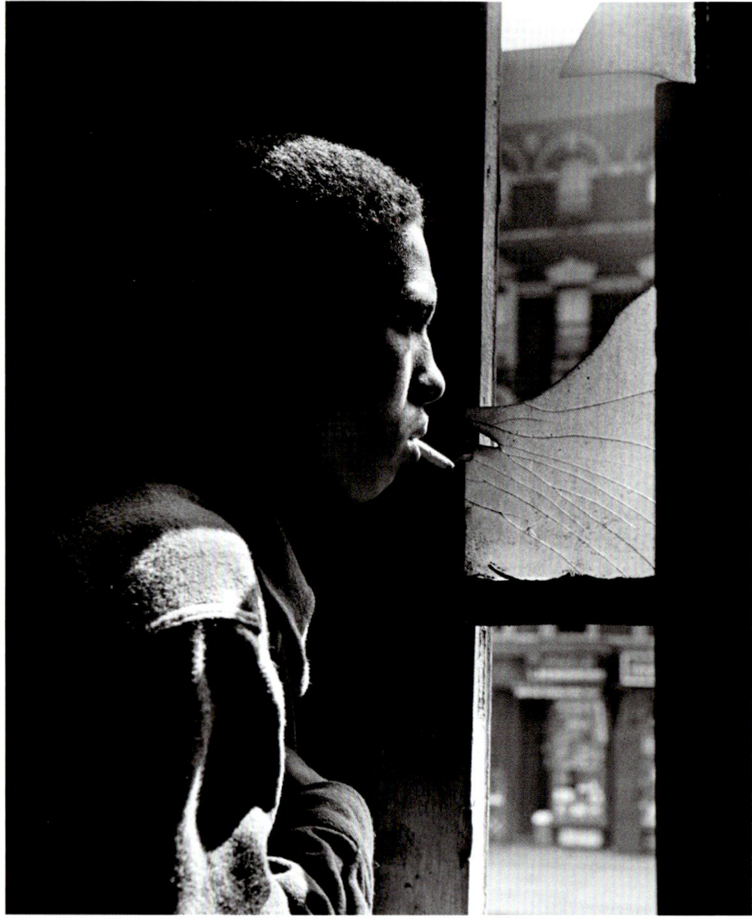

Above: Gordon Parks, *Trapped in abandoned building by a rival gang on street, Red Jackson ponders his next move*, 1948
© the Gordon Parks Foundation and courtesy the National Gallery of Art, Washington, D.C.

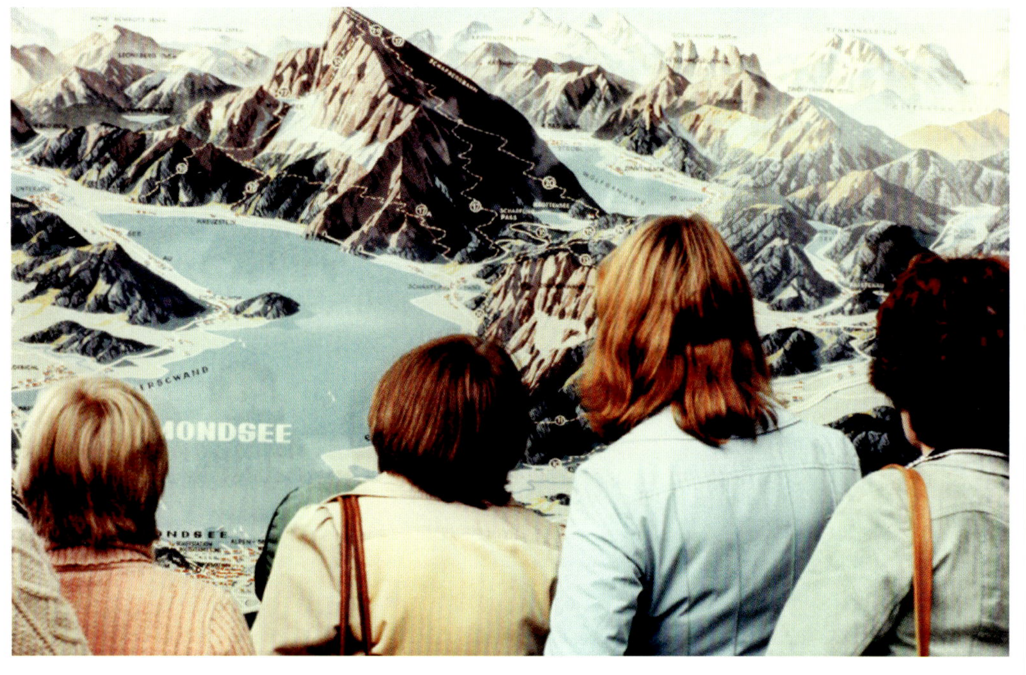

Above: Luigi Ghirri, *Salzburg*, 1977
© Estate of Luigi Ghirri

Luigi Ghirri

In the 1970s, Luigi Ghirri "created a body of color photographs without parallel in the Europe of that time," according to the curators of the first retrospective of Ghirri's work outside the photographer's native Italy since his death in 1992. *Luigi Ghirri: The Map and the Territory* tracks the first decade of his work as a kind of "poetic cartography." The exhibition includes series depicting amusement parks and landscapes from a train, and, significantly, his influential *Kodachrome* images, alongside photographs of people viewing landscapes or representations of exterior worlds. As Ghirri described these surreal interactions, "I wanted to give the person an infinite number of possible identities, from photographer to subject, from being looked at to being an onlooker."

Luigi Ghirri: The Map and the Territory **at Museo Nacional Centro de Arte Reina Sofía, Madrid, September 25, 2018–January 7, 2019**

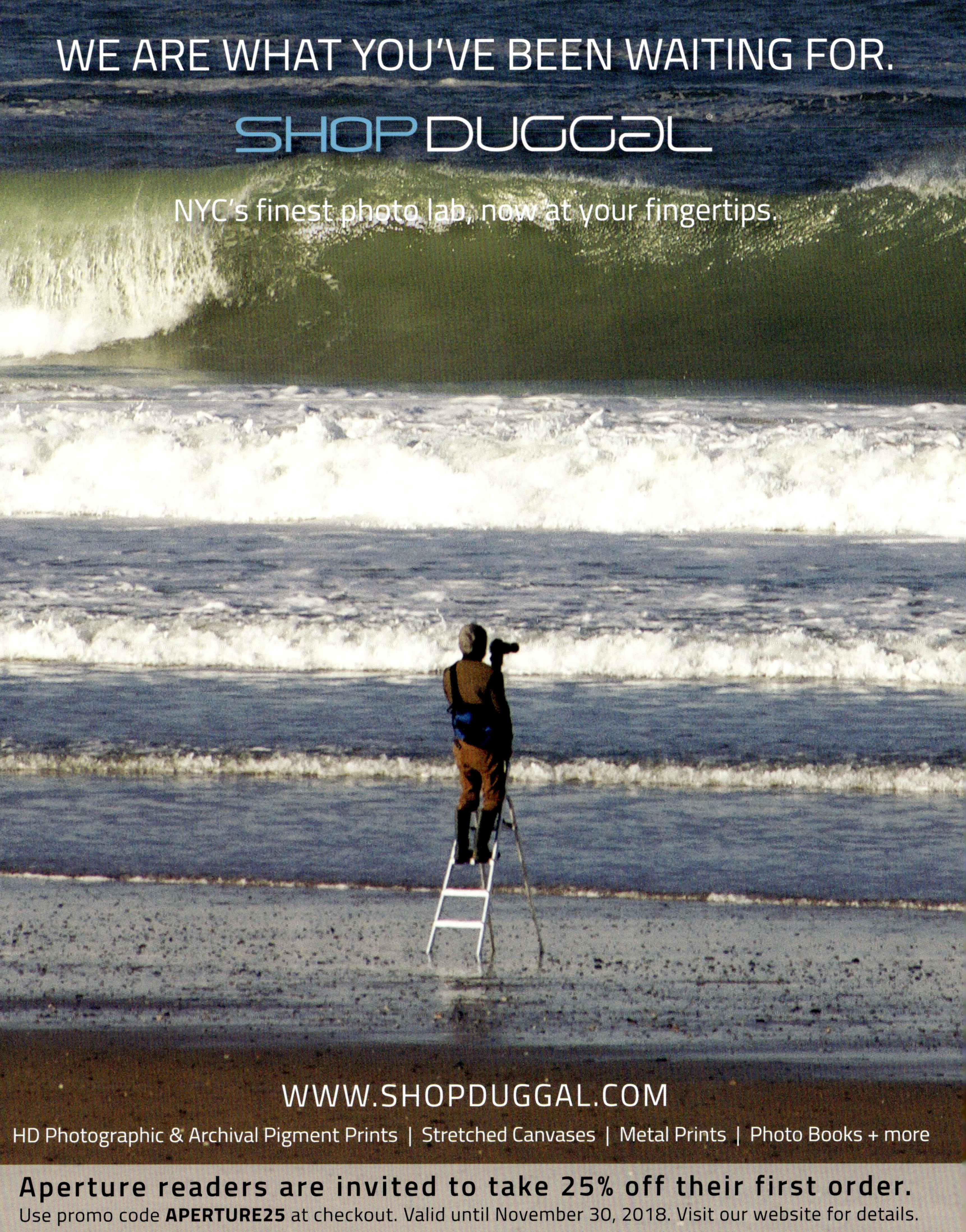

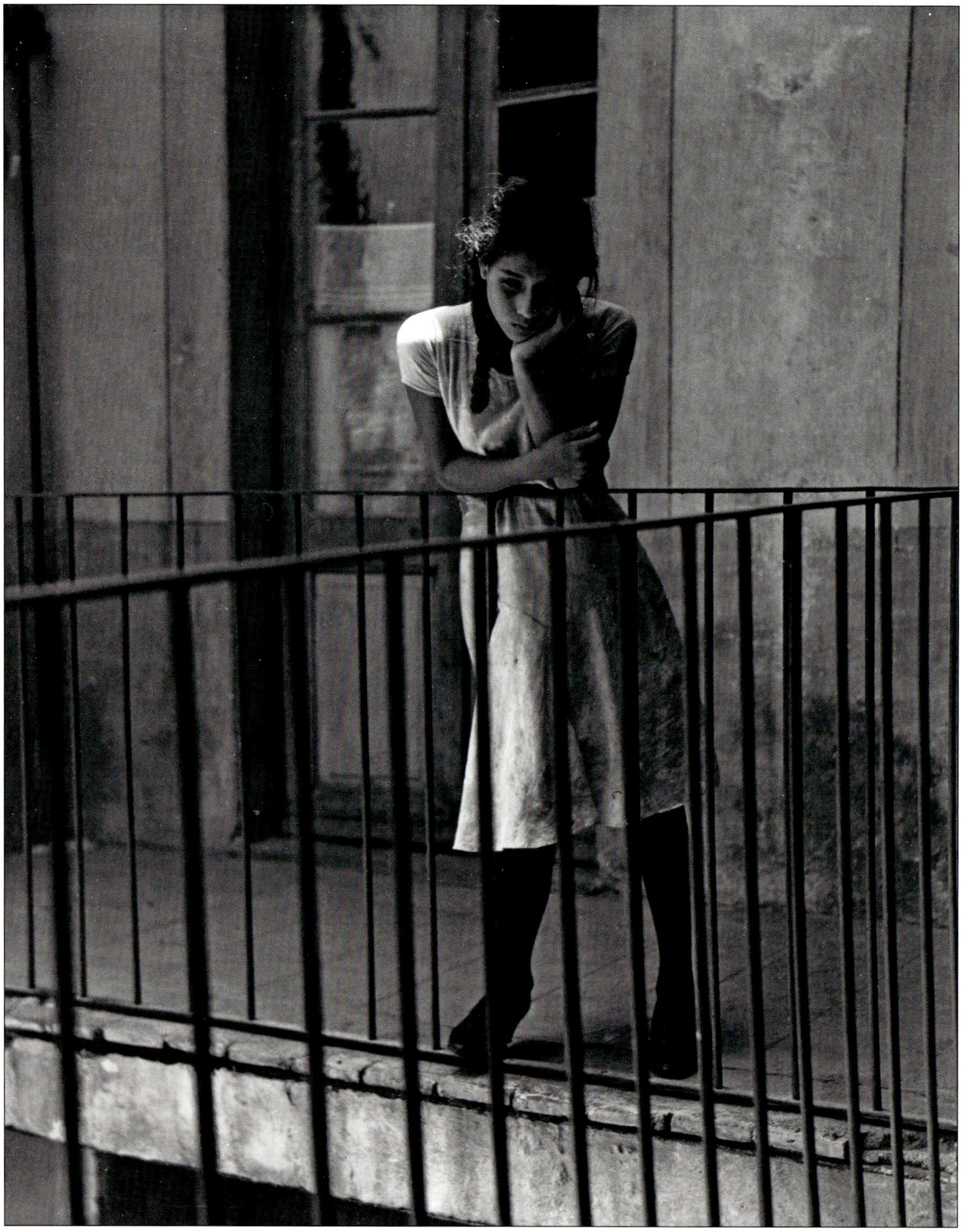

Backstory
Katrien De Blauwer

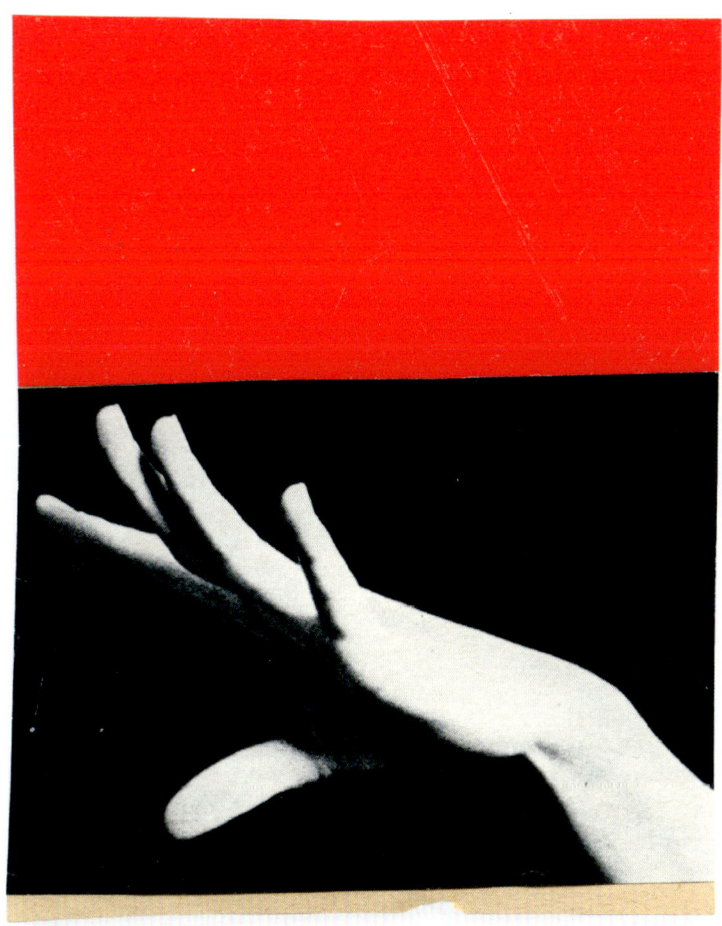

The cinematic collages of a Belgian artist

Diane Dufour

Flaubert said that we only ever perceive the world in disparate fragments. Katrien De Blauwer's work seems to take the French writer at his word.

While studying fashion at the Royal Academy of Fine Arts in Antwerp over the course of the 1990s, this Belgian artist made the collage technique her own. Patiently cutting and assembling images found in magazines from the 1920s to the 1960s, she recomposes scenes imbued with a fragmented intimacy. In them, bits of bodies, buildings, faces, and landscapes come together.

Faced with these silent rebuses, our eyes identify the different fragments, pick out the cuts, reconnect possible links, and search out clues. The influence of cinema—from Italian neorealism to the films of Alain Resnais, Jean-Luc Godard, and, of course, Alfred Hitchcock—is palpable, including in the titles of works such as *Dark Scenes*, *Single Cuts*, and *Rendez-vous* (all 2013–16). The monochromatic blocks of color, infinite varieties of gray interwoven newspaper, and visible marks of amputation reinforce our physical, almost carnal relation to these images. They make us ask about the very nature of the work.

De Blauwer presents herself as a "photographer without a camera." She sees things, which she captures and reassembles. The cutout replaces the snapshot, and the hand re-creates the frame. Is this a collage practice of avant-garde inspiration or a postphotographic process? After meeting De Blauwer in Antwerp earlier this year and digging into twenty years of her work, I realized it is neither one nor the other.

Leaving these recomposed images free from any definitive interpretation, De Blauwer avoids dictating meaning and does not impose any one reading. It is hard to say whether the image is appearing or disappearing, since separation always remains visible or palpable like a tear. Instead, the image's unity comes from these cuts, recalling the duality present in each thing.

De Blauwer's process, avowedly interior, has reparative aims: "I don't use my works as a diary, but as a form of therapy." Talking with her, I sense a painful childhood dominated by the feeling of abandonment. Through her practice, De Blauwer seems to let her unconscious give form to desires and fears. We may think of what Serge Daney has said: "If there is any merit in art after all, it is impure, it is a hybrid of conscious courage—to work—and conscious submission—to be worked."

Sharp as a blade, De Blauwer's cuts say much about the ghosts that inhabit her. The gaze of the other has disappeared, as if sucked away out of field. Dialogue among the images falls on deaf ears, and the impossibility of language marks the body with the brunt of its violence. The delicate and dissociated sensual elements of a hand, a few locks of hair, or a neck evoke a woman's body and its secret wounds: "That's the paradox of my work; I use anonymous images from magazines to question my personal history, my body, and my sexuality. I act almost as a neutral intermediary between my own history and someone else's."

In this way, the collages offer a narrative in the third person, like an impersonal autobiography. De Blauwer's language, like Michelangelo Antonioni's deserted shots, aligns with a poetics of silence and emptiness. As Fernando Pessoa has said, "The poet is an empty man who, in his distress, creates a world to discover his own identity."

Diane Dufour is the founder and codirector of LE BAL, Paris, which will present an exhibition including Katrien De Blauwer's work in spring 2019.

Translated from the French by Matthew Brauer.

Katrien De Blauwer, *Red Scenes (7)*, Antwerp, 2016

Redux
Rediscovered Books and Writings

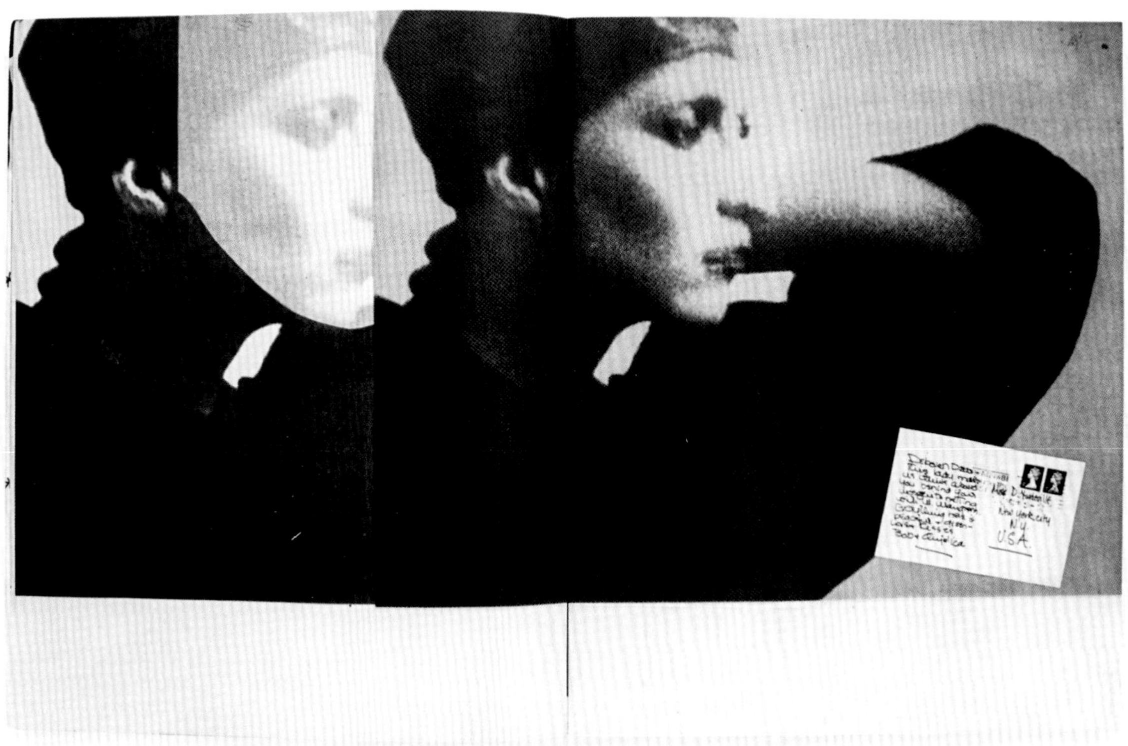

Deborah Turbeville's take on the fashion magazine

Alistair O'Neill

"I'm all for amusing, crazy goings-on," fashion editor Diana Vreeland noted one night, in December 1975, at the launch of Deborah Turbeville's fictitious fashion magazine *Maquillage*, "but essentially fashion is a totally serious business and it always has been." Produced in a limited edition of one thousand copies, *Maquillage* was first shown when the New York bookstore Rizzoli held the exhibition *Fashion as Fantasy*, which presented fifty-two spreads of Turbeville's images on two large boards, as if they were on the wall of an art department.

At the *Fashion as Fantasy* opening, Andy Warhol stood at the entrance next to a Charles James ribbon dress; Paloma Picasso screened a fifteen-minute film about herself; and Rudi Gernreich attended with two models wearing bicycle handlebars on their shoulders, reflectors across their chests, and bicycle seats repurposed as loincloths. For Turbeville, a fashion photographer and former editor at *Harper's Bazaar*, *Maquillage* presented the realities of fashion through the guise of a magazine but with pages that looked like illustrations for a crime novel.

Maquillage exchanges the lacquer of promotion for an introspective view of working life within the fashion industry. Polaroids, handprints, scratched enlargements, and high-contrast black-and-white photocopies, collaged with postcards and letters sent from models and associates to the photographer, outline another view on fashion. Disjointed accounts of aspirations and fears unfold in monochromatic and washed-out tones. One handwritten fragment reads: "I'm working for Guy Bourdin for five days (I think during collections), for which I am happy. I have wanted to work for him for a long time, I hope that he won't be too sinister."

In the same month that *Maquillage* was released, prints of Turbeville's bathhouse series, which had been published in American *Vogue* in May 1975, were included in the first exhibition to survey a history of fashion photography, *Fashion Photography: Six Decades*, curated by Robert Littman. On December 28, the *New York Times* art critic Hilton Kramer published a damning review, describing a Turbeville photograph as "one of the most beautifully composed pictures in the show, yet its 'Marat/Sade' imagery leaves one wondering if we have not moved beyond the boundaries of fashion photography into something more pathological." The review brought Turbeville a *succès de scandale* beyond the pages of the fashion magazine. Yet, *Maquillage* counters Kramer's accusation, suggesting that the deviant social pathology at play in her work is not a thematic import, but merely a reflection of the experience of models working in the 1970s.

Four decades later, in a post–Harvey Weinstein, #MeToo-inflected landscape, *Maquillage* appears prescient in its resonance, for example, with Cameron Russell's Instagram posts of anonymous stories of model mistreatment via the hashtag #MyJobShouldNotIncludeAbuse, and it prefigures the Model Alliance, established by Sara Ziff, in 2012, to raise awareness around harassment, mental health, and eating disorders. But *Maquillage* offers a more nuanced idea of the magnetic pull of fashion. As another postcard notes, "I am dying to do something glamorous."

Alistair O'Neill is Professor of Fashion History and Theory at Central Saint Martins, London.

Cover of *Maquillage* (Millock Press Inc., 1975)
Courtesy the Deborah Turbeville Foundation

Curriculum

A List of Favorite Anythings By Susan Meiselas

For Susan Meiselas, the story always comes first. An influential documentarian, Meiselas came to photo-world prominence with the publication of *Carnival Strippers*, in 1976, and *Nicaragua, June 1978–July 1979*, in 1981. She insists on context: her photographs are often prefaced by an explanation of the political situation as told by her subjects and, when possible, are accompanied by audio or even augmented-reality interviews. Her most recent series, *A Room of Their Own* (2015–16), is a collaboration with victims of domestic violence in the U.K. Meiselas writes that "the stories they had hidden within themselves were no longer invisible"—a manifesto of her life's work.

Richard Rogers, *Quarry*, 1970

This was the first film I saw by Dick Rogers, the man who became my partner for thirty years. Perhaps I was drawn to the graphic portrayal of the life cycle observed through the seasons, which marks the landscape of an abandoned quarry and those who inhabit it each summer. Counter to the sheer aesthetic beauty are the resonant voices of youth at play; suspending their fears, sharing their encounters with the Vietnam War, they were forced to move from teenage lust and into becoming men all too soon.

Edmundo Desnoes, *Memorias del subdesarrollo* (Memories of Underdevelopment), 1965

I met Edmundo Desnoes in 1976, when he was still living in Cuba. His novel, *Memorias del subdesarrollo*, which had been transformed into a 1968 film with the same title, created a powerful character trapped in time and revealed the deep alienation of a bourgeois intellectual. I was an American with no previous context to grasp the complexity of Desnoes's ambivalence to the revolution, but I was deeply engaged by his contradictions and moved by his honesty.

Teju Cole, "Getting Others Right," *The New York Times Magazine*, June 13, 2017

I love to listen to and read Teju Cole, who dares to make work and talk or write about the work of others. Through his voice, my eye delights with new discoveries while my mind remembers to always ask the harder questions.

Telling the stories in which we are complicit outsiders has to be done with imagination and skepticism. It might require us not to give up our freedom, but to prioritize justice over freedom. It is not about taking something that belongs to someone else and making it serve you but rather about recognizing that history is brutal and unfinished and finding some way, within that recognition, to serve the dispossessed.

Abigail Heyman, *Growing up female: A personal photo-journal*, 1974

Abigail Heyman found a highly distinctive style to address early feminist issues: her intimate portrayal in *Growing up female* includes images and handwritten text about the daily lives and perceptions of women in the early 1970s. I remember reading her aspiration "to bring to conscious awareness so many things we do and feel and take for granted as women." She visualized the multiple assumed roles women played, which have not changed significantly since then, despite the many decades in which equal respect has continuously been fought for.

Patricio Guzmán, *La batalla de Chile* (The Battle of Chile), 1975

Probably the first documentary film I saw that traced a transformative political process in such a way that I could imagine myself being present as it evolved. The intensity of Patricio Guzmán's drive to capture a flow of events, each seizing a tumultuous moment in time, brought me to witness a country splitting open. One particularly memorable scene is viewed through the lens of one of the team's cinematographers: his dedicated eye frames the street, determined to take full risk as he faces his own dramatic death.

John Berger and Jean Mohr, *A Seventh Man*, 1975

The subject of John Berger and Jean Mohr's book *A Seventh Man* is as current as it was over forty years ago when it revealed the European economy's deep dependency on migrant workers, and the humiliation endured in their harsh, hidden lives. The book focuses on their search for work and longings for home. Together, Berger and Mohr collaborated and created an exceptional assemblage form, mixing facts and poetry, words and images, not illustratively, but woven together to carry readers along their journey of discovery.

Bieke Depoorter, *As it may be*, 2018

Collaboration in the representation of a community is challenging for any photographer to do with an original and thoughtful approach. I have seen subjects comment on the way they are seen, as well as engage in the process of portraying themselves. What is especially bold and exceptional in Bieke Depoorter's work in Egypt, beginning after the revolution in 2011, is her return in 2017 with an open invitation to have her images written on directly by anyone, not only those framed within a specific image.

Susan Sontag, *Regarding the Pain of Others*, 2003

I cannot fully trace how I was shaped by my first reading of Susan Sontag's essay "Photography" in the *New York Review of Books*, in 1973, but Sontag continued to be a seminal reference as my own work evolved over time.

All memory is individual, unreproducible—it dies with each person. What is called collective memory is not a remembering but a stipulating: that this is important, and this is the story about how it happened, with the pictures that lock the story in our minds.

Opposite, clockwise from top left: Abigail Heyman, *Houma Teenage Beauty Contest*, 1971; cover of *A Seventh Man*, 1975; still from *Memorias del subdesarrollo*, 1968; Teju Cole, *Zürich*, July 2015; still from *Quarry*, 1970; Bieke Depoorter, Tunis, Egypt, 2013

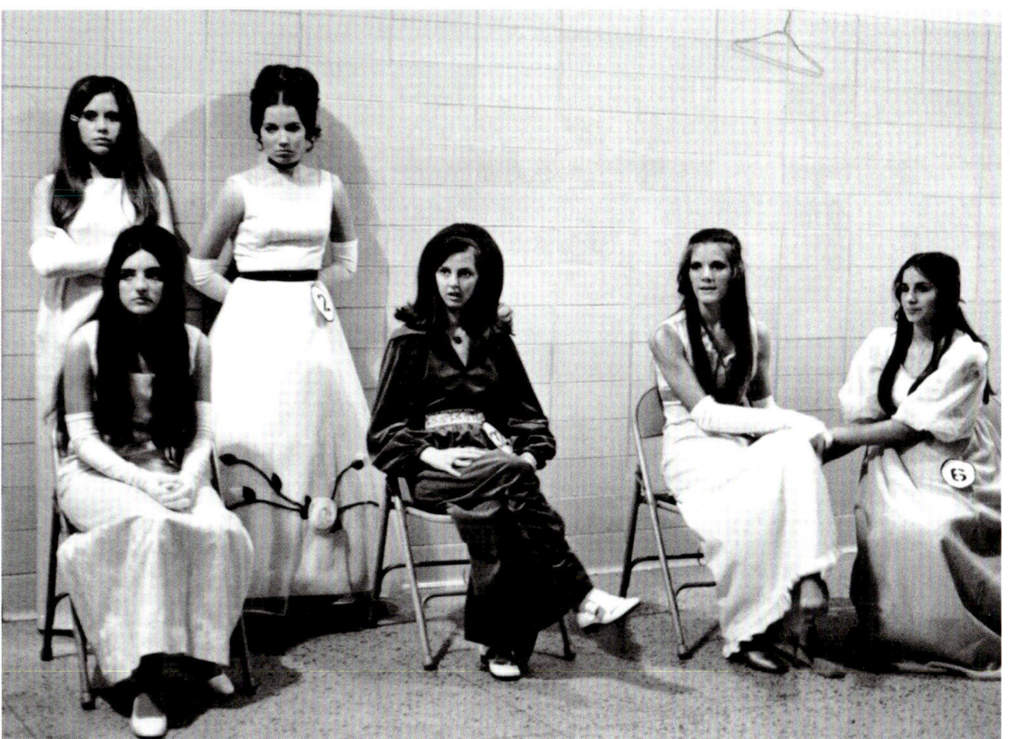

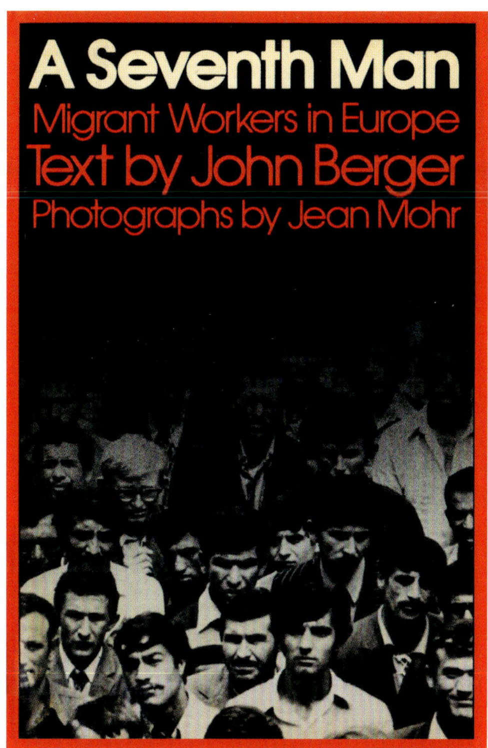

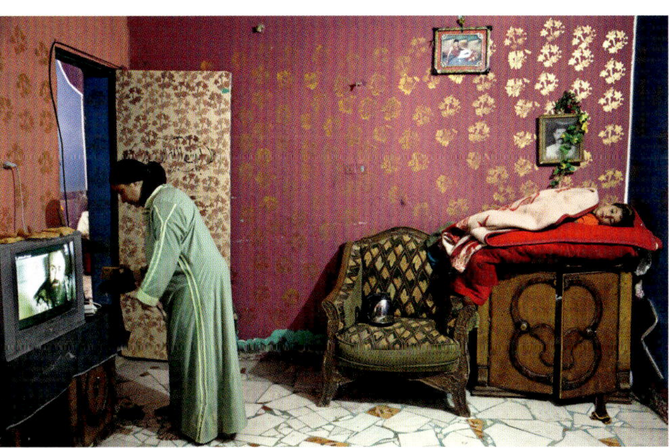

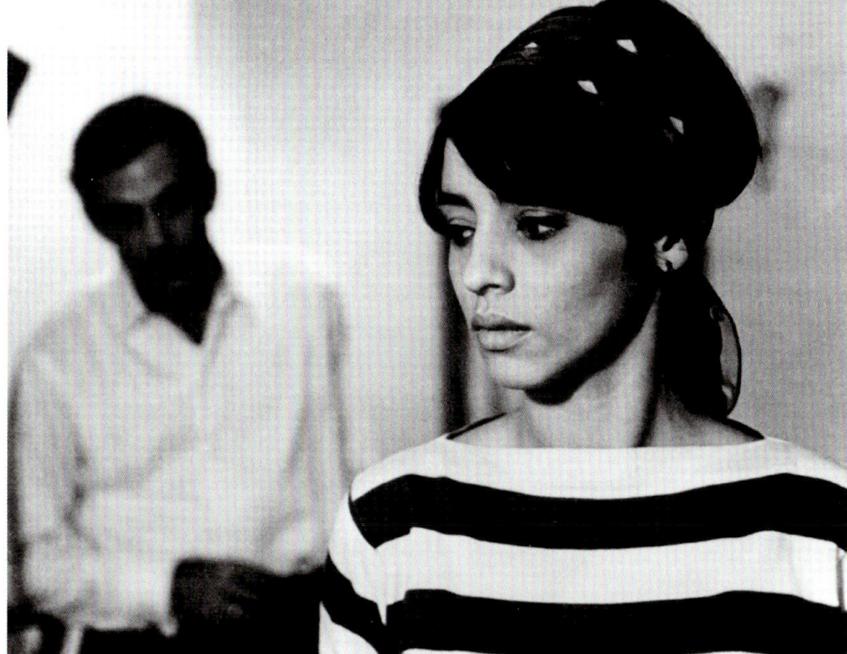

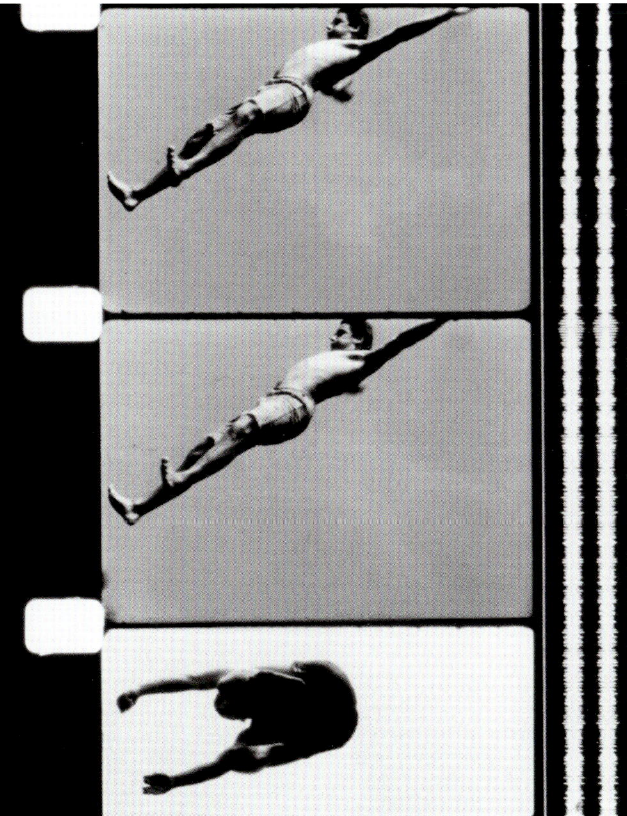

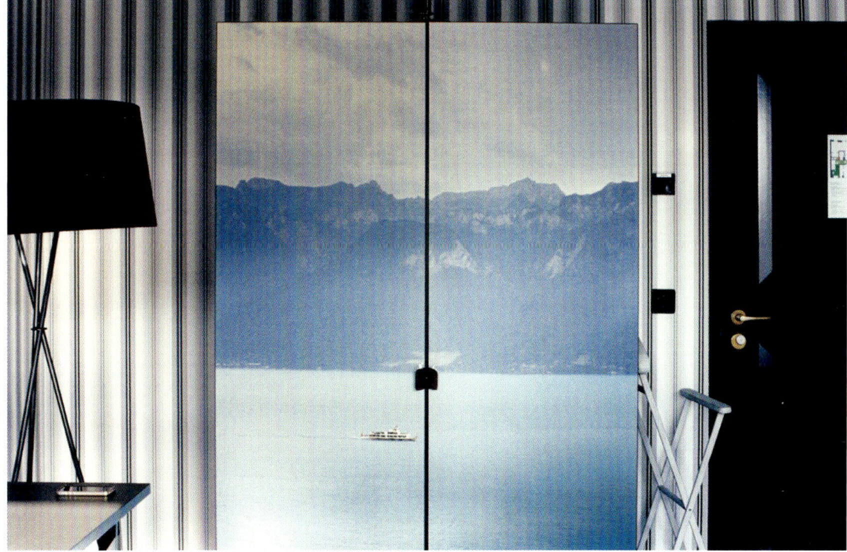

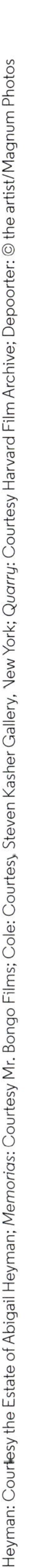
Clockwise, from top left: Heyman: Courtesy the Estate of Abigail Heyman; *Memorias*: Courtesy Mr. Bongo Films; Cole: Courtesy Steven Kasher Gallery, New York; *Quarry*: Courtesy Harvard Film Archive; Depoorter: © the artist/Magnum Photos

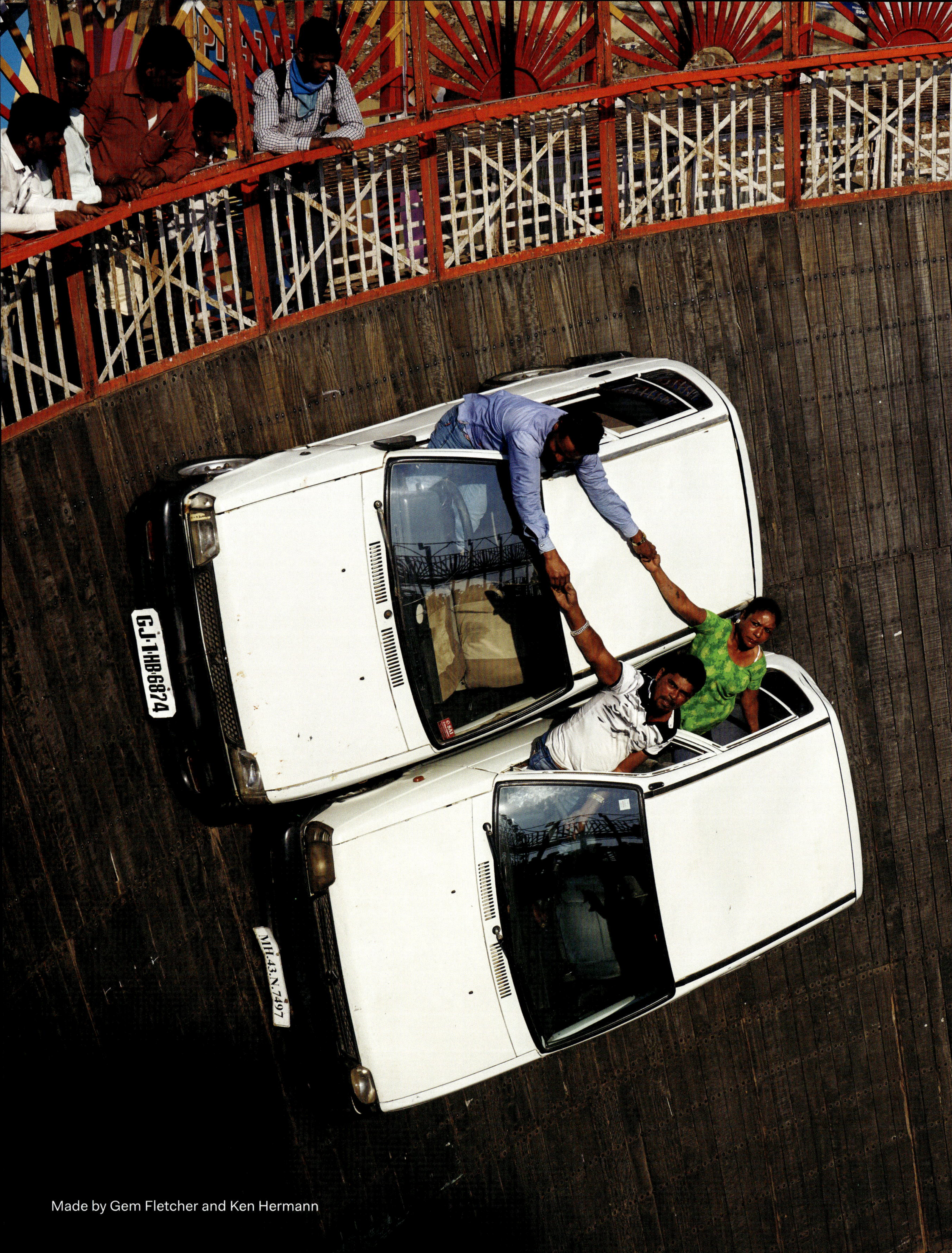

Made by Gem Fletcher and Ken Hermann

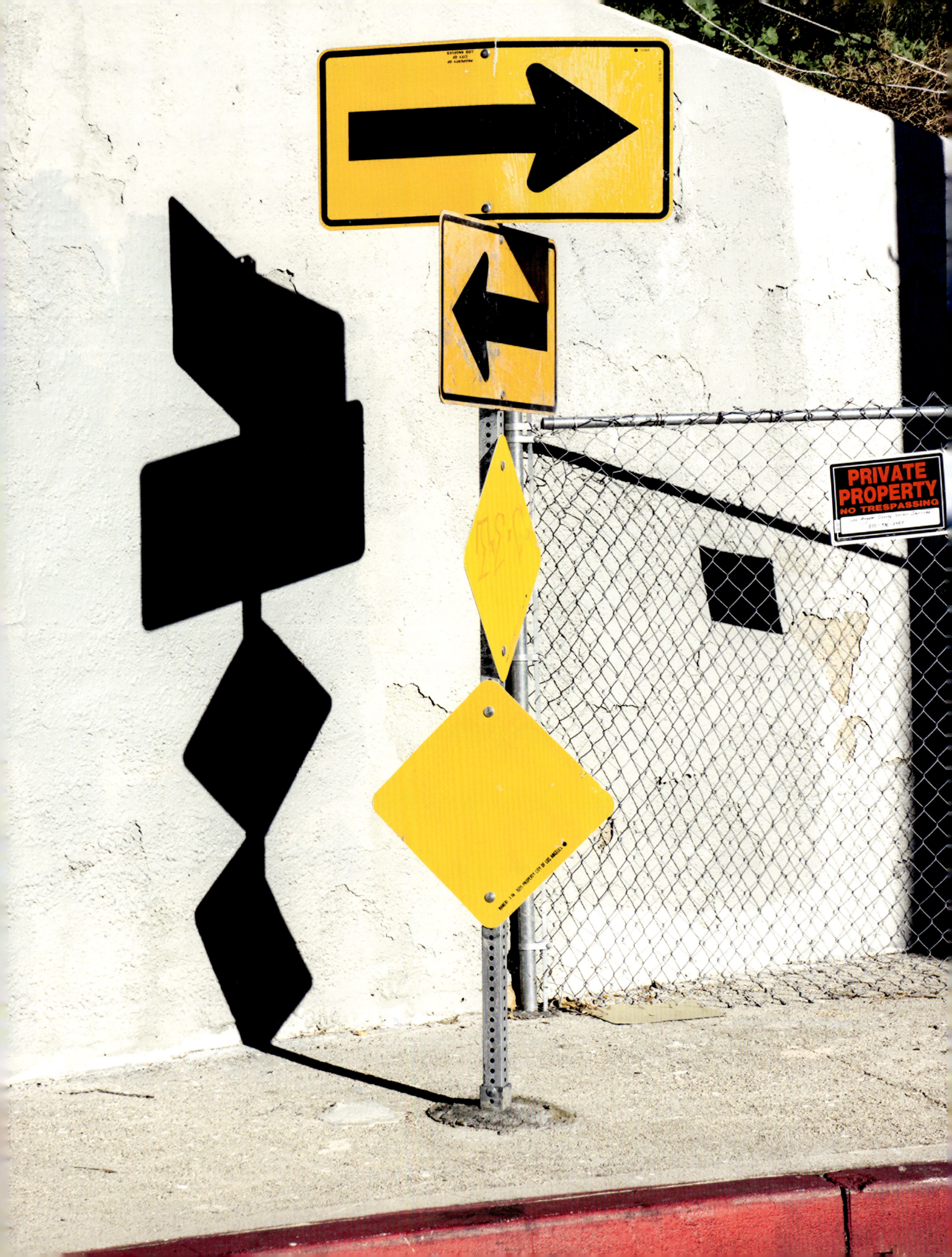
PRIVATE
PROPERTY
NO TRESPASSING

Mike Slack, *Untitled (Los Angeles)*, 2018
Courtesy the artist

Los Angeles

"LA is my big studio," says Anthony Hernandez. "One day I'm in one corner, the next in the middle. It's always interesting."

In this sprawling city, not known for a tradition of sidewalk-wandering image makers, Hernandez might be considered the resident street photographer of Los Angeles. For decades, he has surveyed the city's streetscapes, including its growing crisis of homelessness, and the connections between social position and mobility. In his new series, Hernandez returns to an old subject, bus stops, but now with a formal approach that allows him to see the city in an altered way. For John Divola, too, LA acts as a studio, if in a more literal sense. His projects from the 1970s are improvisations in found, disused buildings. In this issue, Divola and Mark Ruwedel discuss the riches—the plentiful light, the ocean, the desert, the Los Angeles River, the landscapes dramatically altered by wildfire—that Los Angeles and its immediate environs offer to peripatetic, patient observers. "I keep thinking … I'm just going to make the same pictures over and over," Ruwedel remarks. "And then it rains and I think, I gotta go and see what happened."

For artists in LA, a city with no shortage of space despite accelerated gentrification, the private artist's studio, sequestered from the hustle of the outside world, provides its own opportunities for observation and invention. Since at least the 1960s, with Robert Heinecken's founding of UCLA's influential photography program, experimentation, fostered by art schools, has been the norm. "There is not one photographic style here, but a vast pluralism," curator Rebecca Morse observes, as she reflects on Los Angeles as a nexus of photographic traditions and innovations—a city where native-born artists have made their own scene, and where transplants bring fresh energy.

Ilene Segalove grew up in the shadow of Hollywood and became enchanted by the slippages between reality and illusion. She notes that her art was always about the concept and the quotidian, as she cast her mother in projects staged in their Beverly Hills home. Today, the tradition of disregarding boundaries and orthodoxies continues in the work of a younger generation of image makers including Paul Mpagi Sepuya, Carter Mull, David Alekhuogie, and Rodrigo Valenzuela, who each use the studio as a space in which to combine photography with sculpture and performance. Sophie Tianxin Chen directs herself in her Burbank home. Torbjørn Rødland, who likens his process to that of directing a movie, harnesses sublime light that endows his oblique dramas with a curious aura.

Since the city's early days, when the entertainment industry beckoned filmmakers to LA for its light, architects have followed. Among LA's wildly eclectic architectural offerings, from "dingbat" apartments to mini-malls to old stucco houses, are masterpieces of modernism. Mona Kuhn has recently photographed the Schindler House in West Hollywood, while Janna Ireland has embarked on a catalog of the stylish buildings of Paul Revere Williams, an African American architect whose prodigious work dots the city, though many of his designs have been destroyed or radically altered.

Like any metropolis, LA is dynamic, changing, evolving, contested. Photographs often provide some sense of permanence, of telling and holding on to history. In 1948, at the age of twenty, Don Normark chronicled Chávez Ravine, a Mexican American community that three years later would be destroyed to make way for real estate speculators and eventually Dodger Stadium. Would we have a record of Chávez Ravine without Normark's account?

Seven decades later, the artist Guadalupe Rosales began assembling archives of Chicano life in the city, from 1990s underground raves to car culture to groups of young women posing for DIY glamour shots. Through her popular Instagram accounts and installations, Rosales carefully collects and showcases vernacular images that speak to how traditional archives often exclude the stories of underrepresented communities. Her projects underscore the idea that the pluralism, adaptability, and expansiveness of photographs are commensurate with the multitudinous and sprawling character of the city itself. "The reason I started doing this was because so much imagery of LA out in the world was stereotypical," Rosales says. "The archive shows communities in the city that weren't represented. Collectively we are reframing history, retelling the story of the city through personal experiences, reexamining the past through an insider's point of view."

—The Editors

City of Images

Six artists and writers reflect on Los Angeles in pictures.

James Welling: Los Angeles, Twice Lived

I twice lived in Los Angeles: from 1971 to 1978, when I was a student at CalArts, and from 1995 to 2016, when I ran the Photography Area of the Department of Art at UCLA. The first class I took at CalArts was a video workshop taught by performance and video artist Wolfgang Stoerchle. Consequently, some of my early works, and those of my classmates, were video art as documentation. In addition to Stoerchle, John Baldessari was a significant figure at CalArts. Baldessari's work at this time involved documenting activities, from throwing colorful sheets of paper out windows to pointing at green beans. From my perspective, documents of "performances" produced the best work in Los Angeles in the 1970s. The template for using the camera to document performance came via works such as Ger van Elk's *The Discovery of Sardines* (1971) and Bas Jan Ader's *In Search of the Miraculous (One Night in Los Angeles)* (1973).

When I returned to LA in 1995, performance documentation was still in full bloom with Sharon Lockhart's *Auditions* (1994) and Martin Kersels's *Tossing a Friend* (1996). However, in the 1980s and early '90s, the landscape of photography had reoriented itself in the wake of postmodernism and staged photography merged with the documentary tradition. In the beginning decade of the twenty-first century, experimental photography became increasingly viable, in part due to improved chromogenic paper and advances in digital printing. A number of photographers, myself included, began to tinker with the components of the image—working inside the image, as it were, and exploring the physicality of the photographic print. More recently, a hybrid of still life, documentation, and self-portraiture has gained traction in the work of Sophie Tianxin Chen, Paul Mpagi Sepuya, and Rodrigo Valenzuela (all of whose work is featured in this issue).

The bold and uneven legacy of Robert Heinecken, an artist I barely thought about when I lived in LA the first time around, continues to haunt me. At UCLA, I worked inside Heinecken's darkrooms (he had taught at the school years earlier), frequently brushing up against his ghost. What Heinecken bequeathed to me and many other photographers in LA over the past fifty years was permission to manipulate and distort the photograph as much as we wished. All you had to do was try it out and see if you liked it.

James Welling teaches visual art at Princeton University.

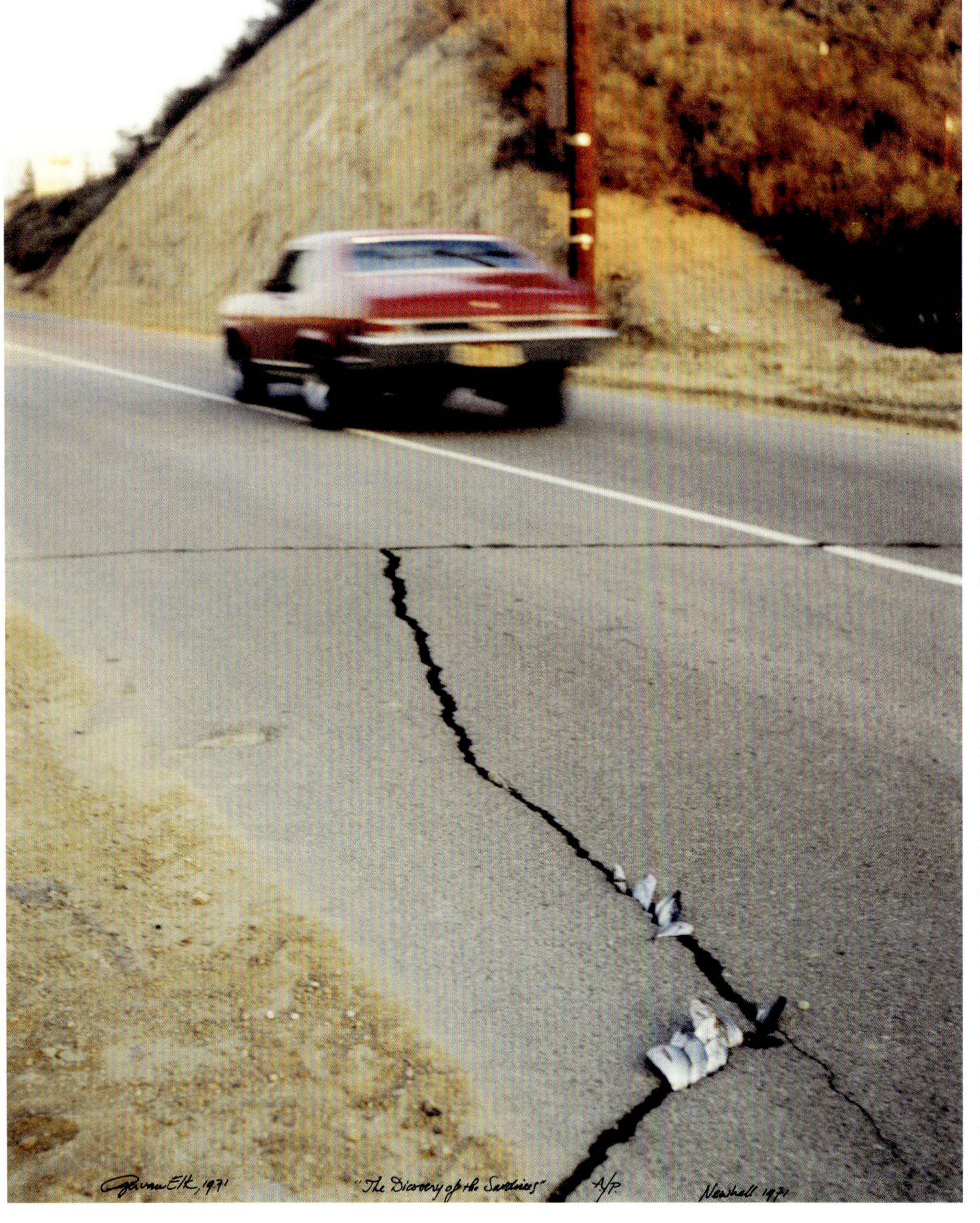

Ger van Elk, *The Discovery of Sardines, Placerita Canyon, Newhall, California* (detail), 1971
Courtesy GRIMM, Amsterdam and New York

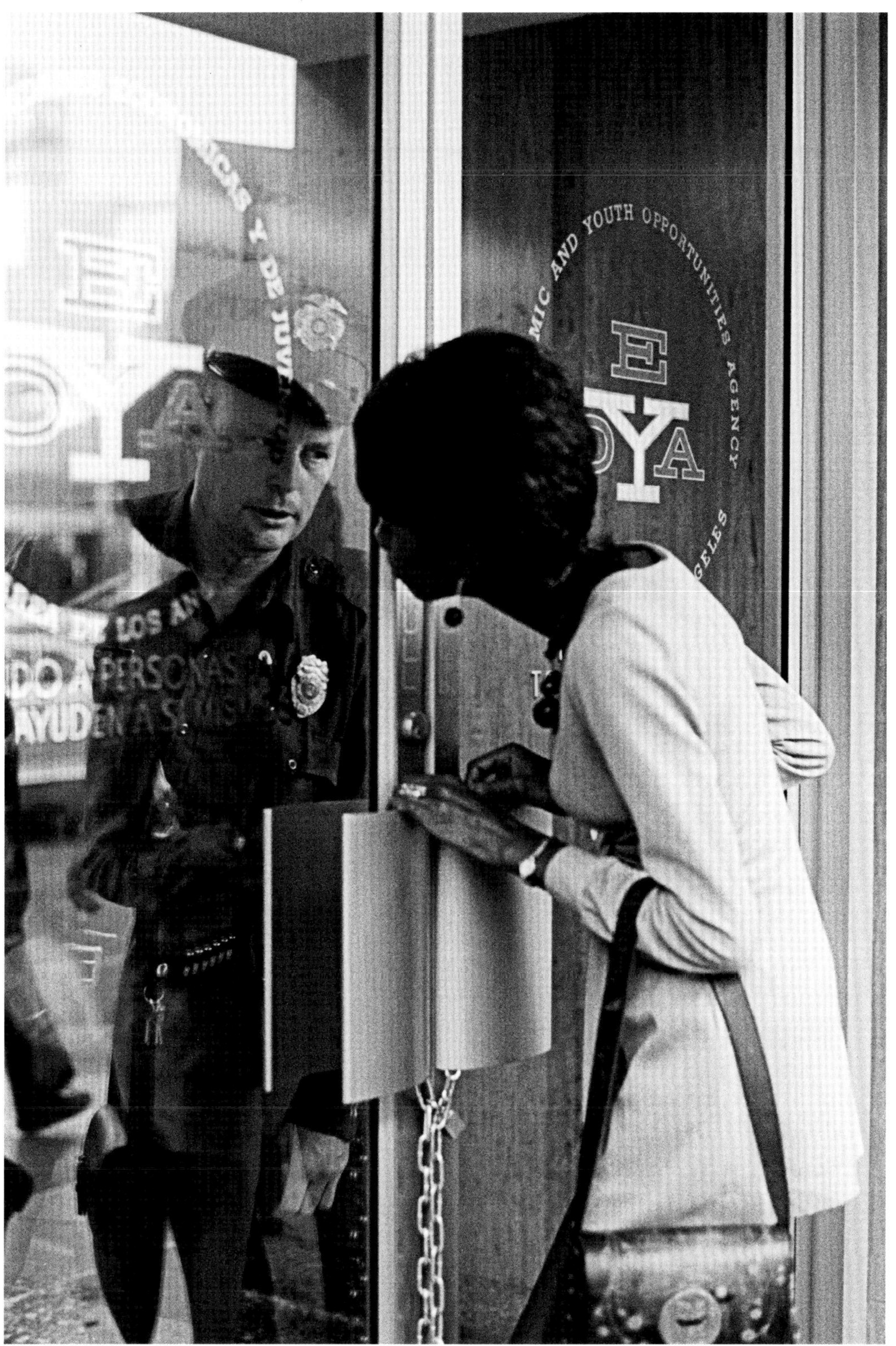

Pedro Arias, ***A woman outside the locked Economic and Youth Opportunities Agency exchanges glances with a police officer inside,* ca. 1973**
© and courtesy the artist and the UCLA Chicano Studies Research Center

Luis C. Garza on *La Raza*

The year 2017 marked the fiftieth anniversary of *La Raza*, the journalistic voice of the Chicano civil rights movement. *La Raza* was an epic Los Angeles publication whose existence, from 1967 to 1977, captured a decade's worth of transformative events. During that time span, a collective of photographers associated with the newspaper set out to document the social, political, and cultural activities of LA's Chicano community.

As a member of the photographer collective and the cocurator of *LA RAZA*, an exhibition at the Autry Museum of the American West, I was provided with access to the twenty-five thousand images from *La Raza* that are now part of the Chicano Studies Research Center at UCLA. It was an extraordinary and insightful opportunity to delve into this powerful image history—a recovery and a rediscovery made fifty years after the events that shaped this LA community. Among the photographs in the archive are thousands of 35mm frames shot by Pedro Arias, a mentor to all through his demeanor and commitment. Arias's images, along with the thousands more by members of the collective, resonate today as distant echoes traversing time.

For example, there are two compositions that contrast with one another. The first, taken in 1971, captures a procession of flag-bearing marchers on a desolate rural road as they enter and exit the frame, silhouetted against a cloudless sky. The view is taken from a low angle, which adds tension to the moment. The second photograph, from 1973, is intimate and confrontational in its reflective depiction of a uniformed white police officer and a fashionable African American woman. The two attempt to communicate through the divide of the locked and tightly chained glass door of a social service center in downtown LA. We curiously lean in as if trying to hear their conversation.

Arias, like most of us in the *La Raza* collective, was not a photographer per se, in the sense of a professional vocation. However, we all accepted wide-ranging assignments and filled in wherever necessary to get the job done; only a dedicated few moved on to careers in the media arts. We taught each other and became photojournalist activists with pen or camera in hand or on the protest line with a picket sign.

We were both witness to and participants in the struggle of the emerging Chicano movement for social justice as it unfolded across civil rights–era LA and on the global stage. As photojournalists, we were dedicated to telling our side of the story, armed with cameras to shoot the day's events. This was in direct opposition to the Spanish- and English-language mainstream media outlets in the US that gave the movement little to no coverage and, when they did report on it, presented it in a negative context. The archive of *La Raza* preserves part of a larger historical record; the images taken by *La Raza*'s collective of photographers went well beyond the barrio borders of LA to influence regional, national, and international news.

Luis C. Garza is cocurator of *LA RAZA* at the Autry Museum of the American West, Los Angeles, which is on view through February 10, 2019.

Awol Erizku on La Brea Avenue

In 2017, I was invited to create a billboard for a site on La Brea Avenue, a main Los Angeles road that I often drive down. The project, for me, became about disruption, about putting blackness in a place where you wouldn't expect it. Saying that sounds ridiculous in 2018, but it's not so often that you see this kind of imagery and symbolism on a billboard. Right?

The still life is composed of objects I picked up while traveling in Egypt. When I travel, I'm getting to understand myself, understand blackness, or understand just being a human in the world. Being black in America is not the same as being black in Japan, as being black in Hong Kong, as being black in Brussels. Partly, this image is about LA as an industry city. The color correction card, which I use during photo shoots, sometimes with celebrities, is a symbol that I've been incorporating into my work. When I lived in New York, I could approach people on the street to make a picture. But, after moving to LA, in 2014, I found it wasn't as easy for me to approach someone on the street, so the still life, made in the studio, became important.

I sometimes went back to rephotograph the billboard, and I'd run into people photographing it themselves. I would ask them, without identifying myself as the artist, "Hey, what do you think about that?" A lot of people were like, "Yeah, man, I like it; I've never seen shit like that." That's kind of my intention: to start pointing at things and get people to notice them. Until I got to Cooper Union, the standard of "beauty" for me was what I saw in classical art books. In high school, I was taught that the representation of beauty in civilization started with Greek and Roman art. In my work, I'm highlighting another history—not only Egyptian culture and Nefertiti, but also African iconography more broadly, which has appeared in my work for some time now. I grew up being slightly ashamed of my culture, because I didn't understand how powerful it was. Now, I want to showcase that power and tell the generations that'll come after me, "Hey, embrace your culture. It's okay."

Awol Erizku is an artist based in Los Angeles.

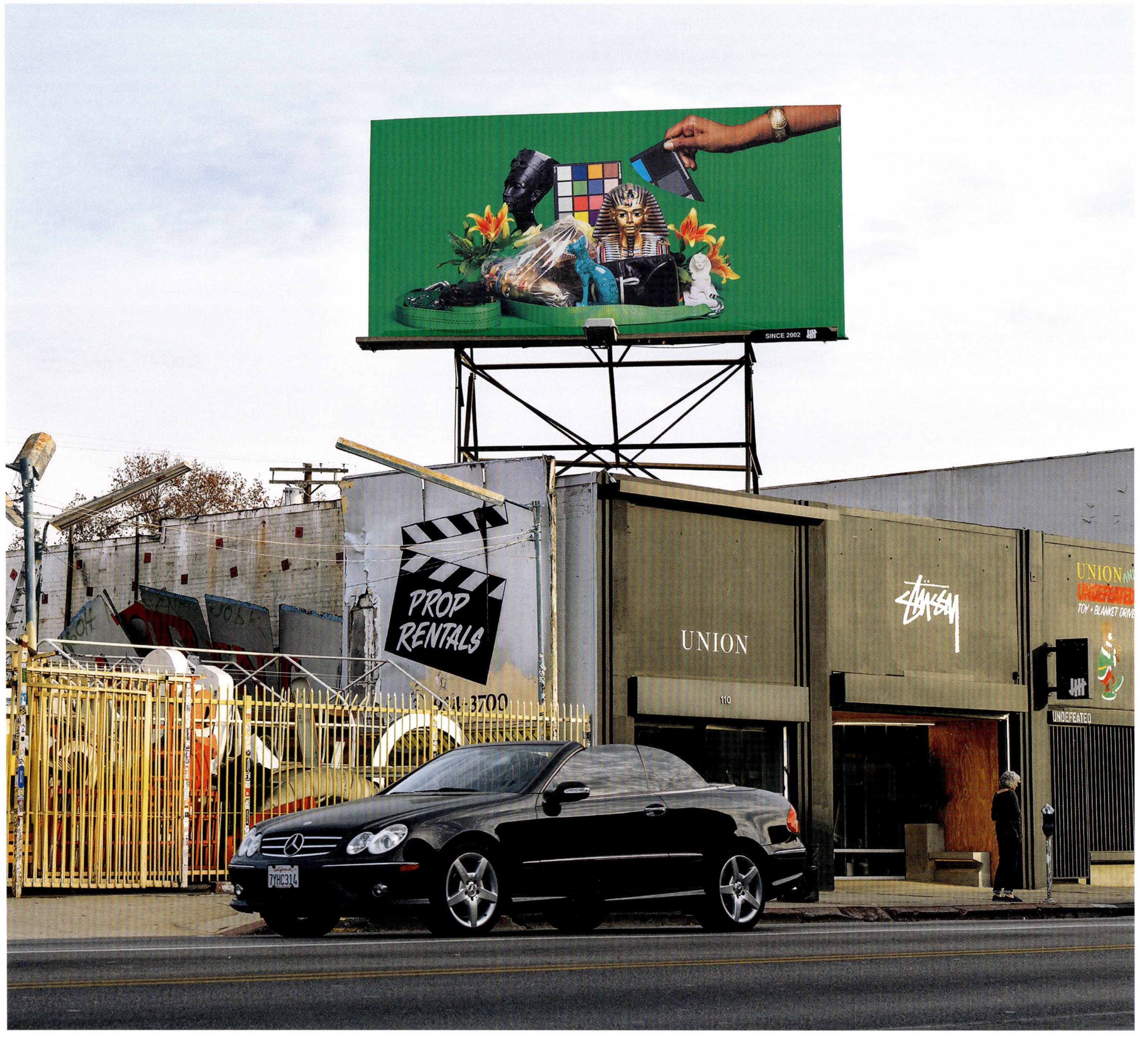

Awol Erizku, *Asiatic Lilies*, Los Angeles, 2017
© and courtesy the artist

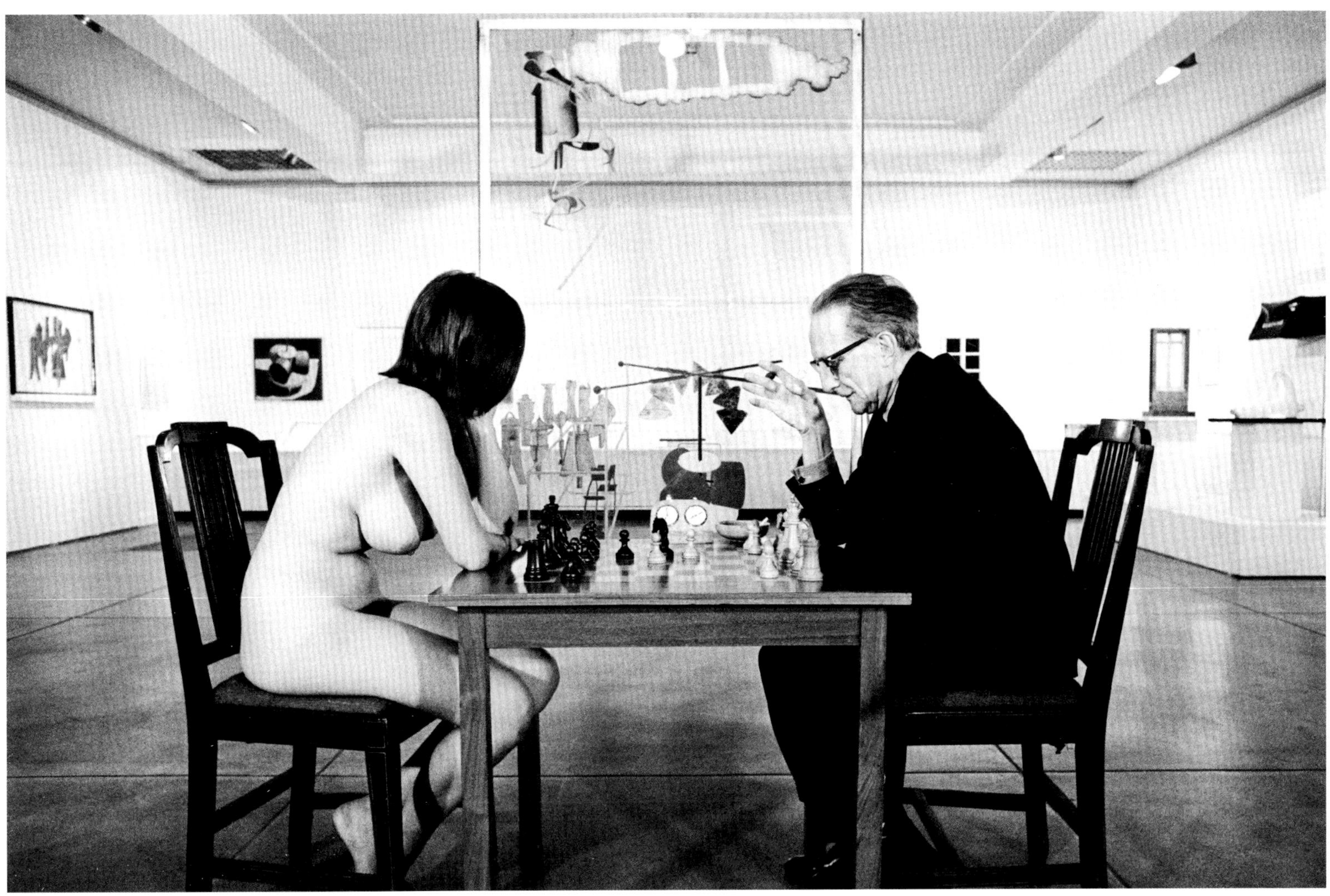

Julian Wasser, Duchamp Playing Chess with a Nude (Eve Babitz), Duchamp Retrospective, Pasadena Art Museum, 1963
Courtesy the artist

Dana Goodyear on Eve Babitz

This 1963 photograph of a marmoreal nude, face occluded, playing chess with Marcel Duchamp was a stunt, the idea of a Contax-toting stalker of the Sunset Strip named Julian Wasser. Later, when the nude was famous enough to make the outing satisfying, she began to be identified in captions as the Los Angeles writer Eve Babitz, author of books like *Slow Days, Fast Company: The World, the Flesh, and L.A.* (1977) and *Sex and Rage* (1979), both recently re-released. Wasser knew Babitz and her circle; according to a 2015 interview in *Vanity Fair*, he was always trying to get them, and the other girls at Hollywood High, to take off their clothes and pose for him. Twenty by the time the picture was made, Babitz was so jittery and reluctant—and Wasser was so greedily eager to see his setup through—that he kicked her smock away so she could not back out.

So, they took their places at the board, before Duchamp's masterwork *The Bride Stripped Bare by Her Bachelors, Even (The Large Glass)* (1915–23). Babitz let her hair blot out her face, like a John Baldessari dot, and they played a few awkward, undistinguished rounds. The resulting image works as a sight gag—the female body as ultimate readymade? a spoof of the emerging language of performance art?—but its jauntiness contains a crueler tone. It's a put-on that hides a put-down, and Babitz is the butt of the joke.

Some images take a long time to resolve. This one, often reprinted, speaks to the giddy, freewheeling time when the rest of the world dismissed LA—art, it was thought, happened in Paris and New York, and artists only came to town to party and gawk. (Meanwhile, Ed Ruscha and company were setting the table for the next course.) So, when Duchamp, who had long ago retreated from the art world and declared himself a chess player and *respirateur*, agreed to have the 1963 retrospective of his work, *By or of Marcel Duchamp or Rrose Sélavy*, at the Pasadena Art Museum, it was both comic (Pasadena, whatever its dowdy Bostonian grandeur, was a suburb of a suburb culturally) and doubly historical—a punctuation point on Duchamp's career and an announcement that LA was a new artistic capital. That shift is captured within the frame, where he appears frail and pinched—five years from death—and she's as naked as the day she was born.

Babitz, who hung out with male artists, designed album covers for rock bands—most famously, Buffalo Springfield—and wrote books. She wanted in, and who could blame her? But more than a record of her arrival, and the arrival of all the other women like her, the photograph is a record of men—men of culture, wearing clothing—having a laugh at a time when a woman's options for stability and success were pretty much limited to marrying it. (Even Joan Didion, Babitz's elder by a decade, whom Wasser shot in front of her Corvette Stingray, advertised in the classifieds in search of a quiet place for "a writer and his wife.")

A few years ago, when I interviewed Wasser, he told me, with a snicker, that the Babitz picture was Duchamp's favorite image of himself. Babitz is the subject—try to imagine the picture without her—devoid of subjectivity. It's a ridiculous photograph. We have to laugh (or scoff) at what it remembers: a time of complicity, exclusion, and exploitation that flourished on the desires of women to claim their seat at the chessboard, a situation that we have finally, this past year, begun to collectively confront. It also, more tenderly, records the end of LA's goofy, outskirts innocence, personified by Babitz. When I look at the picture now, I see it as a warning telling women not to get caught playing fake chess, to come unembarrassed to the board, and to take the queen.

Dana Goodyear is a staff writer at *The New Yorker* and the author of two collections of poems and a book about food in America.

Geoff Dyer on Bevan Davies

Formally, the photographs Bevan Davies made of homes and streets in Los Angeles in 1976 have much in common with those made by Walker Evans in the American South in the 1930s. Often full frontal, they are marked by a similar stillness: a stillness that registers the absence of both physical movement—people, cars, wind—and implied movement or passage of time. Los Angeles is thought of as the quintessential city without a past, where nothing is preserved, where the old makes way for the new without regret or nostalgia. Emptied of time as they are, I am tempted to say that these pictures represent an eternal or unchanging *idea* of Los Angeles. There is none of the sense that we get, as in the work of Eugène Atget, from seeing an old Paris that must be preserved before it makes way for the new. Nor is there the urgency expressed by the title of Berenice Abbott's 1939 book *Changing New York*. But even if these buildings are still there, unchanged, the photographs show them at a very precise stage of their existence. This is emphasized by pictures in which house numbers—1432 or 1517—seem to double as records identifying not only where, but exactly *when* the photographs were taken. That's an illusion, obviously, but the earlier comment about time and its absence perhaps needs to be rephrased, recalibrated. Davies's pictures extend the photographic moment so that we *see* time as experienced by the buildings in them.

Davies's aesthetic has similarities with that of Lewis Baltz and the New Topographics photographers: Each picture is a statement of fact. Taken together, they amount to an inventory of *what is there*, without stylistic embellishment. And yet, at the same time, Davies's work does not have the feel of unflinching rigor or stern objectivity. There is an implied gentleness here, almost—though the focus is sharp—a softness.

Why? How to account for this quality? I think it has something to do with familiarity. Although I've never seen any of these buildings before, I look at the photographs of them not with astonishment, but with the kind of fondness a neighbor might feel. Not a human neighbor—this is not the viewpoint of someone looking through the curtains of the house across the way or sitting on a porch. No, this is the viewpoint of a neighboring building. This is how a given house might appear to one of its kind. We have the sense, in other words, that this is how these buildings might, *in time*, photograph themselves.

Mention must also be made of the black cypress trees against the white walls. In *Twilight in Italy*, D. H. Lawrence wrote that "as we have candles to light the darkness of night, so the cypresses are candles to keep the darkness aflame in the full sunshine." These photographs prove that what Lawrence observed in San Gaudenzio also holds true in the long sunlight of Los Angeles.

Geoff Dyer is Writer-in-Residence at the University of Southern California, Los Angeles. His latest book is *The Street Philosophy of Garry Winogrand* (2018).

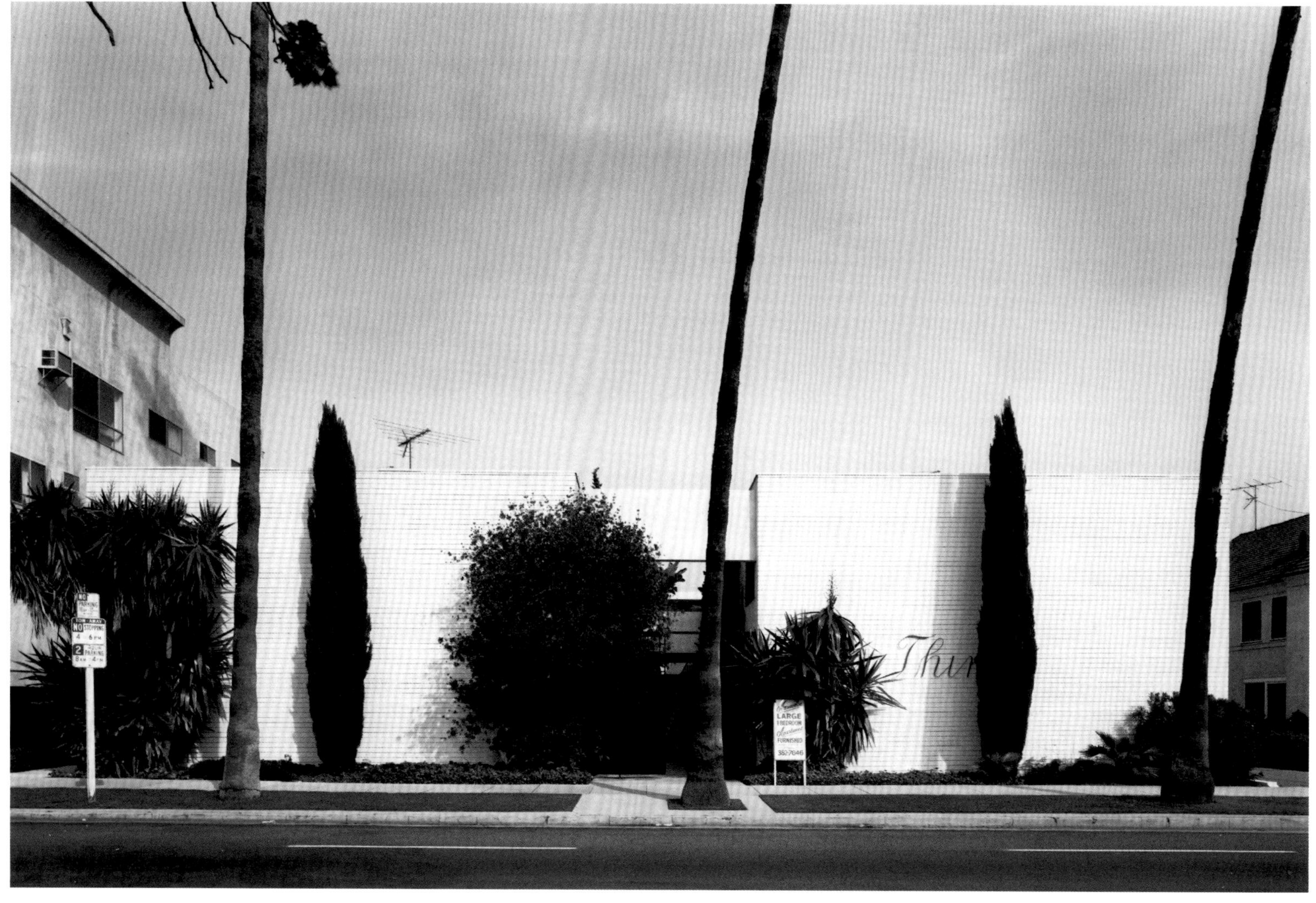

Bevan Davies, *Apartments near Wilshire Blvd., Los Angeles*, 1976
Courtesy the artist and Joseph Bellows Gallery, La Jolla

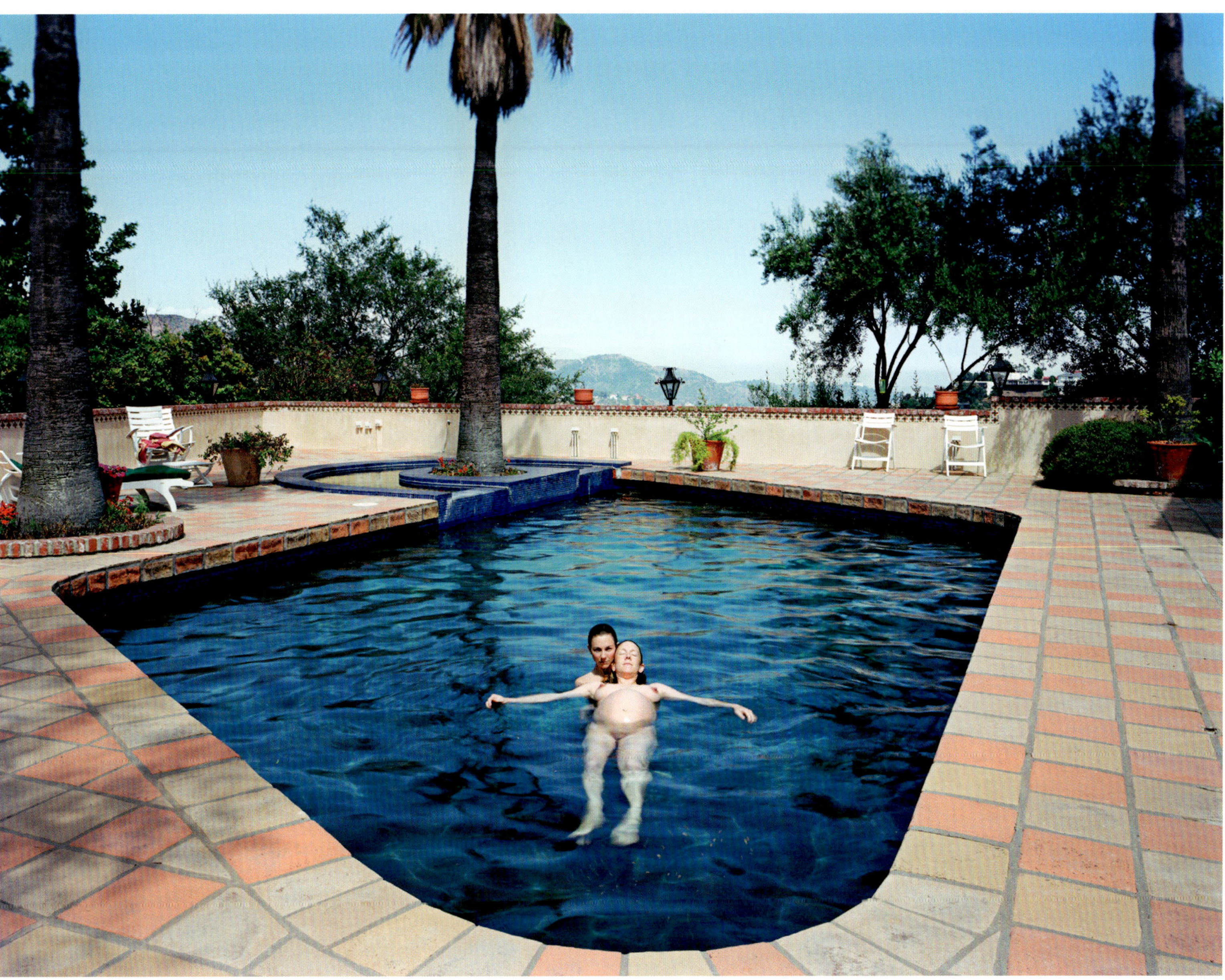

Catherine Opie, *Miggi & Ilene, Los Angeles, California*, 1995

Catherine Opie on Domestic Life

I lived in San Diego from the age of thirteen on up, and then I went away to San Francisco Art Institute. I was perfectly happy living in San Francisco, actually, and didn't even consider moving to Los Angeles because the north kind of hates the south. People would like to secede, I think. But graduate school brought me to Los Angeles in 1986—I came down to go to CalArts and eventually decided to stay there. My friends in San Francisco were utterly shocked that I wasn't coming back home. I just said, "I'm sorry. It's a more interesting city to think about and to be involved in and to be an artist in." So I stayed.

Back then, around 1987, the big game in town was Los Angeles Contemporary Exhibitions (LACE), an alternative space downtown. LACMA was completely sleepy. There was no Hammer Museum, really. And MOCA had just been built. I still remember the shopping bag that had the image of MOCA on the front of it, saying, "Opening Soon." It was an artists' town. I loved wandering around. I loved thinking about the city. I felt that there was an enormous amount of space. There was a sort of anonymity that I was able to have in Los Angeles that I wasn't able to have in San Francisco.

I worked at Pan Pacific, a camera store, making eight dollars an hour, and began a series of images called *A Long Way From Paris* (1989). That was my first body of work made inside LA. I'm somewhat of an observational photographer; I think about ideas, about how things look. I started right away when I moved into the city, with photographing around MacArthur Park, because they were building the first Metro Rail to be underground. I started making those images when I realized the kind of gentrification that was happening with MacArthur Park in relation to the Metro Rail. By around 1992, I was running the photography facilities at UC, Irvine, and it took four to five freeways to get there every day, so my freeway photographs came out of that imagined space.

I've always loved the mishmash of the city, from the mini-malls on up. LA is a very dense place, but it's also an urban sprawl that is suburban too. You have palm trees and stucco houses. LA is always thought of as this place that captures ideas about the division between inside and outside that architecture—like the buildings of Richard Neutra and Rudolph Schindler—has created.

I took this picture of Ilene Chaiken, who was the creator and producer of *The L Word*, and Miggi Hood, an architect at the time, when I was working on my series *Domestic* (1995–98). This was a few days before Miggi had her baby, and the only place she felt comfortable was in the pool, so I said, "Let's do some pool pictures." *Domestic* examines domesticity in relationship to lesbian women. But the series was also about my own desire for the domestic. To make the photographs, I drove around the country for three and a half months, thinking about being domestic in relation to the larger American landscape.

Catherine Opie is an artist based in Los Angeles and Professor of Photography in the Department of Art at the University of California, Los Angeles.

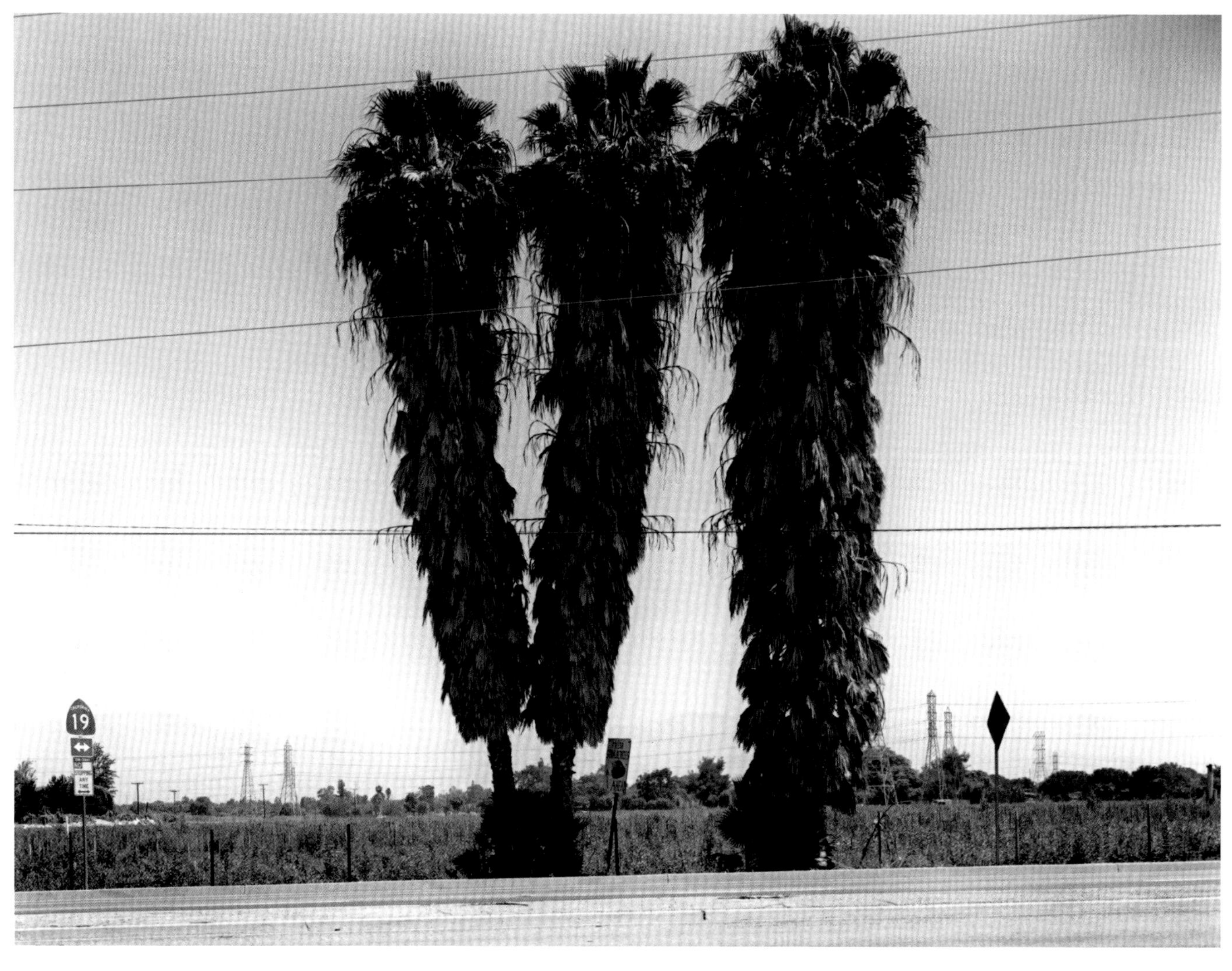

John Divola & Mark Ruwedel

A Conversation with Amanda Maddox

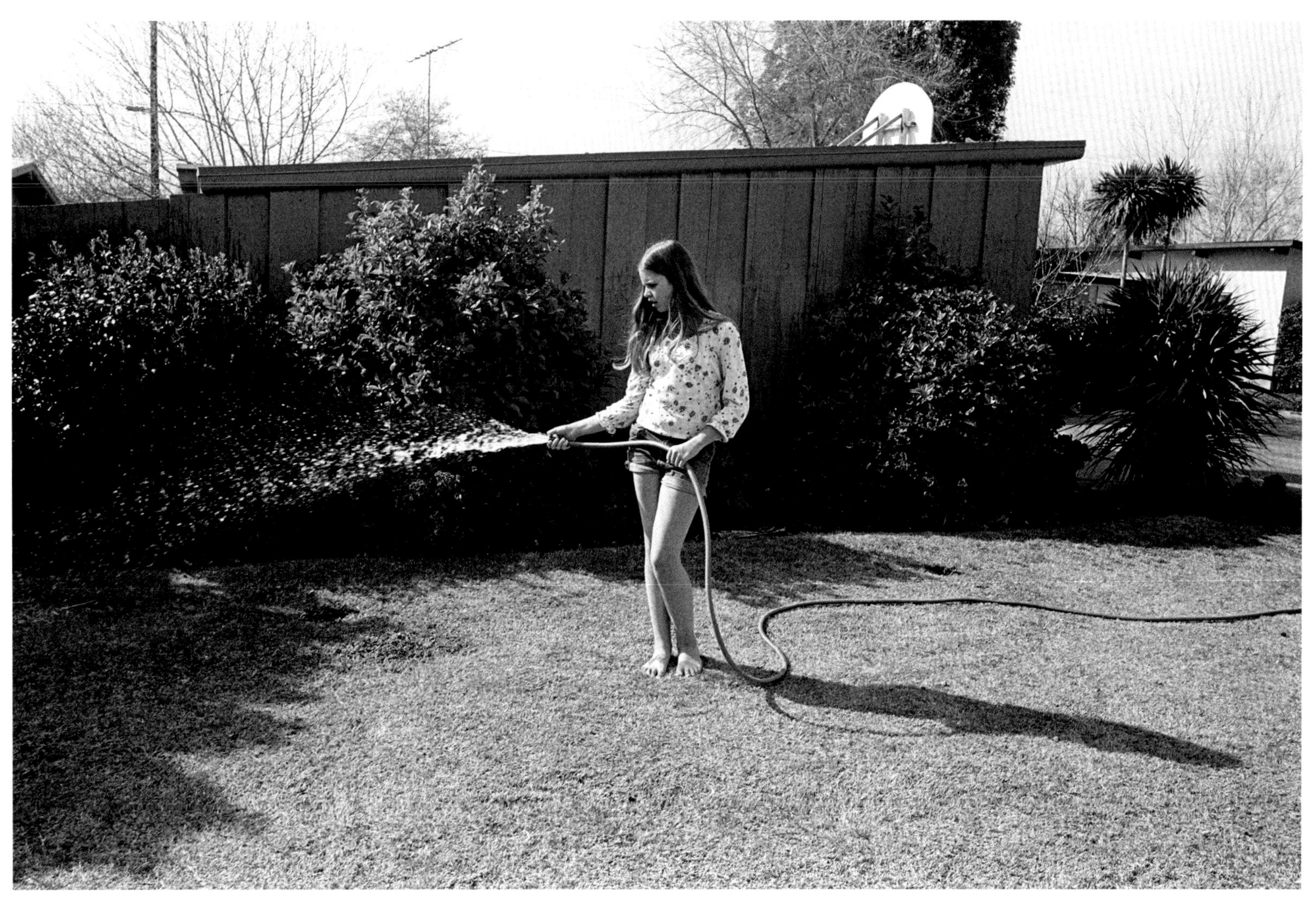

"Los Angeles isn't a city," wrote Eve Babitz. "It's a gigantic, sprawling, ongoing studio." The photographs of John Divola and Mark Ruwedel might just prove her point. A native Angeleno based in Riverside, Divola often utilizes and activates spaces found in his immediate environment—from an abandoned residence on Zuma Beach to derelict desert houses. Since the 1970s, he has incorporated modes of intervention and improvisation (often involving spray paint) into his photographs, a process that reveals his presence while also synthesizing the conceptual and evidentiary quotients of the medium.

For Ruwedel, who moved to Long Beach in 2002, Los Angeles County presents limitless photographic possibilities. Relocation to Southern California put him within proximity of the American West landscapes that feature frequently in his investigations of how human activity and historical events register on the environment. His recent projects address the tension between nature and culture visible across the city.

Last spring, curator Amanda Maddox spoke with Divola and Ruwedel about their distinct but related practices, their attraction to the desert, and their preferred means of traversing Greater Los Angeles (read: Nissan Xterra) in pursuit of compelling subjects.

Page 28:
Mark Ruwedel,
Walk Across LA, Mile 22,
2012

Previous page:
John Divola, *Untitled (woman watering lawn)*, from the series *San Fernando Valley*, 1971–73

Opposite:
John Divola, *N34°11.115' W116°08.399'*, from the series *Isolated Houses*, 1995–98

This page:
Mark Ruwedel, *Walk Across LA, Mile 2*, 2011

Amanda Maddox: **I'm curious about your different perspectives on Los Angeles. John, you're a native who's seen the city evolve over the course of your life. And Mark, you're a transplant who arrived with some idea of the American West. Did that hold up?**

Mark Ruwedel: I grew up with this idea that California was the golden land. My parents, when they moved back to Pennsylvania from National City, regretted it their whole lives.

AM: **Really?**

MR: Yeah. The big family story was how they settled for something less due to family pressure. Having cut my teeth as a photographer in eastern Canada, the fact that I can photograph on any day of the year is really important to me.

John Divola: I like the idea of sitting outside in January. [*laughter*]

MR: I think John doesn't appreciate that like I do.

JD: Probably not to the same degree. I'm the one that doesn't know any better, right? I can tell you it's a place that, as a photographer, as Mark was referencing, is an extraordinary subject.

You've got this combination of people building something next to something else with total liberty and disregard for any kind of architectural vocabulary or coherence. And then by the same token, you've got these later manifestations of just completely homogenous tract homes, which are all mock Italian or French.

There's this kind of subtle line between Disney vocabulary and the vocabulary of architecture, and then it's sprinkled with a few modernist things, but never enough to come to any kind of coherence in relationship to one another.

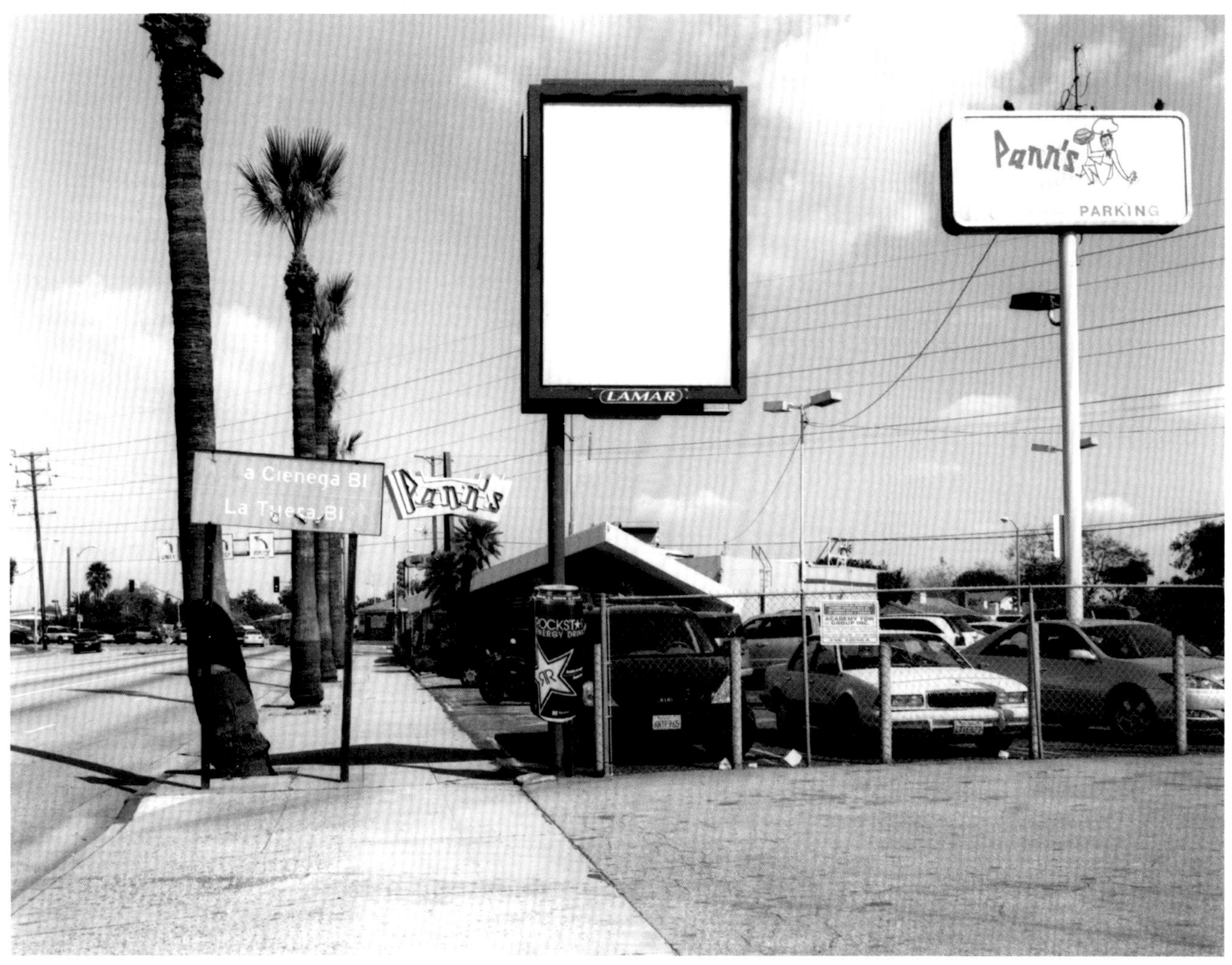

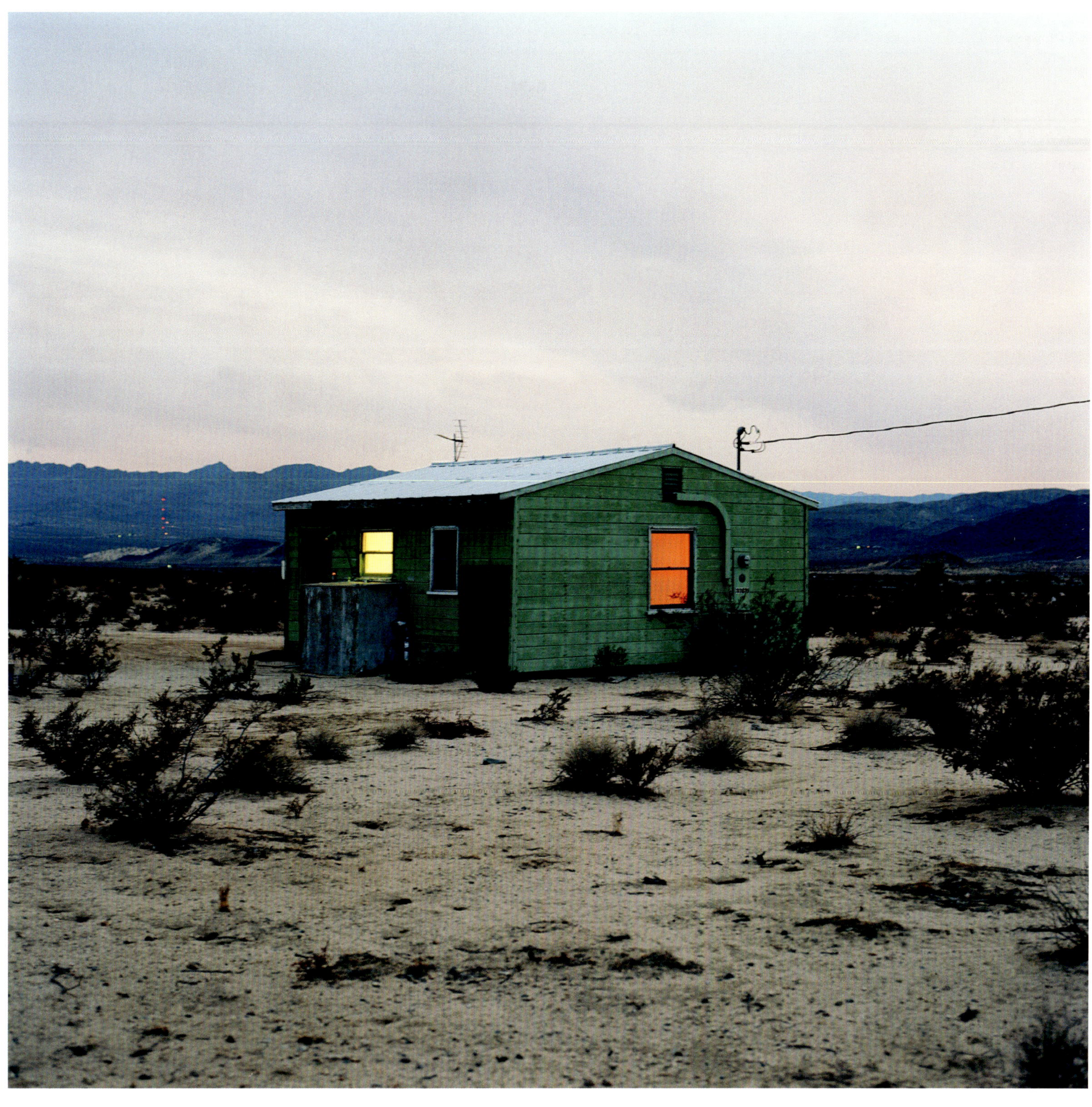

You have a sense that Los Angeles is all temporary, that it's all in flux and changing and dynamic.

And having grown up here, I've always been in a kind of dynamic, changing environment. I think if you grew up in Los Angeles, it's not like you grew up in an old city that's been there for three hundred years. You have a sense that it's all temporary, that it's all in flux and changing and dynamic.

It was kind of spectacular because, as a photographer, you could just take your gear, jump in your car, and go anywhere. You've got the ocean, I've dealt with that; and then you've got the desert, and I've dealt with that; and then you've got the mountains. It's hard to imagine a richer kind of environment in terms of possibilities.

MR: The deserts—it's sort of complicated to get to the bottom of what the desert is about. It represents a lot of things. I'm sure John has a take on that too that probably overlaps but is quite different.

AM: **Let's talk about your attraction to photographing in the deserts here.**

JD: There are classic visual things, like a deep horizon line. I used to teach in the summer at a graduate program at Bard College and would take my camera. I'd go out to photograph, and I couldn't do it. There were all these damn trees in the way. I couldn't see anything. Here there's this incredible light, especially somewhere like Wonder Valley.

MR: And everything that is there is right there. It's not overgrown. The light, obviously, but also the sharpness because of the lack of moisture in the air. That's another aspect that appeals to me, especially those pictures of the houses that I photographed just after sunset—not at night, but in those couple of minutes just after the sun drops below.

AM: **At dusk?**

MR: Yeah. As soon as the shadows disappear, basically. I think, having been schooled sort of in the heyday of Postminimalism and all that, I have an aesthetic that's kind of clean and spare.

There's another attraction to the desert: stuff doesn't disappear really fast there. Things might fall down, but they stay there for a long time. And nobody ever seems to clean up. So it's all out there to be read. I have over two hundred photographs of bras lying in the desert.

AM: **What about the architecture of the desert? Are you drawn to that?**

MR: I guess so. I don't know.

JD: Well, those homestead houses—it's interesting that they're so minimal that they become almost like a logo for the idea of habitation or home.

MR: Yeah, so a Platonic ideal.

JD: Sometimes like a Monopoly house, even.

MR: Which was also why I was attracted to some of the abandoned doghouses. They're just miniature versions of that kind of house. Also, there's an incredible history there. It's sort of imprinted. A friend of mine was looking at my work once, and he said that where I photographed were places where the bones are closest to the skin.

JD: And the people you run into out there, either they want to get away or they've been pushed to the edge.

AM: **So there is an interesting kind of character you find?**

JD: Yes. It's the people that build hurricane fences around their little sheds with klieg lights. There are other people that have been on drugs, and it's the cheapest possible place on Earth you could live.

AM: **There is a kind of pull from the city.**

MR: Well, I guess it's both an extension and a sort of negative. In fact, one of the areas that I photograph that's desert is the Antelope Valley. Half of it's still in Los Angeles County. There are people living out there that work in the city. It's very, very close. And, you know, the earlier literature about Los Angeles always speaks about this kind of struggle to keep the desert out of town in different ways. There's a great scene in one of Joan Didion's novels about the woman sweeping in the high wind, sweeping the dust off the porch or something.

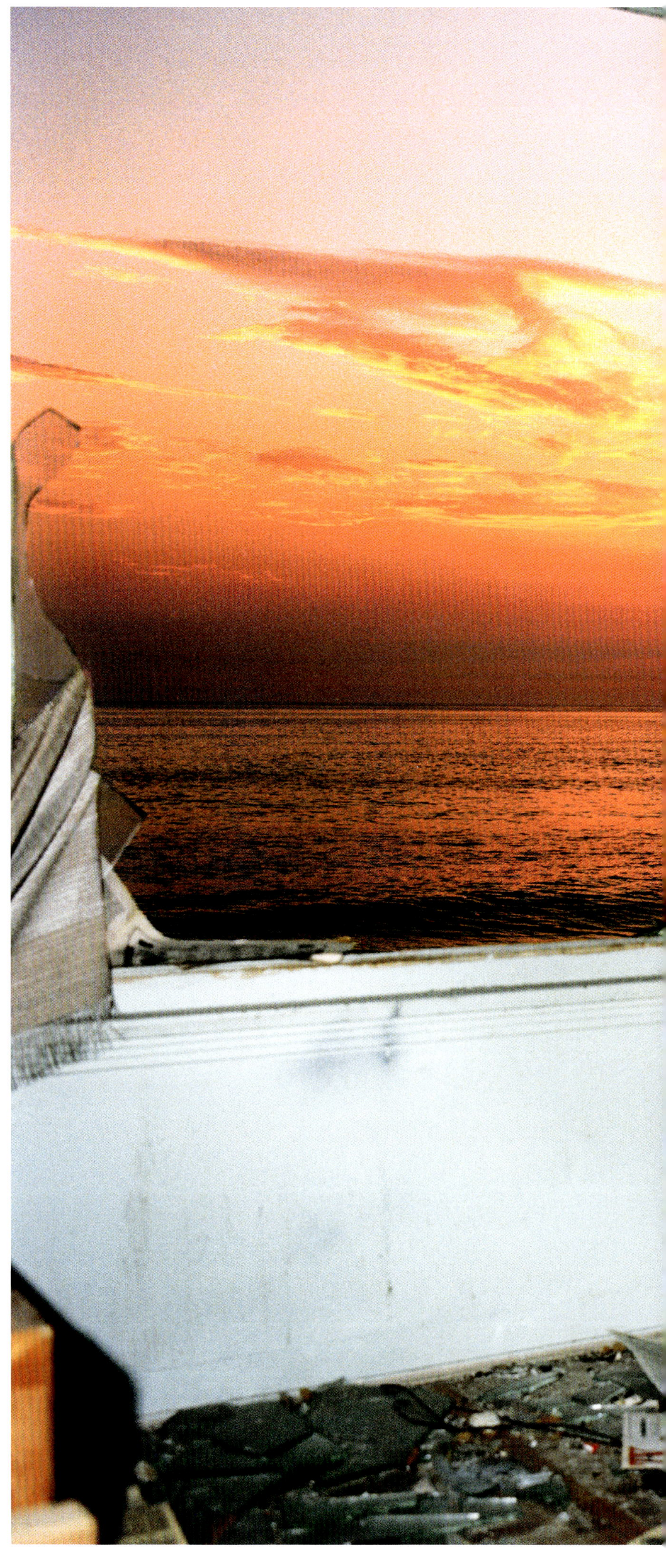

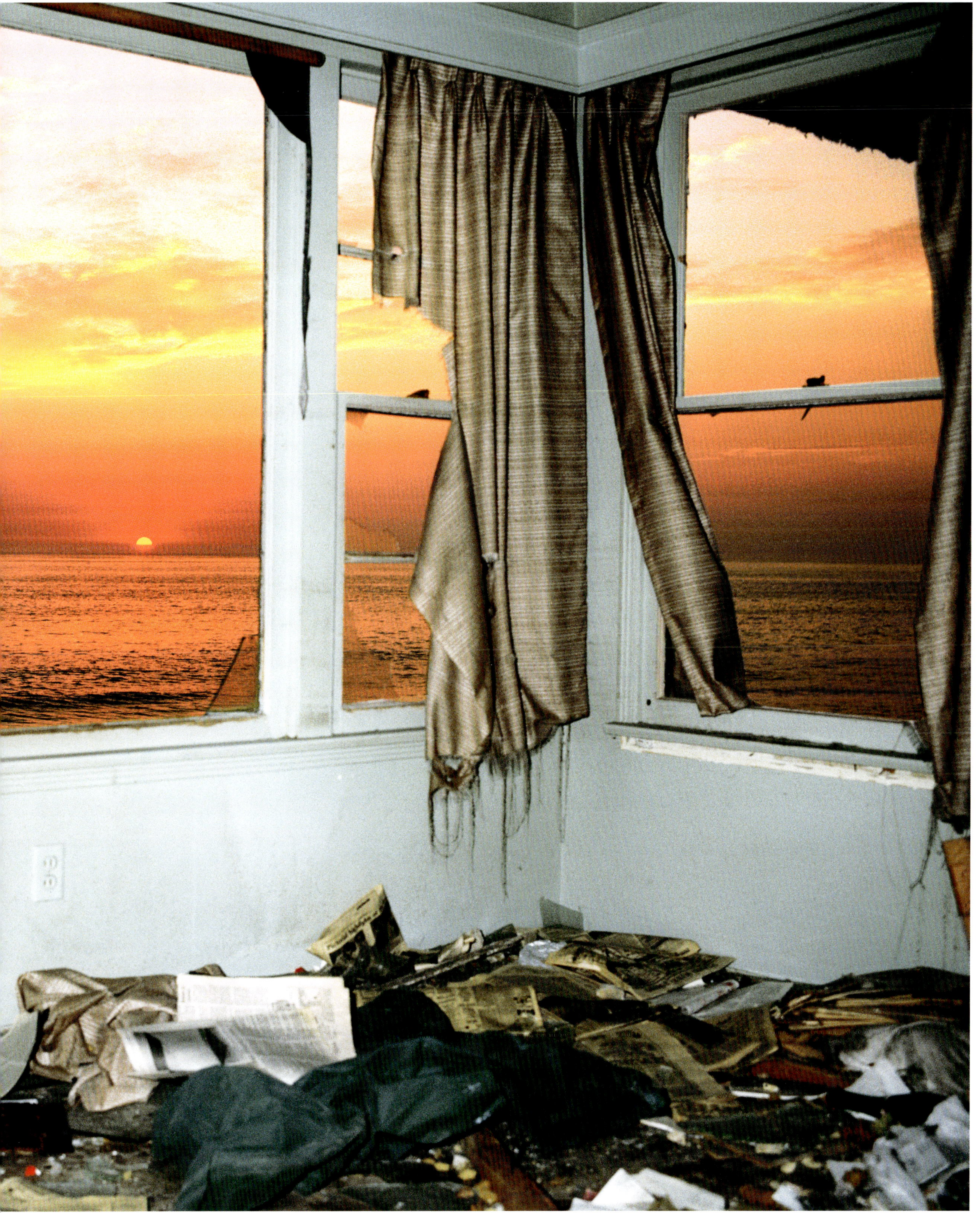

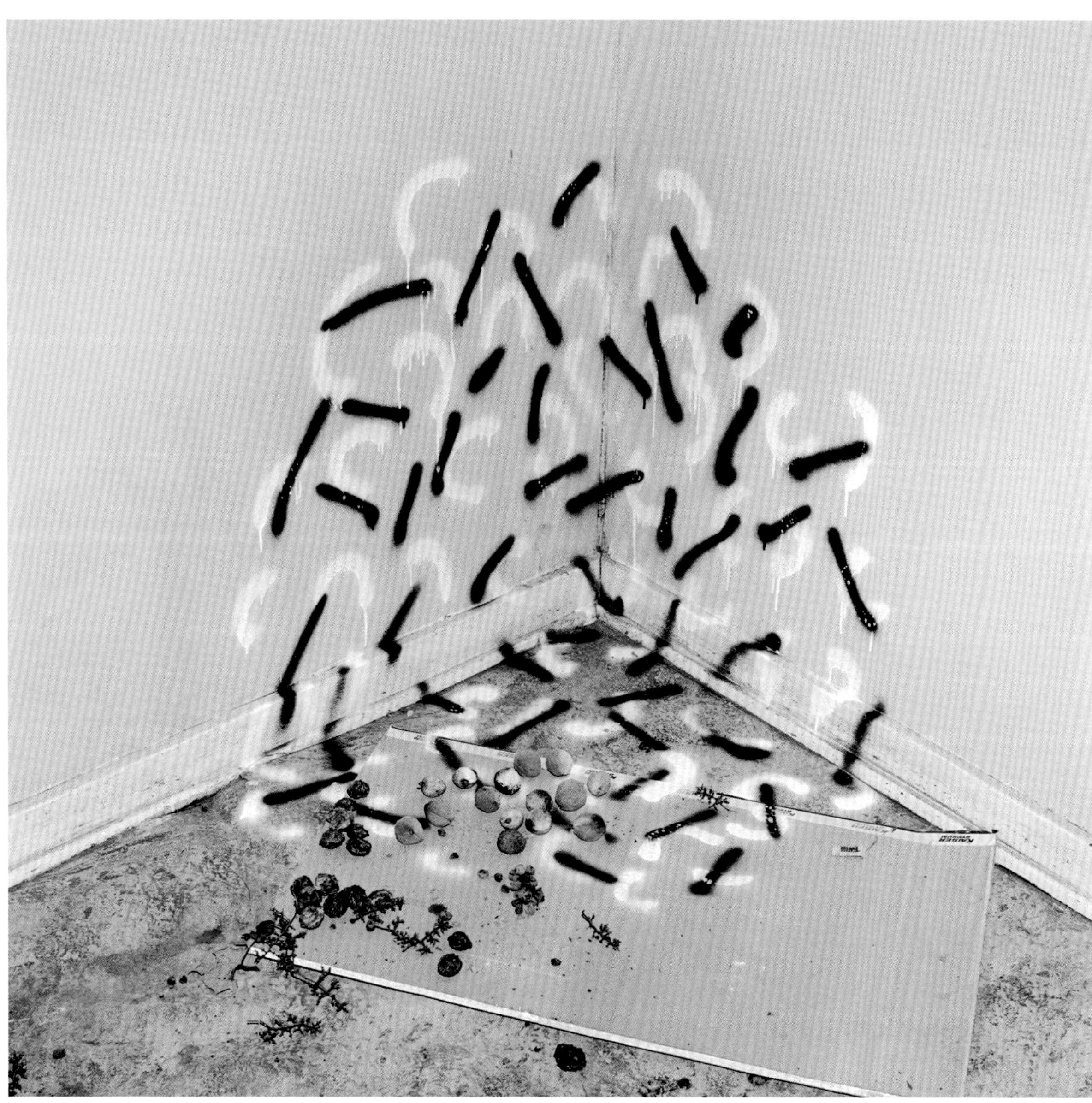

Previous spread:
John Divola, *Zuma #85*, 1977, from the series *Zuma*, 1977–78

This page:
John Divola, *74V54*, 1974 from the series *Vandalism*, 1973–75

Opposite:
Mark Ruwedel, *LA River/ Glendale Narrows #3*, 2015

Overleaf:
Mark Ruwedel, *Sepulveda Fire/Getty View*, 2018
All photographs courtesy the artists and Gallery Luisotti, Santa Monica

AM: **Right, a futile exercise.**

MR: Exactly.

JD: I certainly made some bodies of work that address the nature of Los Angeles as a kind of cultural fact more than others. But when I go out to the desert, for example, I'm often interested in general kinds of existential ideas, not specific historical Los Angeles ideas.

MR: I do think of my desert houses in relationship to Los Angeles. The places I've photographed in the desert form this big arc around the city. For me, they have something to do with this diminished, but still active, notion of the frontier in American culture. The frontier isn't in Los Angeles anymore. You define that edge—that, I think, still speaks to that ideology and to the history of expansion and colonization of the American West. You go east, head north.

AM: **You both produce work that demands a certain level of physicality—walking and driving.**

JD: Yeah, it's physical. I tell my students all the time: You get in your car, and you've got the gear in the back, and you start driving around. And you say to yourself, Well, that's pretty interesting, but I'd have to get out the tripod, I'd have to set up the camera. It's not that interesting. So you drive.

And finally you say, Okay, I gotta get out of the car because I've been driving forty-five minutes. You stop somewhere no more interesting than where you were the first few minutes, and you set up the camera, and you look at the thing you stopped for. But then all of a sudden you look behind you and you go, Oh, wait a minute, look over there, and so you start moving through the landscape.

And there's something about moving through the landscape with a kind of visual concentration that is really almost addicting. There's something about it that's not quite the same as going for a hike. I always tell them the hardest part is getting out of the car.

MR: Yeah, especially for LA kids. It's always a challenge. And I would agree with that addiction thing. For some of the photographs I've taken of the Los Angeles River the last couple years for this project *Rivers Run Through It* (2014–present), I've been back at least twenty times. I keep thinking, I can't go again because I'm going to just make the same pictures over and over. And then it rains and I think, I gotta go and see what happened.

AM: **Right. That relates to notions of chance and improvisation, which come into play in your work.**

JD: When you talk about the collective nature of Los Angeles, it's all about a form of chance in relation to coming across things that are kind of predestined or figured out in some way.

If I go into a building and somebody's kicked holes in the wall looking for copper wire, where the holes and the wire are going to be is up to chance. It's chance in relation to where the sun is oriented when I walk in, and how the light's coming in there. It's all chance.

You're probably not a photographer if you're not looking to embrace it. I'm clearly improvising when I decide what color spray paint to use [as in the series *Vandalism* (1973–75) and *Zuma* (1977–78)].

MR: And you're painting based on something that's there.

JD: Yeah, I'm responding. I go into a room and go, Okay, I've got a few spray-paint cans here, what can I do when I activate this space, or what might I do? So it's purely improvisational, but always in relationship to the language of the photograph. I'm not trying to make the room interesting. I'm trying to make an interesting photograph.

AM: **I'm curious about the initial impulse you had to paint.**

JD: I had been photographing silver butane tanks, and I looked at the photographs, and there's just something unique about when you photograph something silver on a silver print. It's literally silver. I thought, This phenomenon is interesting. Why should I drive all over and look for a bunch of silver butane tanks? I could just paint anything.

This was in 1973. There were lots of abandoned houses. There was a big recession in Los Angeles. People would buy a house, and like one room would burn off, and they owed more than the house was worth, and they'd just leave. So they were available. I didn't have money for a studio, so I would just go into abandoned houses.

MR: A studio wouldn't have worked anyway because there would have been nothing to create.

JD: No, but I might have been making another kind of work and not been out driving around.

In the late 1960s and early '70s, I would photograph in the San Fernando Valley—people watering their lawns and bushes, and garage doors. I was frustrated by the reading of those images as documentary. I was interested in process. I was interested in the fact that I would move through these environments, make these imprints, and bring back these remnants of an engagement.

And people always looked at them and read them as, somehow, a commentary on the subject. In fact, I think that dissatisfaction or frustration probably led me to experiment with moving into *Vandalism*. Now I look back at that work, and I am totally interested in the documentary because time does add to that kind of work.

AM: **Mark, your engagement with the city began more recently.**

MR: I started photographing the city as a city, as opposed to the desert, roughly ten years ago. This has something to do with this very long relationship I've had with Ed Ruscha's books, which goes back to my undergraduate painting years.

When I first moved here, I'd be driving around doing this or that. I'd see some particular apartment. I'm fascinated by all of the vernacular architecture here, but it just reminds me of those little books. I'd say, I should do something about that.

And then somebody gave me a Yashica Mat twin-lens camera, which was the exact same model camera that Ruscha had used for all those books. Actually, I took it as a sign from God that I should do this work.

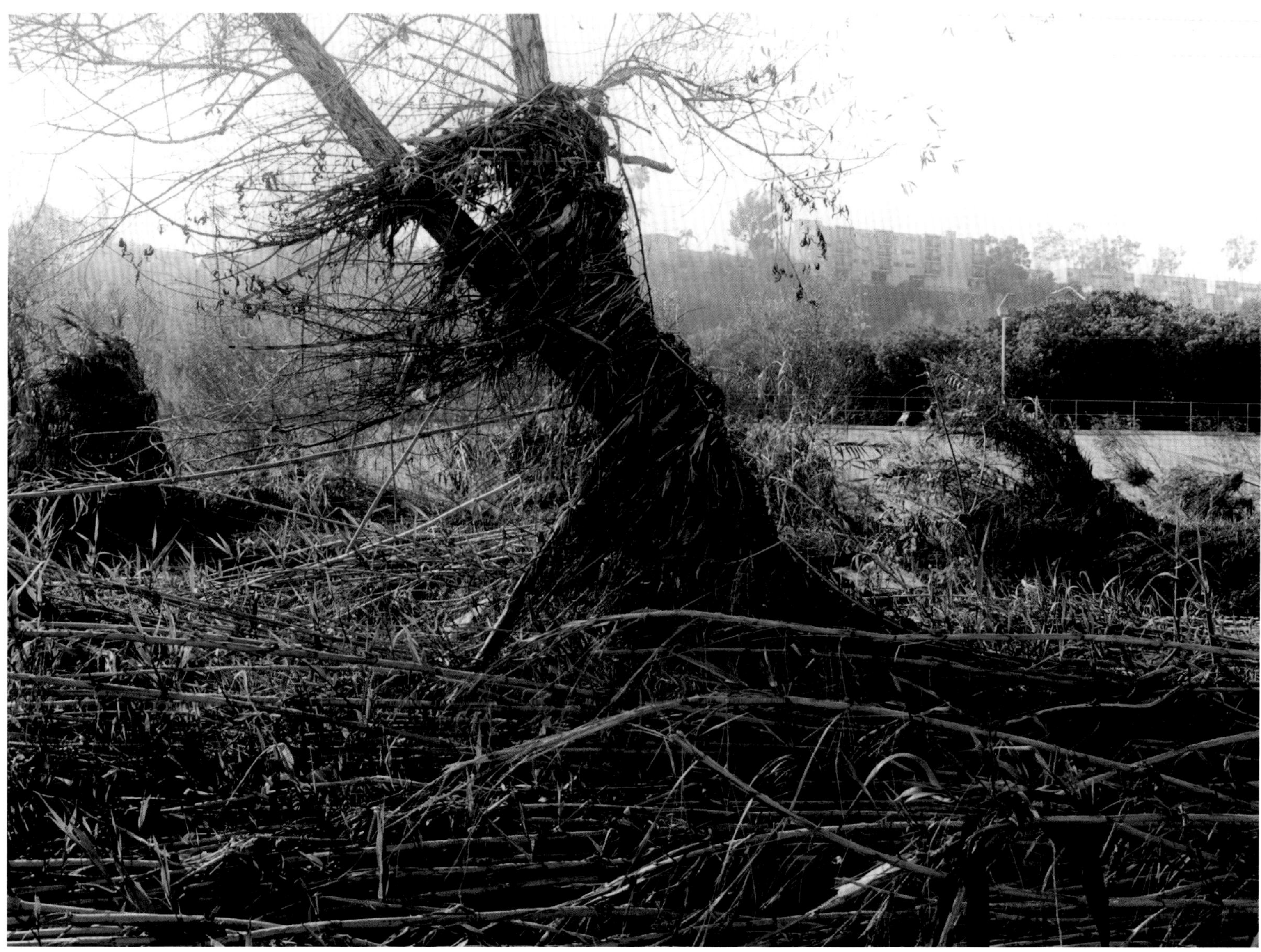

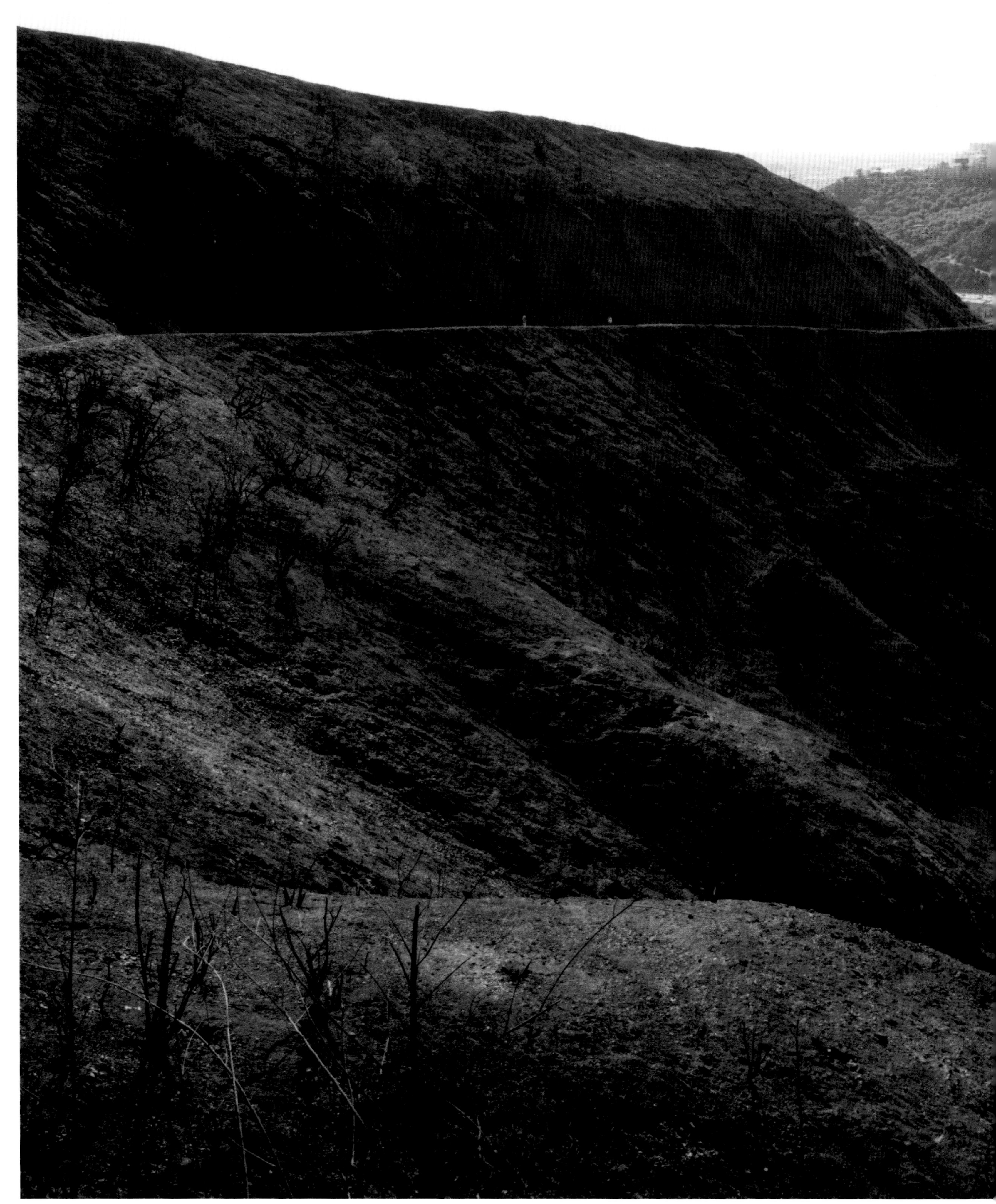

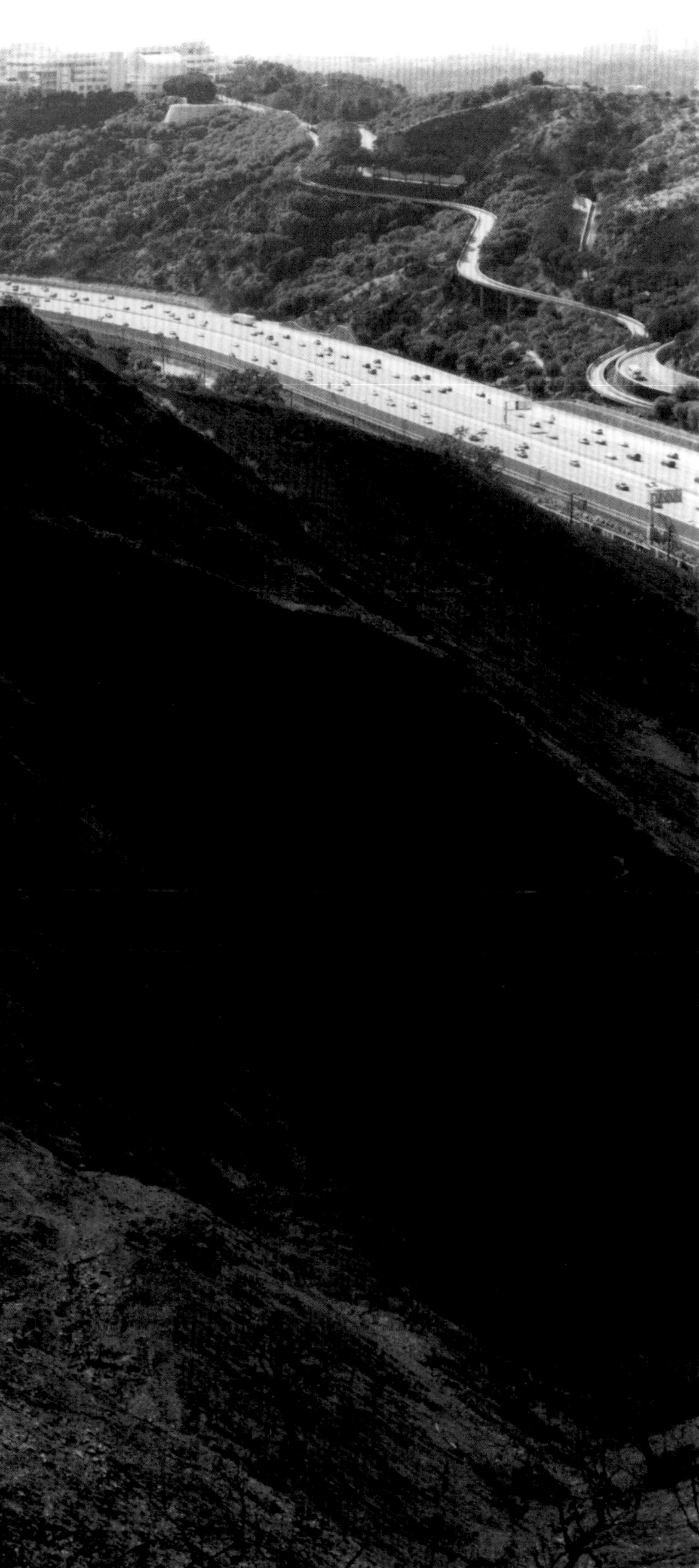

JD: God is Japanese? [*laughter*]

MR: And of all of the tens of thousands of funky, interesting, and odd apartment buildings, how would you choose? But I wasn't choosing.

AM: **It's constrained.**

MR: It's almost like a map, you know? Anyway, shortly thereafter I was asked by a friend who had just walked across Los Angeles—seventy-two miles from Westchester to the San Bernardino Metrolink—if I wanted to photograph the route. I sort of entered that idea quite slowly but became totally addicted to it.

He walked that path for over four days, and I photographed that same line for over two years. And of course, again, in this case, I was literally following a map. Partly through just the nature of the geography, but also as a result of very careful planning. The route was chosen to cross boundaries and borders—natural, economic, cultural, et cetera. I learned a lot more about Los Angeles and the visual tapestry of it.

More recently, I've devised a large project that would be in four parts, dealing with what I thought were four really significant landscapes that define Los Angeles physically and geographically, if not culturally as well. I made pictures of these places in the Palisades where houses are missing. There's just a concrete pad and a kind of slide ... or the street is buckled.

Then we have these amazing fires. Like the fire across from the Getty. I photographed that landscape just weeks after the fire, and it was all black. And I go up now, and I look, and it's all green already. I'm photographing in black and white; I could still make it look black. But it's now fuzzy instead of hard.

AM: **Has anyone photographed LA in a thorough way?**

JD: Google. [*laughter*]

AM: **The Google vans.**

MR: Maybe it's an impossibility.

JD: There's this thing about LA, which is its fictive representation. It's really been the center of contemporary visual culture for the last one hundred years. It is a kind of fictive ground for all kinds of notions of this place.

And, I think, kind of more substantially—not to get all Baudrillard on you—even if you live here, it's the direct experience of having driven through LA. I think that's an interesting idea as well, to see how it's constituted in culture.

MR: My favorite series by Robert Adams is *Los Angeles Spring* (1986), but almost none of those pictures were made in Los Angeles. A lot of them were made in Los Angeles County, but even that's a bit of a stretch for some of them.

JD: Yeah, some are of San Bernardino County.

MR: There's Redlands, Upland, Riverside, and then, weirdly, Long Beach. When somebody asks me about this landscape project when I say it's about Los Angeles, they'll ask, "What do you mean by that?" There are different ways I can define Los Angeles. There's a city, there's a county, there's a culture.

Amanda Maddox is Associate Curator, Department of Photographs, at the J. Paul Getty Museum, Los Angeles.

Anthony Hernandez

Glen Helfand

There are truthful stereotypes embodied in Los Angeles. Two are particularly instructive for looking at Anthony Hernandez's recent photographs: The first is how your social position in this vast metropolis is defined by mobility, through your movement through the sprawl. The second is that this is truly a city driven by images.

Back in the late 1970s, Hernandez, a native Angeleno, created a series called *Public Transit Areas* (1979–80) in which he photographed bus stops with varying numbers of passengers waiting for the RTD (Rapid Transit District). The black-and-white images, very much a Southern California version of street photography, capture the barren expanses of four-lane boulevards, desolate sidewalks in front of appliance dealerships, litter-strewn embankments, stained concrete, and billboards advertising brands of bargain booze. It's a romantically drab vision of a city where nobody walks.

Except that people do: old people, poor people, people of color. They wait for the bus, braving the unrelenting UV rays, the gray filter of smog, and the uncaring whoosh of vehicles, steered by oblivious air-conditioned drivers listening to pop songs on the radio. These are pictures of social vulnerability and unloved urban landscapes, which Hernandez photographed with a five-by-seven camera, sometimes strapped to the top of his Volkswagen van.

This was a period before Hernandez moved on exclusively to color, before he started to capture well-heeled, teased-haired, 1980s shoppers on Rodeo Drive, before he began to photograph spaces with a formal quietude that would betray their contested use and reveal the surprising chromatics of a homeless encampment or abandoned real estate. He has taken pictures in all corners of his hometown. "LA is my big studio," Hernandez says. "One day I'm in one corner, the next in the middle. It's always interesting."

Indeed. Los Angeles is also a city in constant flux, full of teardowns and makeovers. For decades, the transit system has been in steady overhaul. Now there's even a workable subway, with stations augmented with brightly colored public art, and bus stops that shade from the sun even if they have design tricks to discourage long-term lingering. Hernandez's recent series *Screened Pictures* (2017–18) finds him revisiting places he's been before, picturing public transit areas from a contemporary standpoint. What was once a seeming wasteland is full of pixelated color and lush abstraction. Street life, it seems, is currently kaleidoscopic, though still uncomfortably complicated.

Hernandez took these pictures through the metal mesh that forms the permeable walls of these outdoor waiting rooms, capturing the landscape from the position of expectant passengers. The perspective offers a startling contrast to his earlier pictures—arid breezes pass through the perforations, which give the images a digital appearance (despite the fact that they were shot on film, using a Hasselblad with 120mm, 150mm, 180mm, and 500mm lenses, and are not digitally manipulated photographs). "It's like having a filter to see LA in a new way," he says.

Some of the images, including the earlier bus stop pictures, are wildly colorful: they reveal a playground across the street, a verdant corner park, the blue stripe of branding on gas station architecture, palm tree silhouettes, stylish outdoor furniture, and art-directed advertisements for luxury watches.

It wouldn't be LA if there weren't abundant ironies butting up against it all. The visual filters cannot obscure the continued presence of people who could never afford a Tag Heuer, much less rent. Through the metal screen you can still make out a slumping pup tent and bracing, unmistakable evidence of disenfranchisement.

Hernandez is quick to point out that the images break up into abstraction the closer you get to them. It's an optical illusion. But it's real. Just like LA.

Glen Helfand is Associate Professor at California College of the Arts, Oakland.

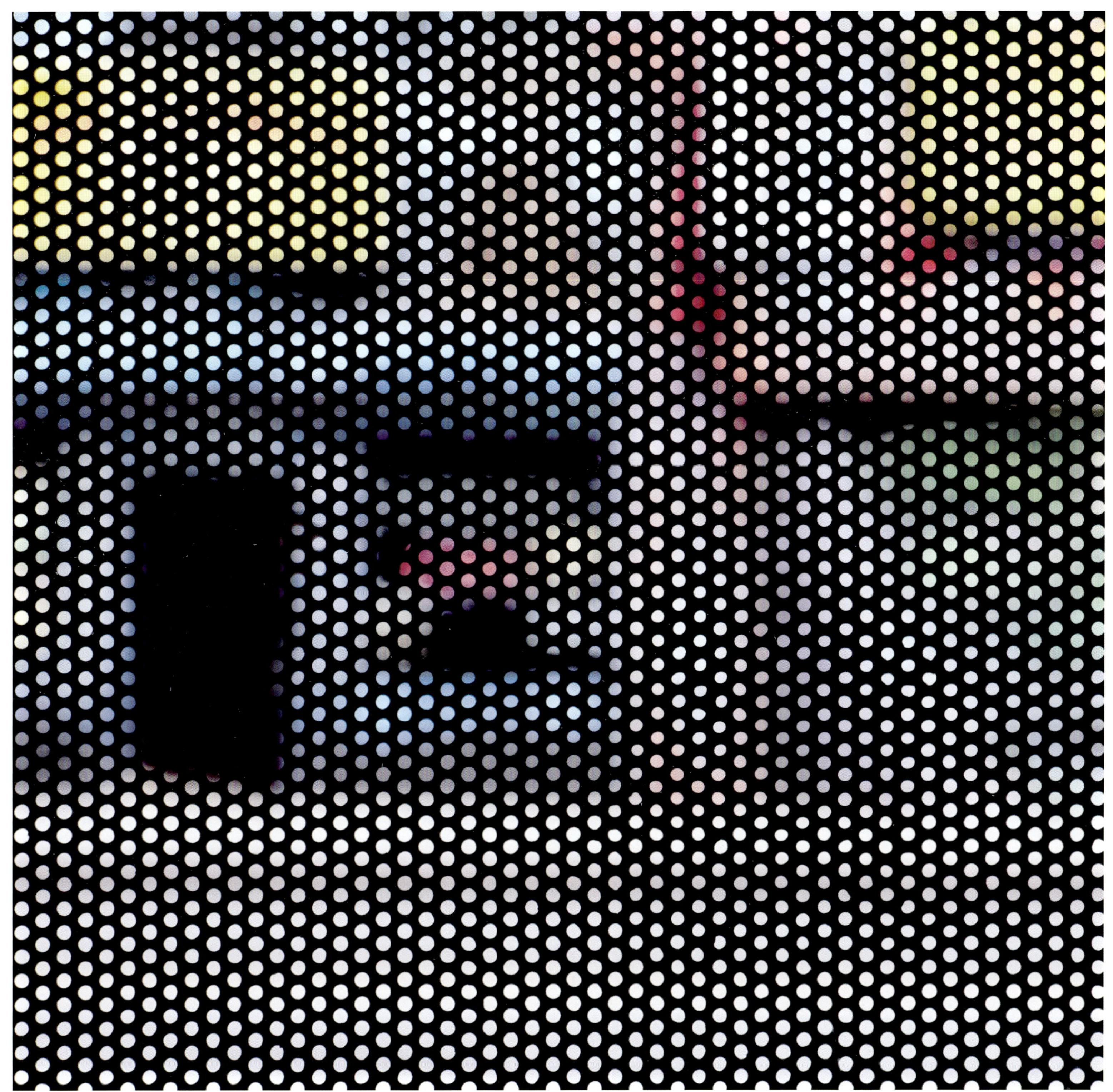

Screened Pictures #1, 2017

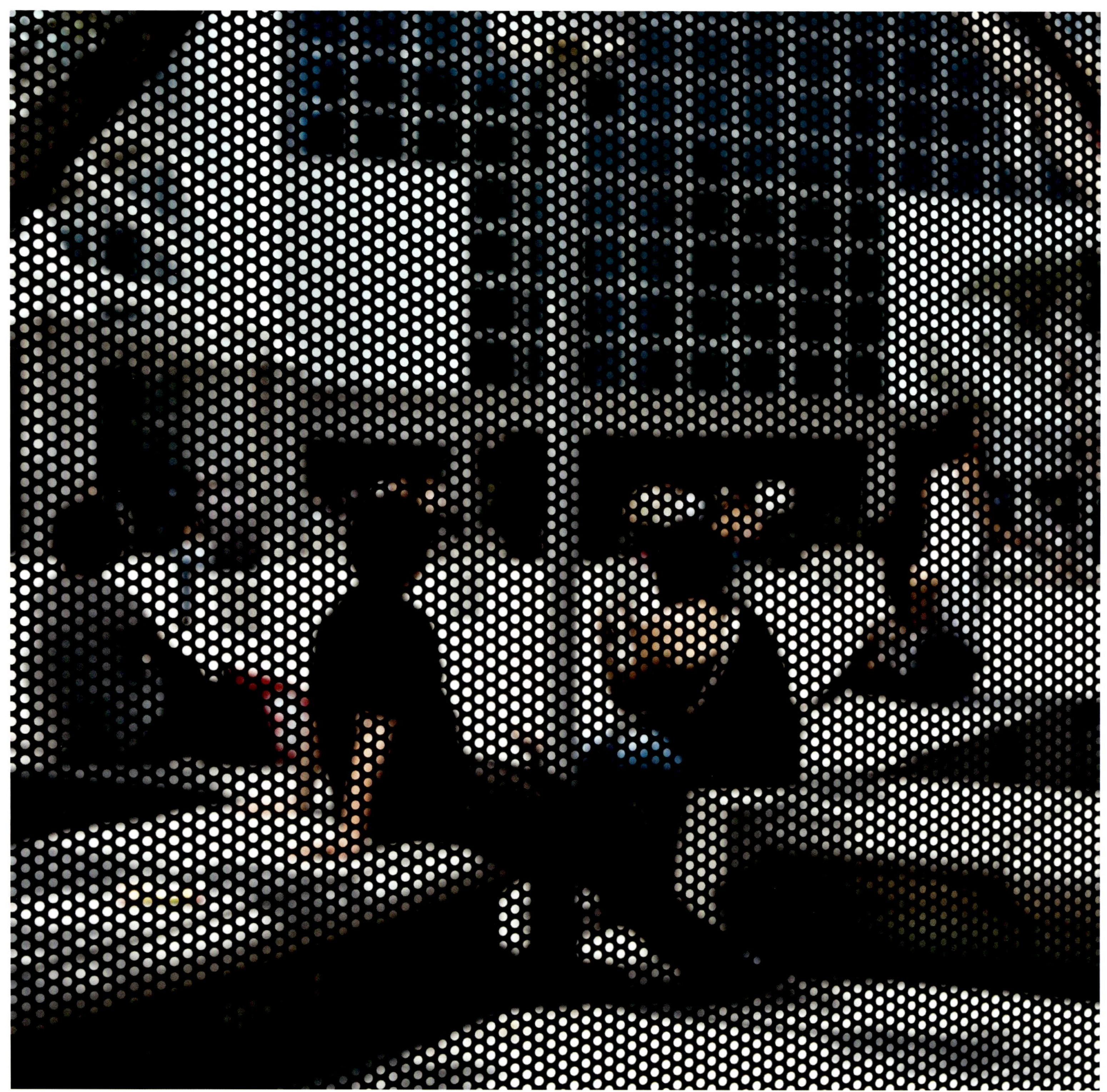

Screened Pictures #19,
2017

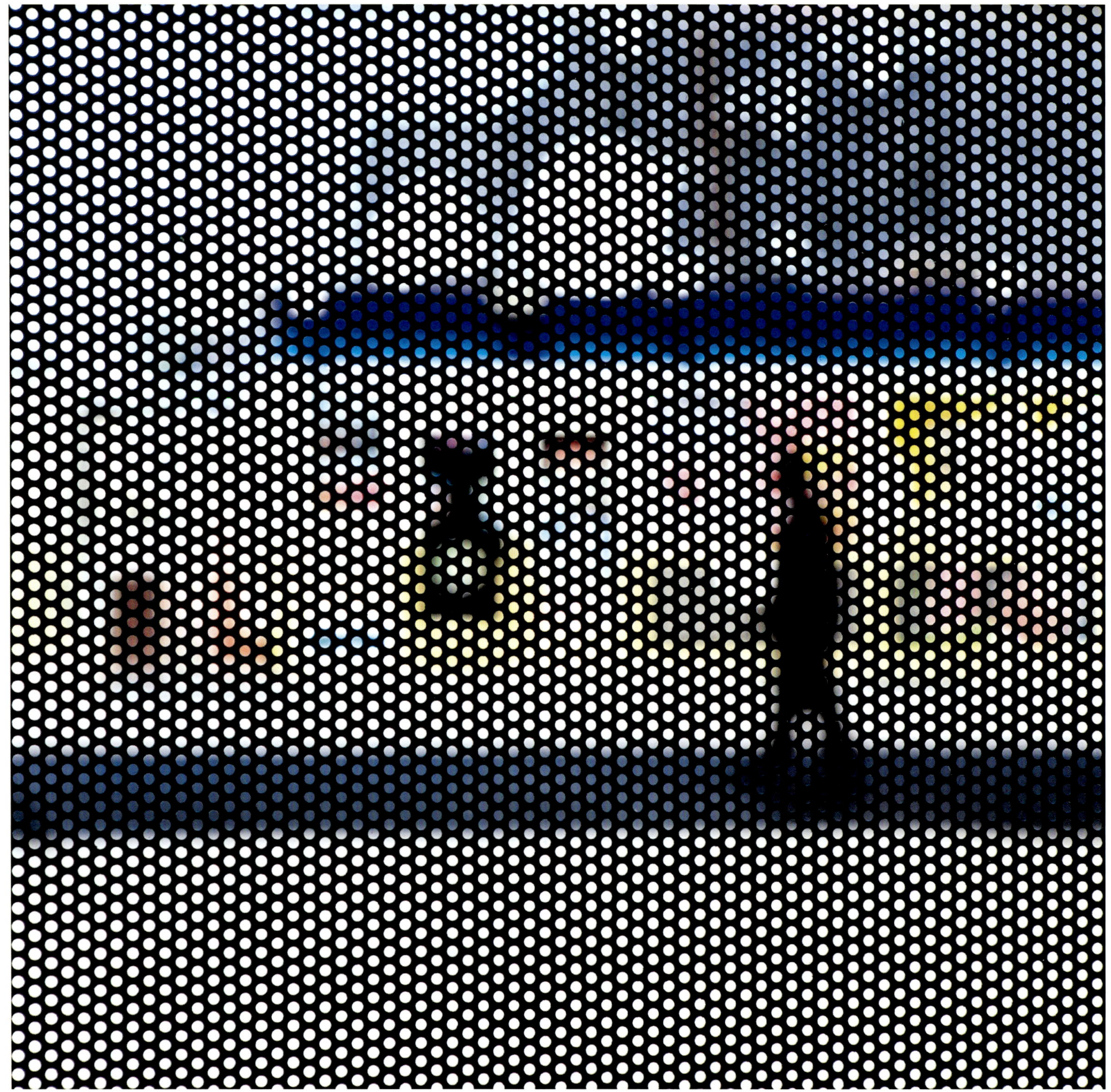

***Screened Pictures #37*, 2018**
All photographs courtesy the artist and Thomas Zander Gallery, Cologne

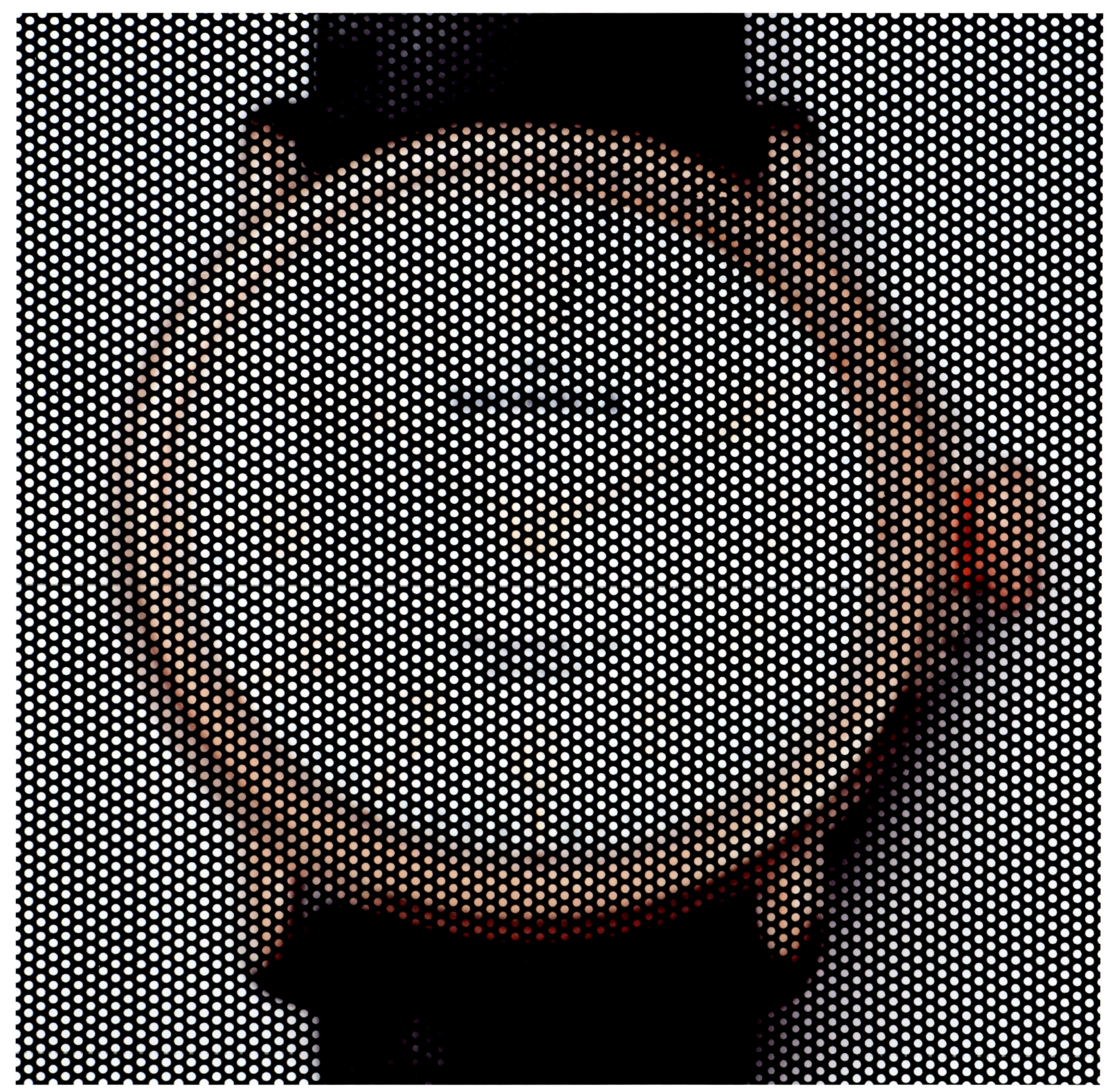

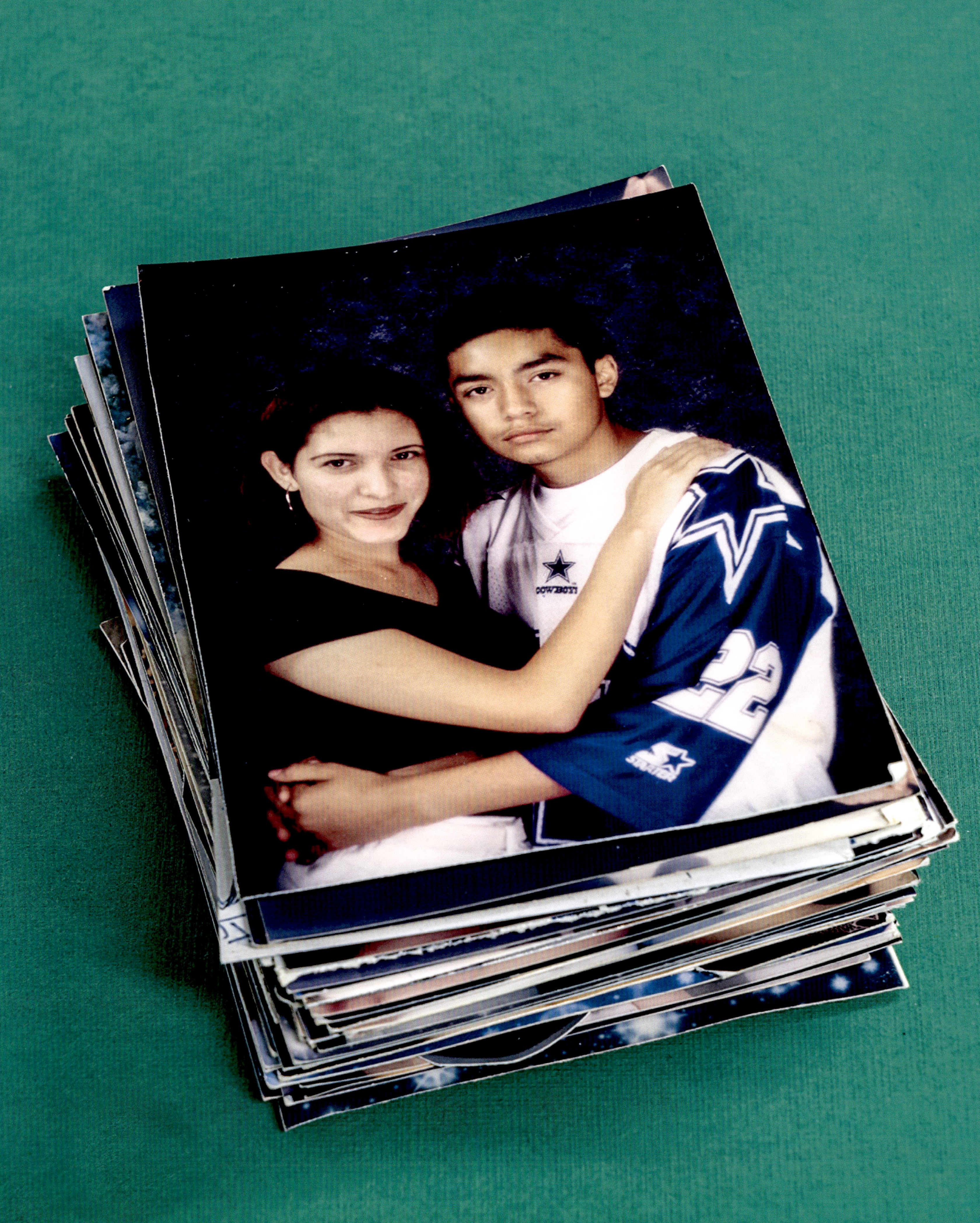
22

Back in the Days

Guadalupe Rosales and her archive of Chicano life in Los Angeles

Carribean Fragoza

Guadalupe Rosales moved to New York with little more than a stack of wallet-sized photographs to remind her of home. She'd left Los Angeles in 2000, a few years after her cousin, Ever Sanchez, was stabbed to death at a party. Nearing her twenties, at the beginning of a new millennium, she decided to relocate her life to New York, where she'd remain living for over a decade. During that time, as she came of age away from the violence that had marked her youth, she held on to those photographs not only as reminders of unresolved trauma, but also as important links to her past.

The photographs, given to her by family and friends she had grown up with in the Los Angeles neighborhood of Boyle Heights, were all made in a similar "glamour-shots style" using hazy filters. In the pre-selfie era, young people would flock to their local malls wearing coordinated outfits, sharply outlined lips and eyebrows, and meticulously teased perms to pose with friends in front of ambient backdrops. The diffused lighting spared them from blemishes, including emotional ones, and saturated the images with sentimentality that with time would turn into acute nostalgia.

Photographs in Guadalupe Rosales's studio, Los Angeles, 2018
Photograph by Mike Slack for *Aperture*

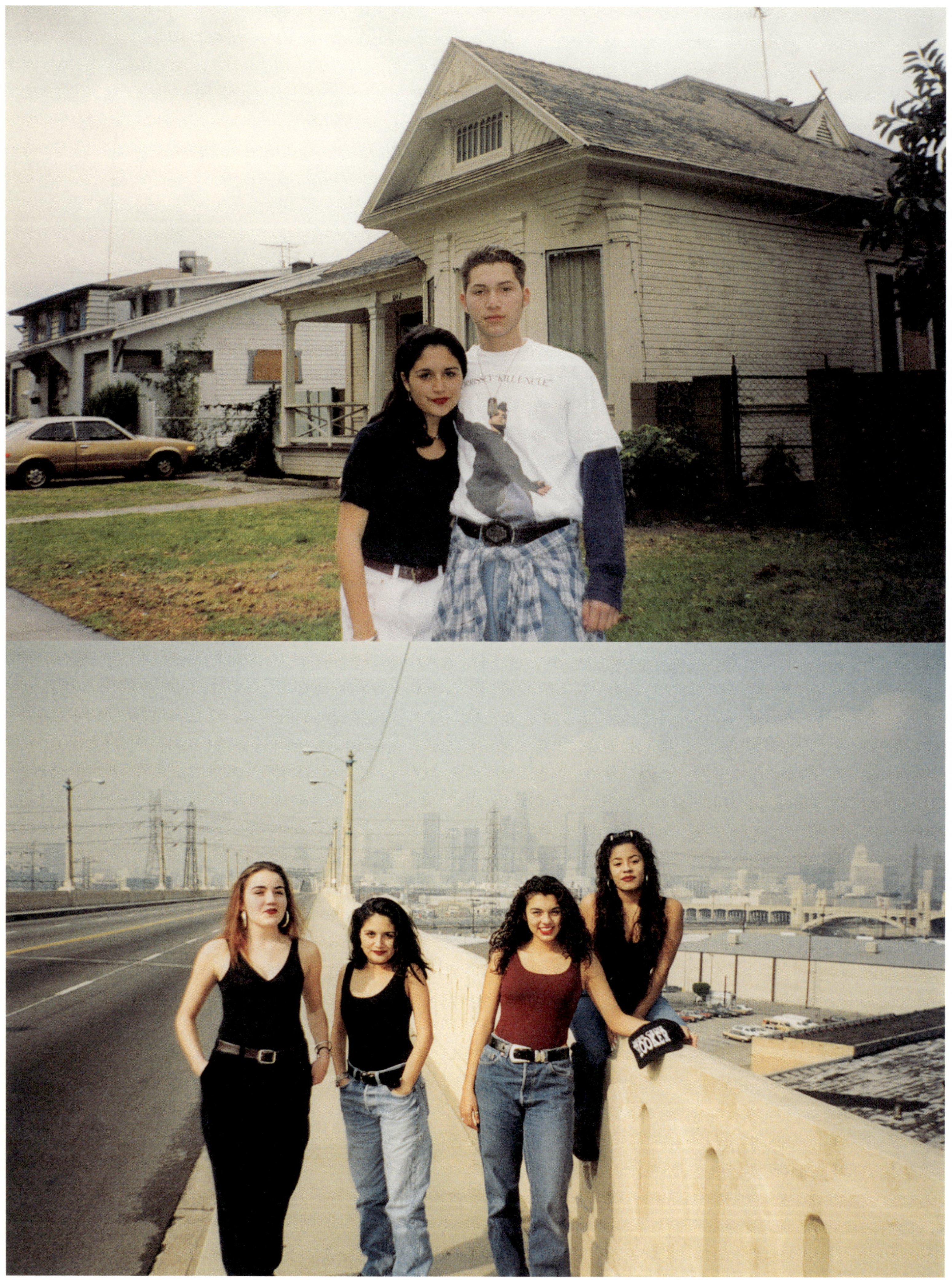
"KILL UNCLE"

For Rosales, these photographs were placeholders for a history that had yet to be told. Their pull eventually compelled her to come back home to LA. "I was thinking a lot about my crew days," she told me. "And I was always attracted to photographs not just for their images, but also for the notes written on the back. They were like relics; they reconnected me."

In 2015, Rosales started Veteranas y Rucas, an Instagram archive focused on youth culture in LA's Latino neighborhoods. Its point of view is from the women's perspective. She posted photographs from her own collection, along with brief anecdotes, in hopes of eliciting feedback. Before long, she had a steady stream of followers that eagerly shared photographs and memories of their teenage party days in LA in the 1990s. Then, in 2016, she developed a second Instagram project, Map Pointz, to collect images and memories of Southern California raves and party crews.

Rosales's project is twofold: The physical collection of objects that she keeps in her studio consists of thick binders and albums filled with hundreds of party flyers, photographs, and party paraphernalia such as glow-in-the-dark beaded necklaces, pagers, and customized backpacks, along with stacks of magazines that document various youth subcultures. But it's also her Instagram projects, Veteranas y Rucas and Map Pointz, that have quickly grown into expansive and generative digital archives of photographs that document scenes of LA. Both have become multigenerational as followers share photographs of family members and themselves, tracing as far back as the 1910s. In all of the images, we see young women and men expressing and embodying Mexican American culture through fashion and posture in their homes, in the streets, and, of course, at parties. The photographs and comments in combination begin to shape the narrative of these deeply rooted communities that have largely remained unrecognized at best and criminalized at worst.

However, Veteranas y Rucas, says Rosales, was not originally conceived as an archive. While in art school at the University of Chicago and far from home, she began with the idea of creating an installation of a teenage raver's or party crew member's bedroom. But she was also thinking of her work as a broader historical project, using photographs and other objects as documents to show what it was like to grow up in 1990s LA as a young woman of color. "I started the work with the intent of finding material on my own time in the 1990s," says Rosales. "But if you don't have the material, you can't use it."

Though Rosales's process of collecting photographs of these unrecognized communities has largely been guided by instinct, it is in step with the work of radical historians such as José Esteban Muñoz, who called for building an "archive of the ephemeral." In his groundbreaking 1996 article "Ephemera as Evidence: Introductory Notes to Queer Acts," Muñoz posits that contrary to traditional archives that exclude marginal communities—the poor, queer, and colored—an ephemeral archive allows us entry into transient spaces, such as dance floors and cruise spots, where we can begin to find their stories.

While the invisibility of these and other marginalized communities, especially youth, has all but erased them from official history, it also once protected them. The 1990s were dangerous times for young people of color in LA. It was a decade of increasing economic disparity, police brutality, and social turmoil that led up to and followed the 1992 LA riots, along with gang violence and rampant anti-immigration policies that prompted days of student walkouts.

"Kids went underground. At raves and parties, we were creating safe spaces for ourselves when everything like the riots and Prop 187 was going on," Rosales recalls, referring to Proposition 187, a 1994 ballot initiative that would prohibit undocumented immigrants from accessing public services such as education

Opposite, top: Photographer unknown, Booker (right) from the Together We Stand crew and friend (left) from Mind Crime Hookers, Whittier, California, ca. 1993
Courtesy Guadalupe Rosales and Eileen Torres

Opposite, bottom: Photographer unknown, Mind Crime Hookers party crew on 6th Street Bridge, Boyle Heights, 1993
Courtesy Guadalupe Rosales

This page: Photographer unknown, Guadalupe Rosales's cousin, Ever Sanchez (right), and unidentified woman, East Los Angeles, 1995
Courtesy Guadalupe Rosales

The photographs begin to shape the narrative of these deeply rooted communities that have largely remained unrecognized.

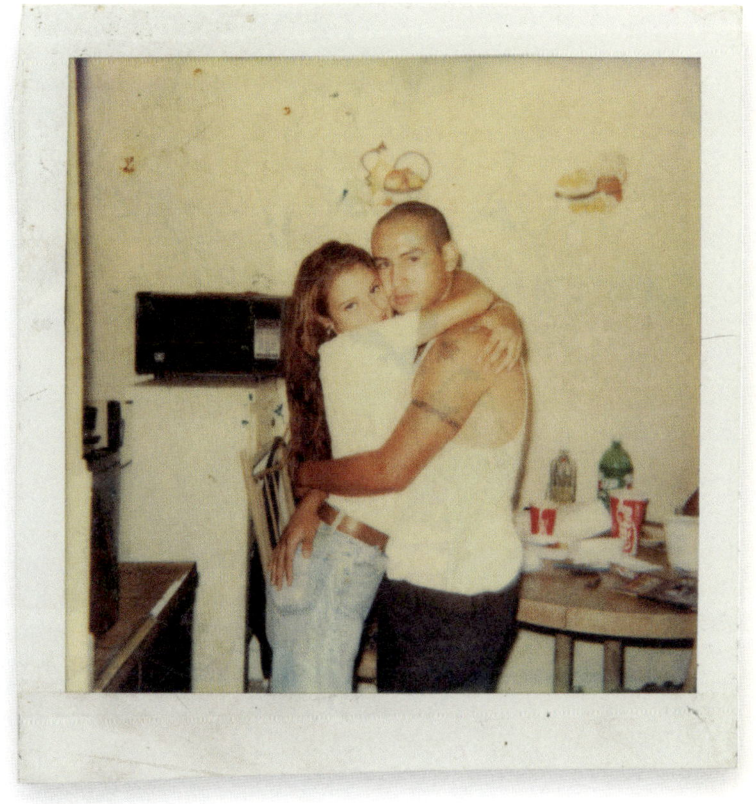

This page:
Photographer unknown, Alma Diaz, Latin Union Car Club, Norwalk, California, 1977
Courtesy Alma and Jash Diaz

Opposite:
Shrine to Ever Sanchez, Guadalupe Rosales's studio, 2018
Photograph by Mike Slack for *Aperture*

and health care. Rosales attended many of these parties when she wasn't going to protests and marches with her mother and sister. Effectively, it was in the underground that youth like Rosales created a world of their own, away from the institutional establishments that had betrayed them.

Map Pointz focuses on the rave party scene. The name refers to what in the 1990s were the coordinates of a party location that could only be accessed by following a specific set of instructions. Flyers often directed partygoers to call a phone number to learn where they would receive an address for the event, usually only hours before the doors opened. The purpose was to keep the location secret from unwelcome party crashers, including police, parents, and rivals.

Party crews would often drive out into the far reaches of Greater Los Angeles, even venturing into Southern California's Inland Empire. "Sometimes we didn't even know where we were going. We'd just carpool and end up in places," recalls Rosales. Very naturally, party culture intersected with Southern California's distinct car culture. Veteranas y Rucas includes many photographs, from across several decades, of young Chicanxs posing with cars, as if this recurring shot marked a coming-of-age or, for women, a display of empowerment. Photographs of young people cruising along LA's Eastside boulevards in customized cars show a weekly urban pageantry of polished chrome, jewel-toned fiberglass, sculpted hairstyles, and the finest hoochie garb. They were parties on wheels.

Veteranas y Rucas includes many photographs of young Chicanxs posing with cars, as if this recurring shot marked a coming-of-age or a display of empowerment.

As these underground parties proliferated and became more sophisticated, they developed an ephemeral infrastructure that suited LA's decentered and transient character. According to Rosales, partygoers became party-promoters who created entrepreneurial opportunities for themselves; amid a barren landscape, they took warehouses gutted by deindustrialization

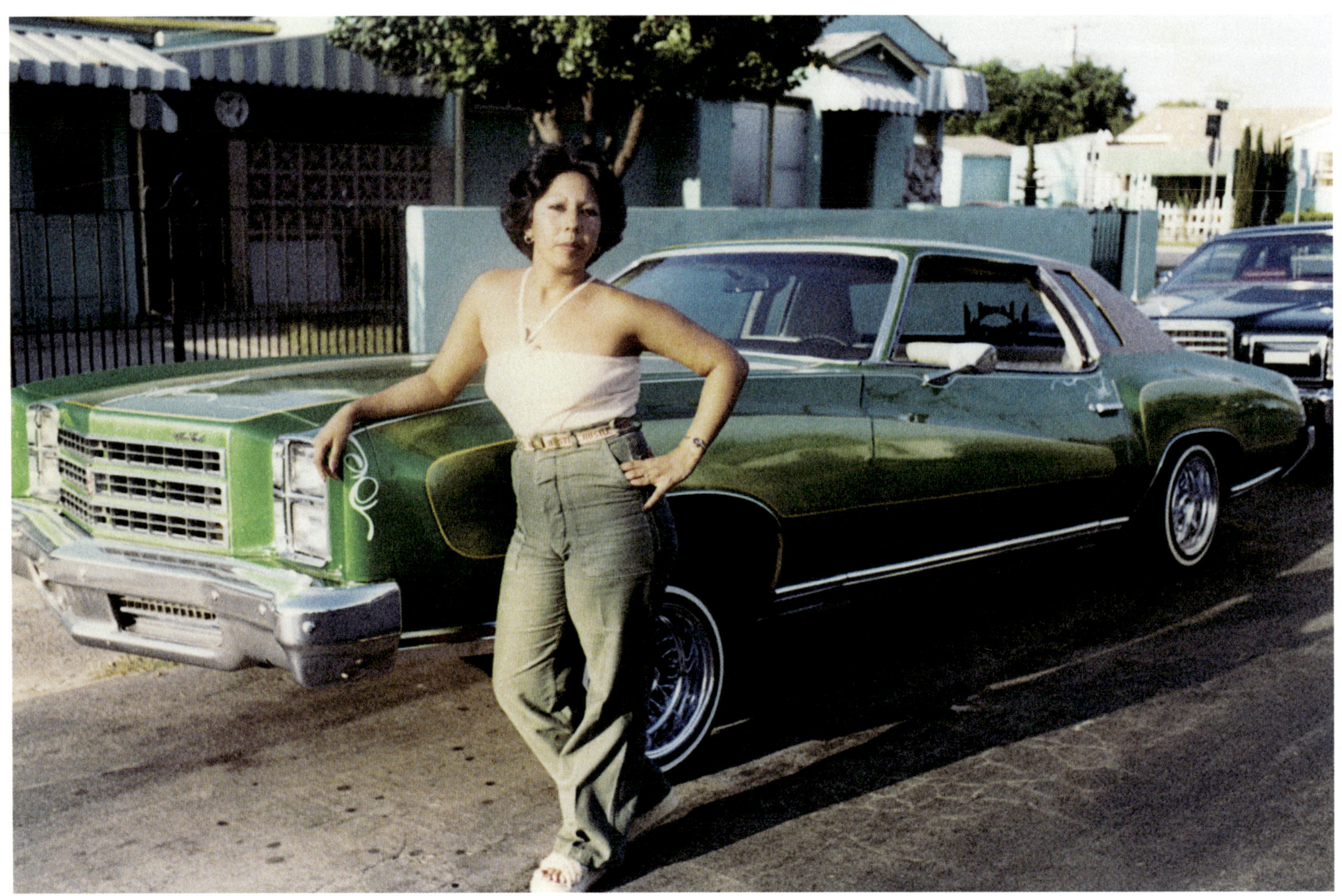

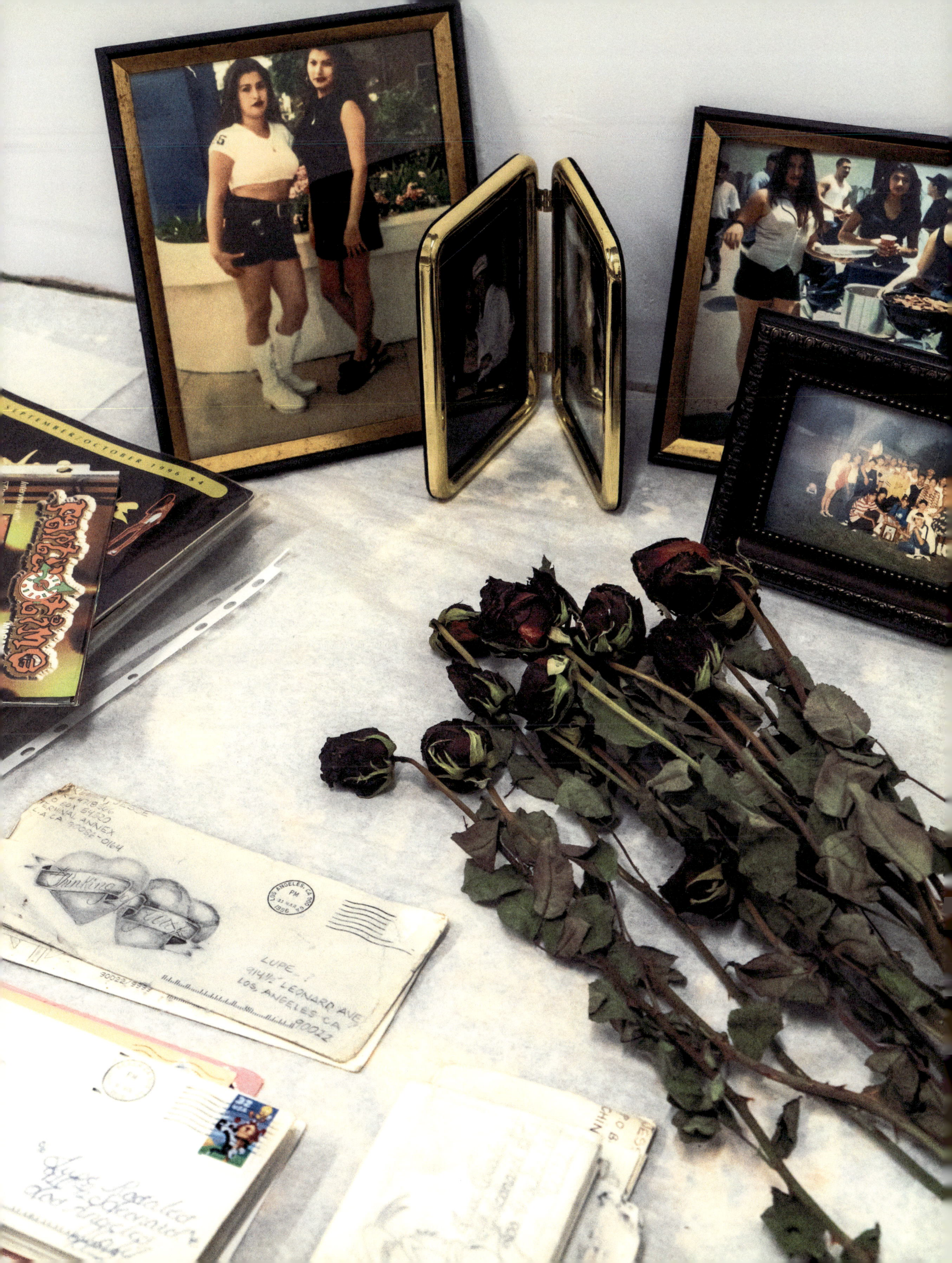
SEPTEMBER/OCTOBER 1996 $4
Thinking
TERMINAL ANNEX
LOS ANGELES, CA
PM
1996
LUPE
914½ LEONARD AVE
LOS ANGELES CA
90022

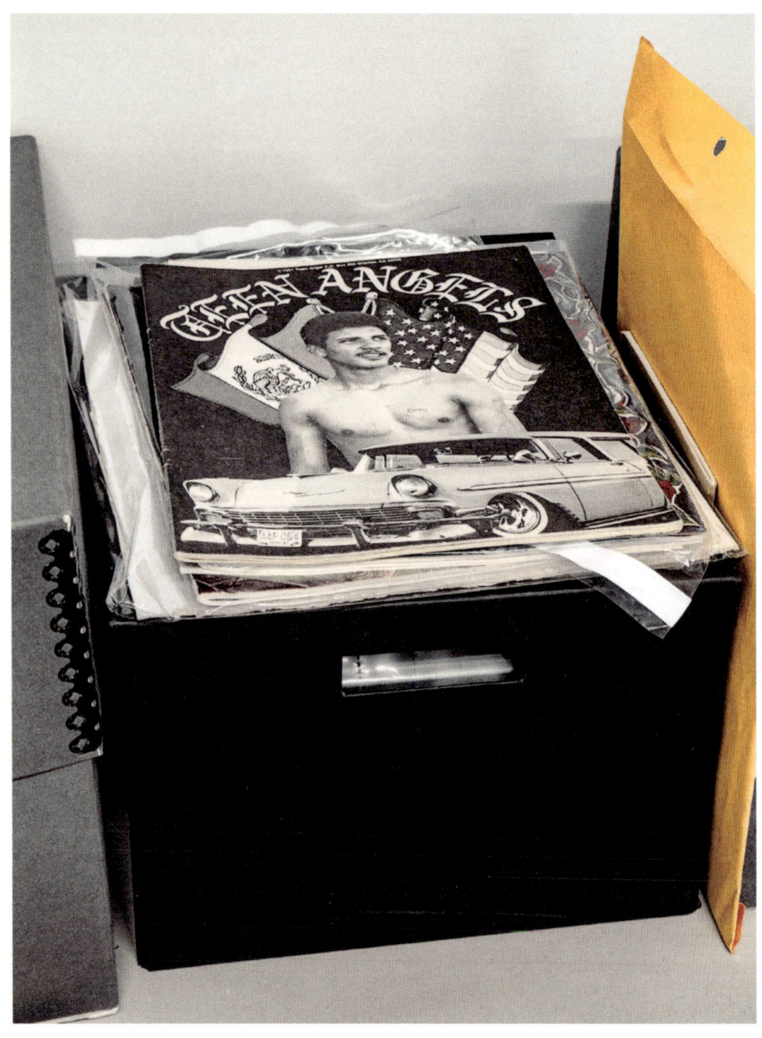

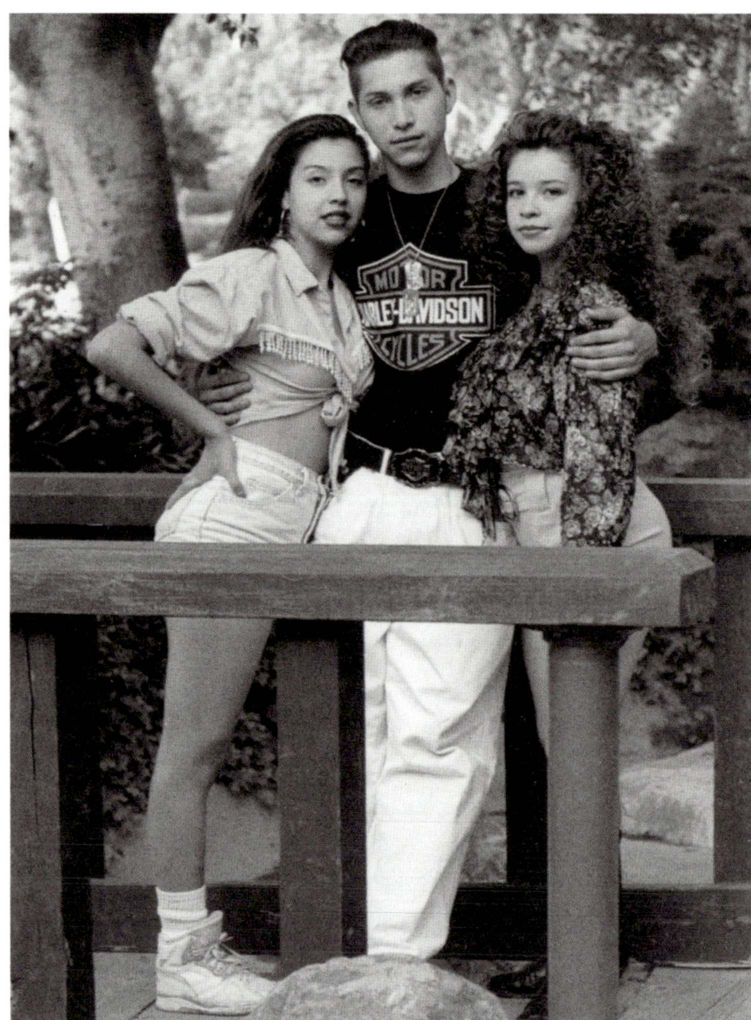

and transformed them into temporary venues for large-scale events, turning these underground scenes into businesses. They taught themselves, and each other, skills as they photographed, laid out, and published their own magazines. They designed their own flyers, booked venues, and found creative ways to promote carefully planned events. "These parties were being organized by teenagers using their own resources," Rosales says. "Schools were not providing us skills. The party scenes allowed us to develop these skills."

Concurrent with the rise of these cultures, print magazines like *Low Rider*, *Street Beat*, *Teen Angels*, and *Urb* thrived as they documented the various scenes and effectively trained new generations of publishers and photographers. Rosales met one of these photographers, Eddie Ruvalcaba, on Instagram and soon began collaborating with him on an installation project at Commonwealth and Council, a gallery in downtown LA. Ruvalcaba was a self-taught photographer for *Street Beat*. His portfolio extends beyond party scenes, including photographs of daily street life, as well as striking images of the 1992 LA riots and their aftermath. This collaboration is an example of how organic partnerships can grow out of collective archive-building processes such as Rosales's, which are, in fact, part of a growing movement of nontraditional, DIY archive projects dedicated to recovering lost histories.

Rosales and Ruvalcaba held one other thing in common: they were both still coming to terms with the trauma of violence and drug addiction that came to afflict so many of their generation. This is also what brings so many Instagram followers to share their experiences with Rosales, as they attempt not only to ruminate on memories of times past, but to make sense of the chaos they experienced. More than just Instagram projects, Veteranas y Rucas and Map Pointz also involve a process of healing, which is why Rosales continues to hold onto them so closely. She says that though she feels some pressure to conserve the objects in the collection she is building, she is not ready to hand them over to a formal or institutional archive. "The project is still evolving, and it's still a part of me. I feel responsible for these things."

Even today, Rosales guards the stack of wallet-sized photographs, keeping it within arm's reach in her studio as if it were a deck of tarot cards. The ink of the neatly written notes on the back of the photographs is now smudged but still clearly says, again and again, "Keep in touch." And she does.

Carribean Fragoza is a writer from South El Monte, California. Her fiction, poetry, and essays have been published in *BOMB*, the *Los Angeles Review of Books*, and *LA Weekly*.

This page, left:
Magazines in Guadalupe Rosales's studio, 2018
Photograph by Mike Slack for *Aperture*

This page, right:
Photographer unknown, Booker and friends, 1992
Courtesy Guadalupe Rosales and Eileen Torres

Opposite:
Swing Kids party crew from San Gabriel Valley, 1994
Courtesy Guadalupe Rosales and Deborah Meza

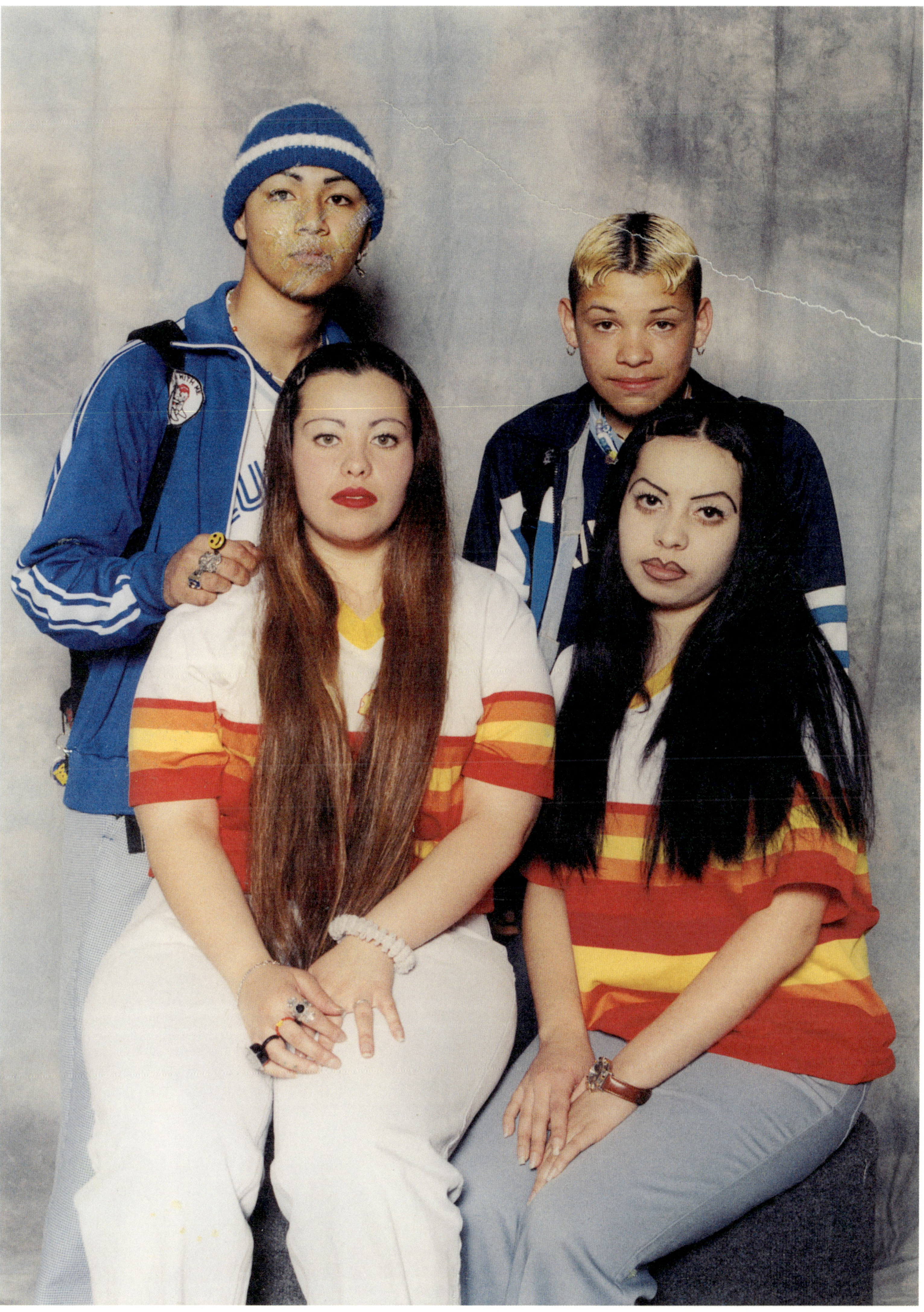

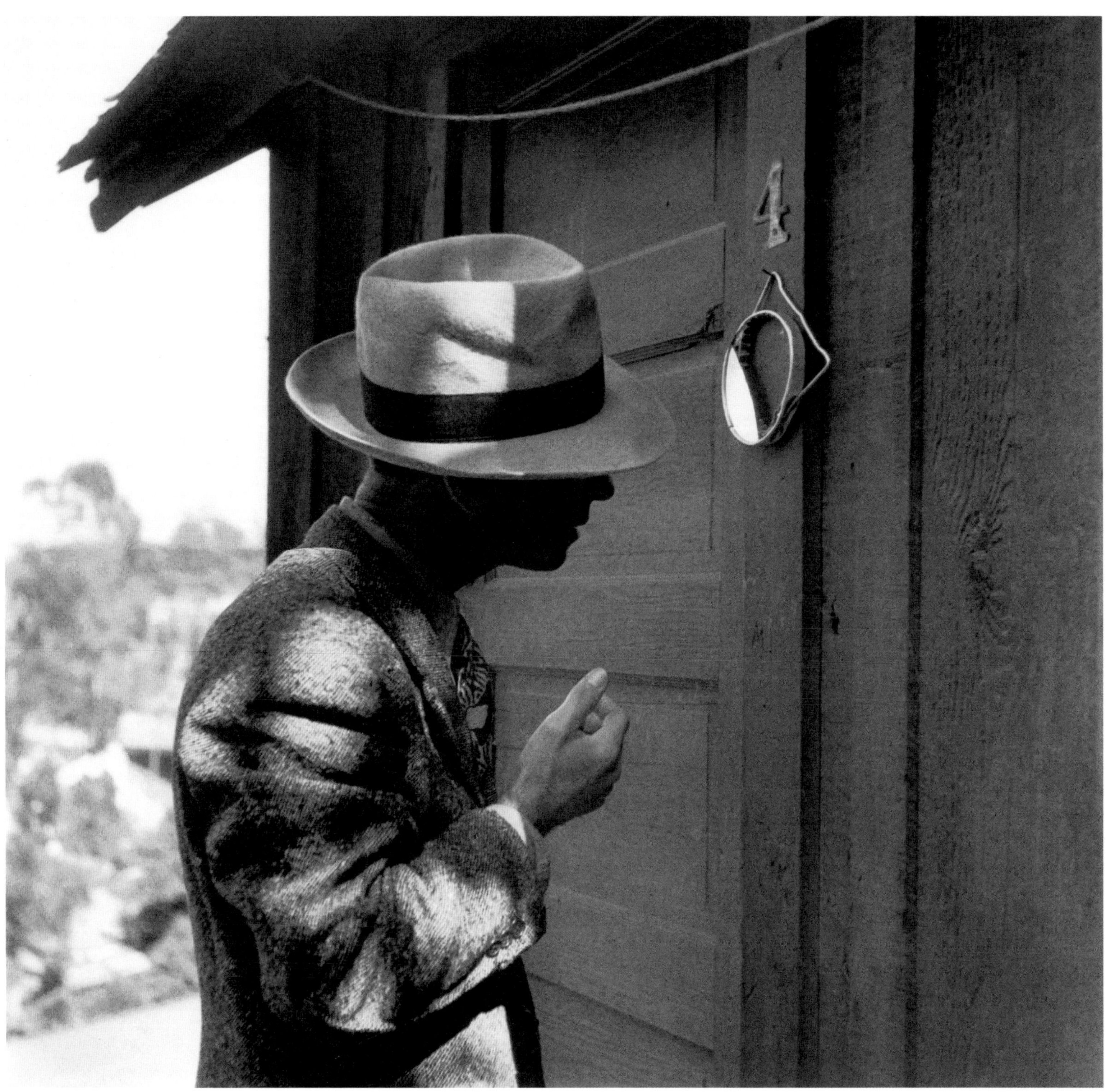

World War II veteran dressed for job search, 1949

In postwar Los Angeles, a young photographer chronicled Mexican American life—in a settlement that would soon be destroyed.

Chávez Ravine

Yxta Maya Murray

In November of 1948, twenty-year-old photographer Don Normark stumbled across a canyon north of Los Angeles and discovered there a pastoral community of Mexican Americans. Born in Washington state and of Swedish stock, Normark would later study in New York under *Harper's Bazaar*'s Alexey Brodovitch, show alongside Dorothea Lange, and, for a short while, live with Edward Weston. Perhaps predictably, when he hoisted his Ciro-flex camera up to the California valley, he saw through its lens a bedraggled paradise: "I began to think I had found a poor man's Shangri-la. It was mostly Mexican and certainly poor, but I sensed a unity to the place, and it was peacefully remote. The people seemed like refugees—people superior to the circumstances they were living in."

Not exactly. The canyon had gone by several names through the years, including Stone Quarry Hills, Cemetery Ravine, and Chávez Ravine, as it would finally be known. Its more than eighteen thousand resident families divided the territory into three parts and called them La Loma, Palo Verde, and Bishop. Many inhabitants had built and owned their own homes, and they fostered a diverse culture; the ravine housed a mix of naturalized and undocumented folks—Latinos, Anglo "bachelors," black people, and Asian Americans.

Lugging his camera from the ravine's lonely paths to its wilderness of vacant lots and bulwarks of tended gardens, Normark spent the next year taking scores of almost unendurably beautiful black-and-white photographs. He found a boy and a girl, both preschool age, who look gilded with sunlight as they plough through a muddy yard. He lensed calla lilies and hydrangeas bedecking a busted house. He snapped two men with expressive eyes, broad-lapelled suits, and abstract-patterned ties, and also a tiny-waisted woman wearing dark lipstick and a victory-roll hairstyle as she arranged a Corpus Christi altar. He captured a World War II vet cooking dinner, a lavish-lipped beauty dressed up in a frothy skirt, a man in a fedora hesitating on a dappled porch, and an effulgent young girl modeling a confirmation gown.

Three and a half years later, two thirds of Chávez Ravine's "peaceful" inhabitants were gone. The government bulldozed the region for a housing project that was never built. Most of the residents sold their properties and scattered, but others watched their houses get taken by eminent domain. The city, particularly LA councilman Edward Roybal, soothed homeowners' anger with promises of the first pick of apartments once they were built. Those who weren't persuaded fled the area because of official intimidation. The remaining unregenerates stayed, locked in a struggle with the city that would later become violent.

The conflict surrounding the community's erasure would be known as "The Battle for Chávez Ravine." The clearance process began in August of 1949, when the Los Angeles City

Johnny Johnson (right) rehearsing Gospel songs, La Loma, 1949

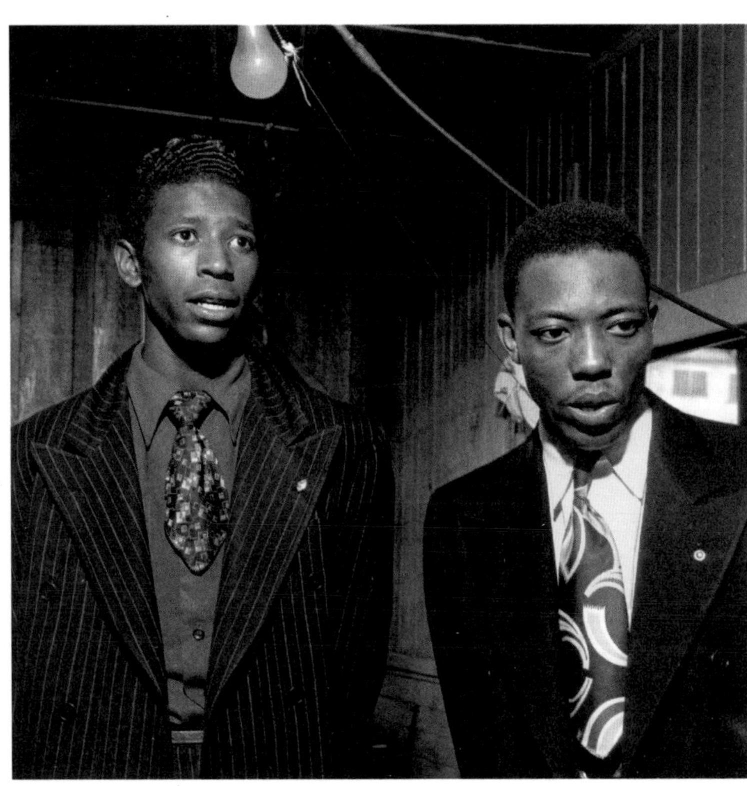

Many inhabitants of Chávez Ravine had built and owned their own homes, and they fostered a diverse culture.

Council approved eleven public housing projects, funded by federal monies authorized by the 1949 Housing Act. Officials declared La Loma, Palo Verde, and Bishop "blighted" and ordered that the neighborhoods be evacuated and renamed Elysian Park Heights. None other than Richard Neutra came on board to plan replacement two-story buildings and thirteen-story apartment towers. Neutra filled his sketchbook with drawings of sleek and featureless designs, and wrote a memorandum describing the area as being full of "human warmth and pleasantness," and inhabited by "Aztecs." He also called it a "slum."

Whether esteemed as romantic refugees by Normark or ornamental obstructions by Neutra, Chávez Ravine's citizens could not escape the aesthetics of *la mission civilisatrice*. Still, the expected pushback did not focus on class or race subjugation: the Neutra projects fell victim to the post–World War II red scare. LA's conservative real estate lobby paired up with the anti-Bolshevik *Los Angeles Times*, and together they railed against the Housing Authority's "creeping socialism." In 1951, the LA Planning Commission held a boisterous series of public hearings on the projects. A year later, the California Senate Fact-Finding Committee on Un-American Activities investigated top brass at the Housing Authority, and then pro-business Norris Poulson was elected mayor.

Normark's serene outcasts did not live up to type during this fracas. Many of the ravine's residents sided with the reactionary real estate lobby, even issuing vague threats at the 1951 hearings. Bishop resident Mabel Hom stressed that "if this plan goes through, I assure you there will be 1,100 families that will not be as American, with attitudes they should possess." Her neighbor, Agnes Cerda, said plainly, "Take our homes away from us and you are taking away our incentive to be good American citizens."

Some of the eleven projects survived this strife, but in 1953 Poulson canceled the contract for Elysian Park Heights, eliminating hope of the promised homes. The land lay fallow for six years. A few stalwarts dug into the canyon. Meanwhile, Brooklyn Dodgers owner Walter O'Malley scoped out LA as a new base for his team. In 1957, the city signed a contract with O'Malley that gave him 315 acres of Chávez Ravine. After two more years, officials extirpated the holdouts: *Los Angeles Mirror-News* photographer Hugh Arnott shot sheriff's deputies hauling a barefoot and disgusted Aurora Vargas down her front stoop. The city broke ground on September 17, 1959.

Normark would later find such success that *Aperture* featured his work in 1964, but his postwar photographs remained dormant until 1999. Over seventy of his images, as well as interviews that he conducted with former residents in 1997, were published by Chronicle Books in *Chávez Ravine, 1949: A Los Angeles Story*. The book reads like a gorgeous time capsule of an innocent and untroubled Latinx indigeneity.

This interpretation proves especially unsettling today, when Eastside Los Angelenos struggle with the gentrification and anti-immigrant policies razing atmospheric Echo Park, Highland Park, and Boyle Heights. Just as realtors' contemporary promotions of East LA's arcadianism need to be corrected with facts about local tenant exploitation, Normark's luminous shots of punched shacks and Catholic beauties cannot be understood without referencing Hom's belligerence or the sight of Vargas getting manhandled by deputies. Absent the balancing information about the residents' protests, a study of *Chávez Ravine, 1949* might convince certain readers that the neighborhoods had been populated by gentle and obedient castaways.

Still, the book hints at these necessary counterreadings. Some of Normark's 1997 interviewees insistently reframed his photographs with their memories. When examining the depiction of the two children in the muddy yard, Henry Cruz said, "You know, a picture like this might look a little depressing to other

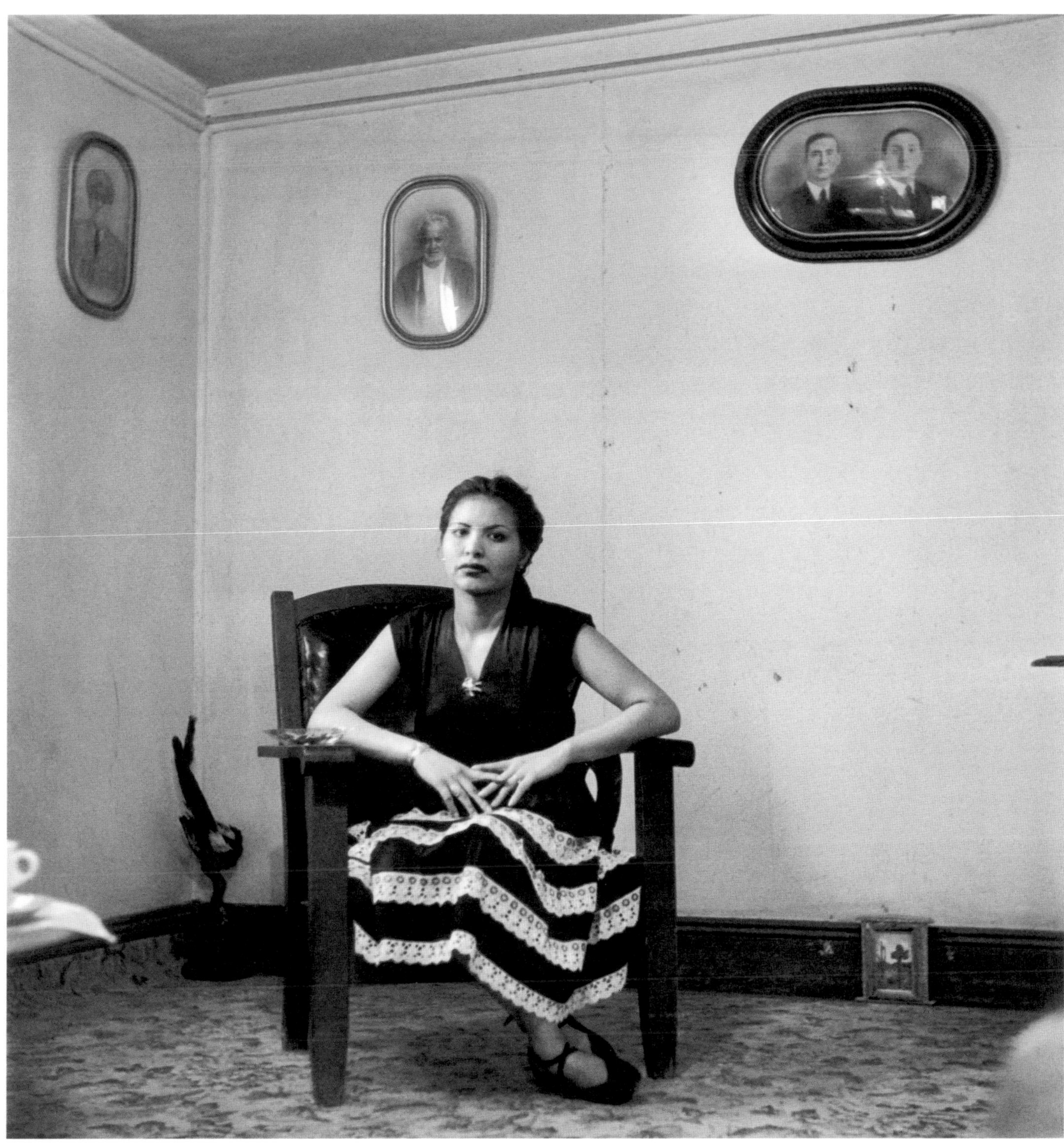

Unknown woman, La Loma, 1949
All photographs courtesy Roselynne Duavit Pasion

people, but not to us.... Look at the expression on those kids." And Sylvia Moyer, while gazing at the image of the calla lilies and hydrangeas foregrounding a home with a tin roof, complained that, in black and white, the picture made La Loma look "sad and grim." But, she said, "On a rainy day you'd hear the rain pounding, while all around it were beautiful flowers and things growing wild. It was just there and suddenly you would notice how beautiful it was."

Every time we describe another person we make a mistake. Perusing a record like Normark's causes equal measures of pleasure and confusion. In the end, Normark's interviewee Rudy Flores probably said it best: "I knew the room I was born in. My mom said, 'You were born in that corner.' ... Once you start selling, it breaks the chain.... What the people were mad about more was the way they went about it. First they wanted to build projects, and we'd get first choice. Then they said an airport. Roybal was our councilman. He would come and tell us one thing and then go down and tell them another."

Yxta Maya Murray is Professor of Law at Loyola Law School, Los Angeles, and the author of the novels *The King's Gold* (2007) and *The Good Girl's Guide to Getting Kidnapped* (2010).

Brian Sholis

Lise Sarfati

Almost a decade ago, French artist Lise Sarfati began photographing young women who had dreamed of life in Hollywood but ended up passing their days on its shabbier corners. Gathered together in her 2010 series *On Hollywood*, the pictures radiate a peculiar intimacy. The stories these photographs punctuate are ambiguous, but Sarfati clearly made them in concert with her subjects—and the women, often seen in close-up, are unquestionably the key protagonists of these narratives.

While that series has much in common with *Oh Man*, completed in 2013, their divergences give the newer pictures a distinct emotional and psychological register. It's not just that these photographs depict men. It's also that "the relationship of the character to the exterior world," which the artist claims as an ongoing preoccupation, is both different and harder to define. These men are enveloped within interior lives we cannot access, and Sarfati underscores the fullness of their solitude by keeping her distance from them. While they are at or near the center of each composition, they seem to slip from the pictures' bounds.

It can be difficult to separate her protagonists from our presumptions about them, especially the class connotations of having to walk under a California sun so pitiless that it plays its own role in these quiet dramas. Sarfati, however, is clear about her intentions and how her formal choices convey them. Though she spent two years wandering downtown LA just before the current wave of gentrification, she didn't want the work to be perceived as a commentary on Skid Row. "It was about the man, the walk, and the buildings." She sees in her subjects' movements a nobility, even a kind of freedom—and, by lowering her sheet-film camera, she subtly grants them a dignity we might, on first glance, be disinclined to.

To dwell on the men, however, is to neglect Sarfati's talent for framing them. She uses street corners to great effect, causing our lines of sight to recede in serpentine patterns. Every surface is flooded with light. As Sarfati notes, it both "creates volumes" and is a "sort of revelation"—not unlike its role in recent California portraits by Bay Area photographer Katy Grannan. The best pictures in Sarfati's series bring this specific light together with the formal ingenuity of the architectural photographers who have shaped our understanding of modern LA. What results are images powerful enough to make you briefly forget, then become all too aware, that these lives—and this place—were on the cusp of great change.

Brian Sholis is the founder of And Others and an independent curator and editor based in Toronto.

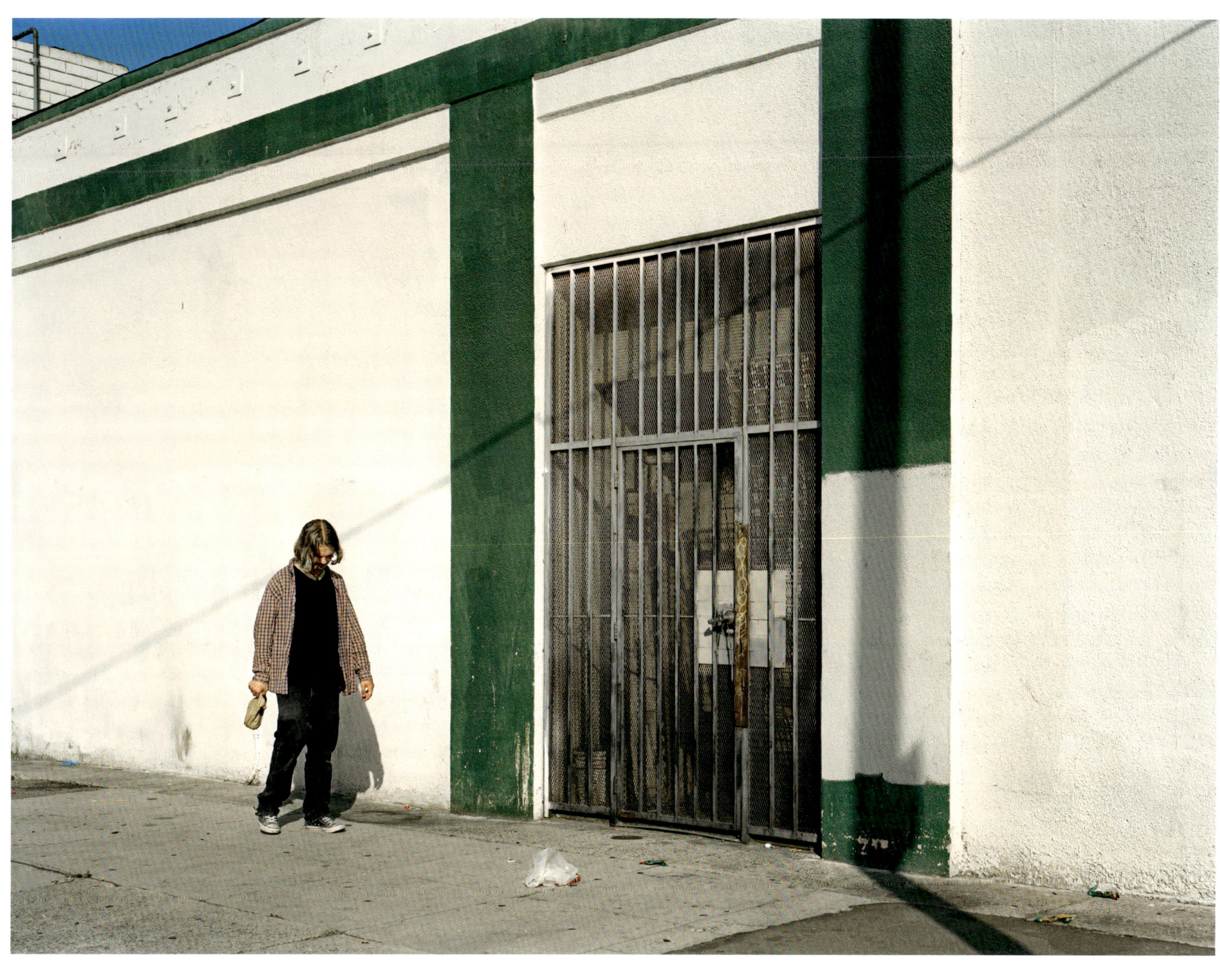

oh man.phg7_07 2013

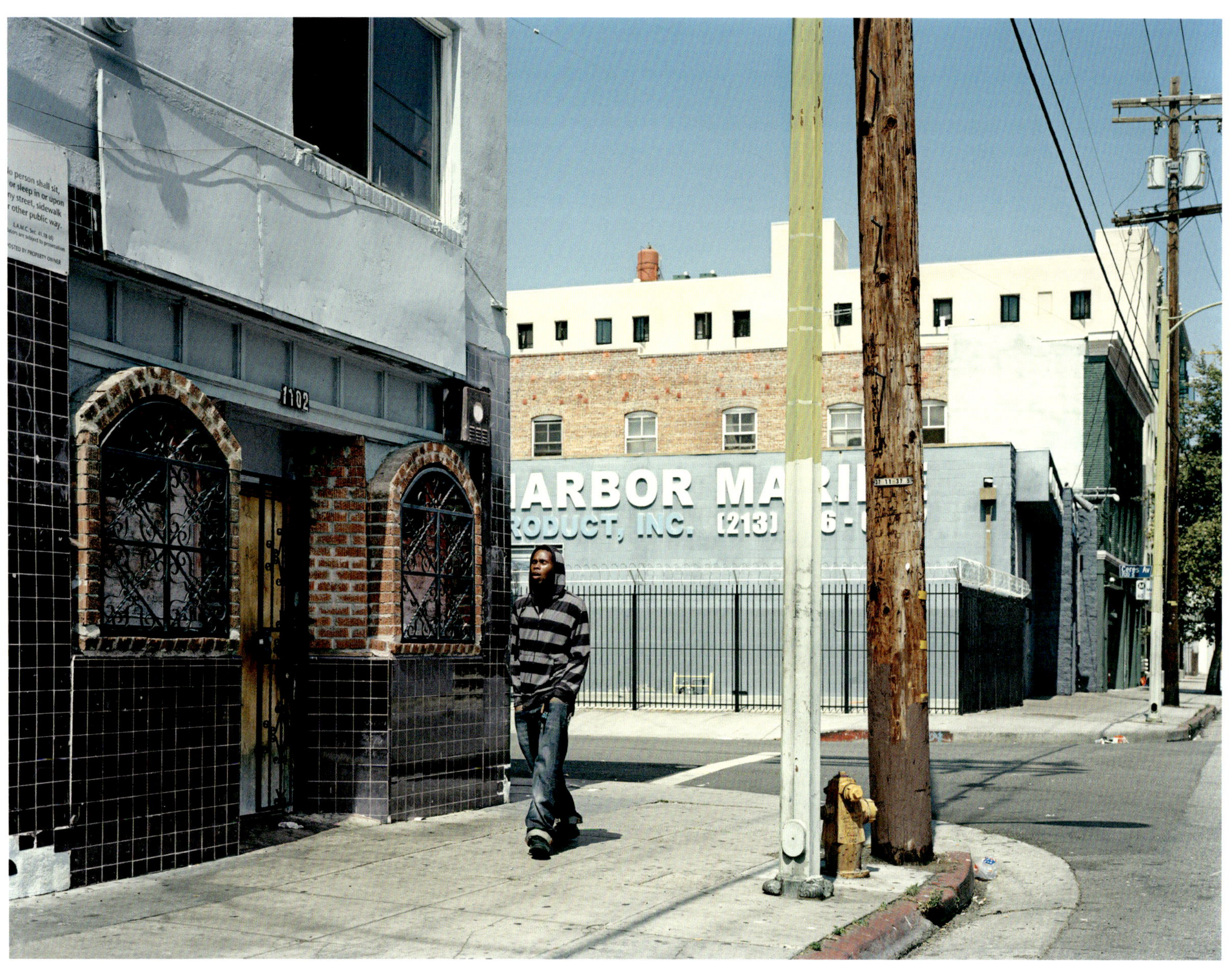

oh man.phg9_08 2013

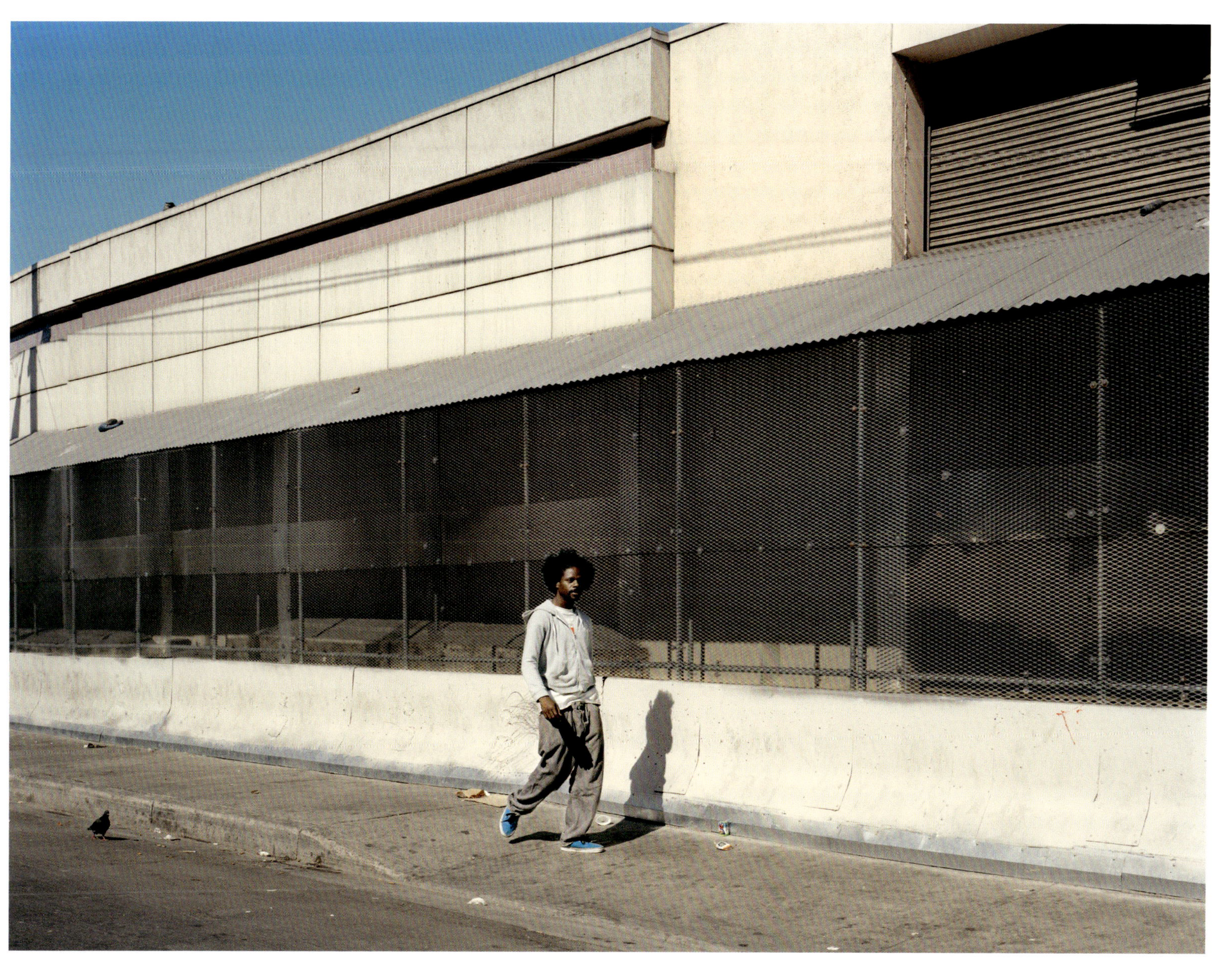

oh man.phg14_08 2013

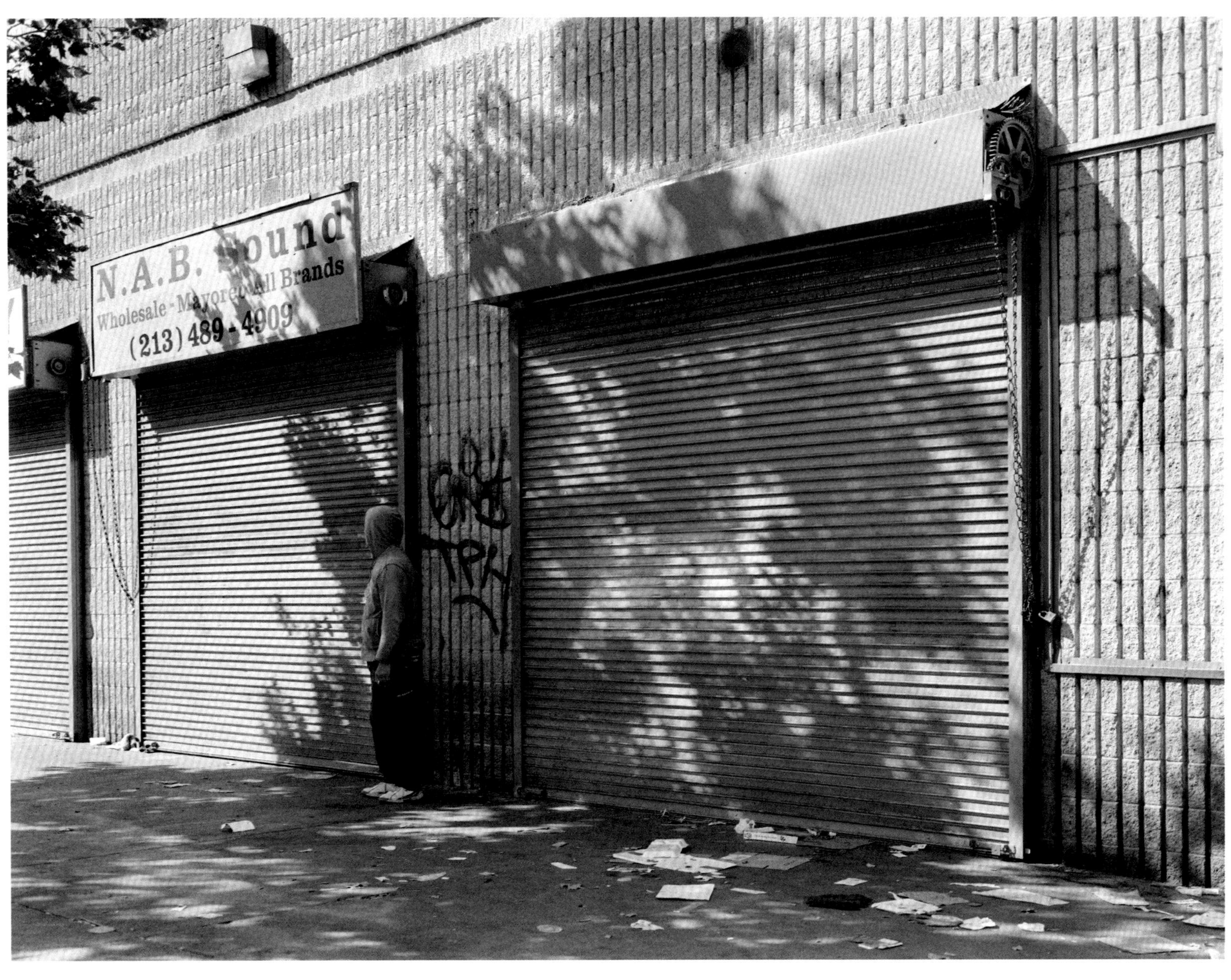

oh man.phg20_06 2012

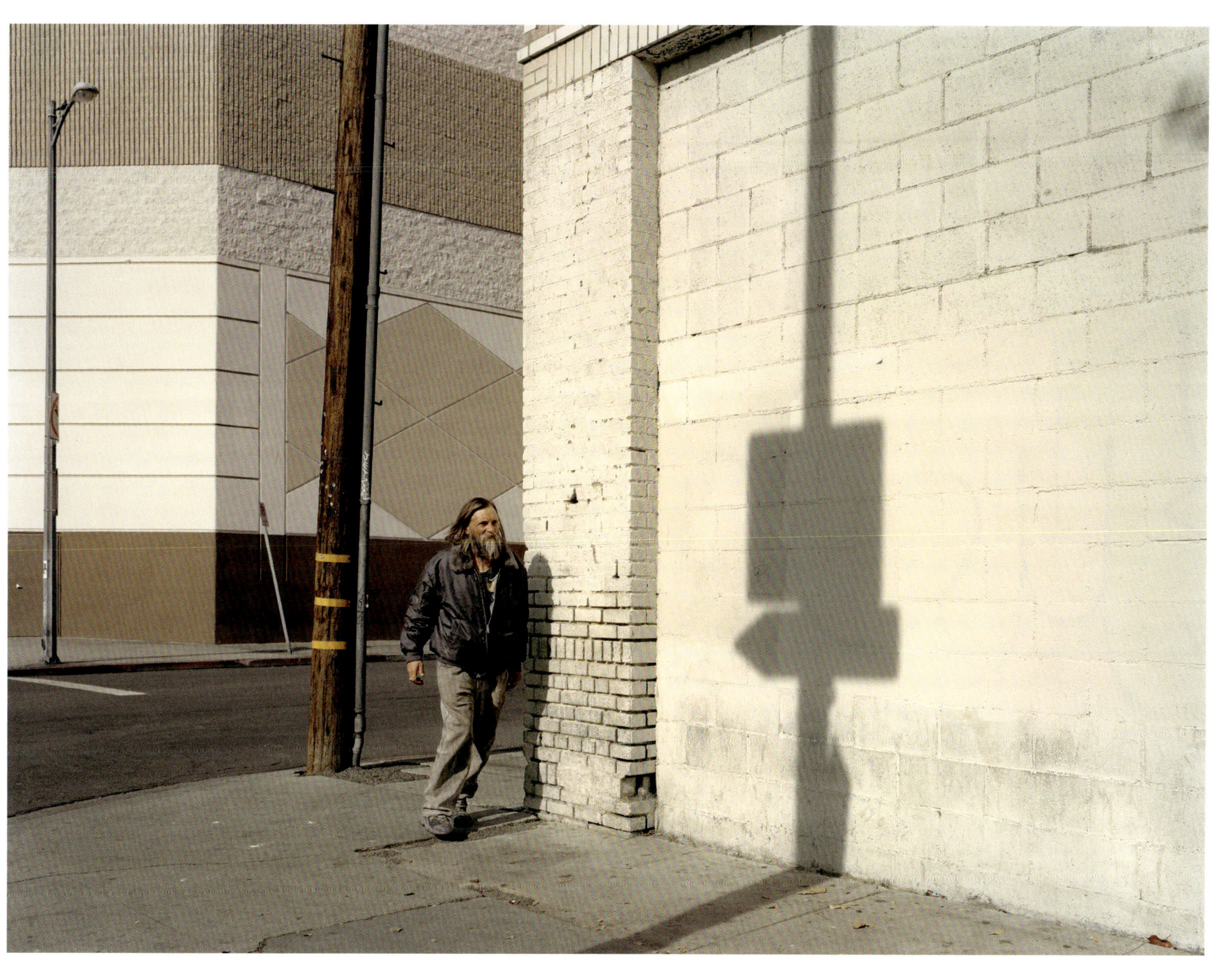

oh man.phg10_12 2012

Kate Palmer Albers

Barak Zemer

How do human beings—and human bodies—experience a culture that is structured around separation? How many ways can we be outside, looking in? And what are the consequences, conversely, of occupying inner spaces? Bodies in states of transition, and subjected to degrees of impermeability, are at the heart of Barak Zemer's photographic interests. The title of his recent body of work, *Aquarium* (2012–16), sets the tone for a range of disorienting states of looking, states of containment, and, often, states of incongruity. Those dark and luminous spaces of immersion and separation act as metaphors both for his experience of Los Angeles and, more broadly, for a heavily structured and mediated experience of daily life in the twenty-first century. As he puts it, "The aquarium is how we live, encapsulated."

Zemer was born in Israel, in 1979, and relocated to LA for graduate school, in 2011, where he found the flux of his encounter as a foreigner echoed and mirrored in the basic structure of this most decentralized city. The rich sensory porousness that had characterized Zemer's daily life in Jerusalem and Tel Aviv was abruptly replaced by an isolation fostered by LA's urban infrastructure and pervasive car culture. The contrast was initially—and to some degree remains—a shock. Of his experience in LA, Zemer says, "I'm trying to deal with it. We're closed in a car, we're all bubbled from each other. It's as though someone planned it for us to be unable to look at or experience somebody else. And the camera fights that. It recognizes the closed thing."

As a result, Zemer photographs prolifically, finding his subjects in the course of daily life, on his travels around the United States and internationally, and at tourist sites like zoos and aquariums that he habitually seeks out wherever he goes. For *Transit*, his 2018 exhibition at LA's Night Gallery, Zemer culled a tightly conceived edit from some fifteen thousand images he's made in the past few years alone. In those photographs, one feels again and again the sense of something just out of reach, a consciousness in which disorientation has become routine. In *Passenger* (2015), an older man's face is partially lit by the blue glow of flight—an inverse of the aquarium. In *Ramp* (2014), the white industrial haze of a Los Angeles morning fails to fully mask the slight oddities of street life. *Aquarium* (2015) depicts a seated woman with her cellphone, appearing comfortably, if incongruously, submerged. Is she taking a photograph, looking out? Or is it a selfie? In *Lotus* (2014), lacquered and bejeweled fingernails offer a closed bloom from the darkness, and in *Head* (2016), a statue seems to have shed a lifetime of tears. The organic and the artificial repeat and replay, in ever-shifting configurations.

In both the vast archive of his images and the radically reduced selection that has become *Aquarium*, the current U.S. political environment is never pictured directly. However, as Zemer comments about the series as a whole, "If it succeeds in being about the human experience, then it's always about politics." In Zemer's work, that feeling finds its way into moments of disconnect, of uncertainty, and of absurdity.

Kate Palmer Albers is a professor of art history at Whittier College, Los Angeles.

Opposite:
Aquarium, 2015
Overleaf:
Passenger, 2015;
Ramp, 2014
Pages 66–67:
Lotus, 2014; *Red Hair*, 2015

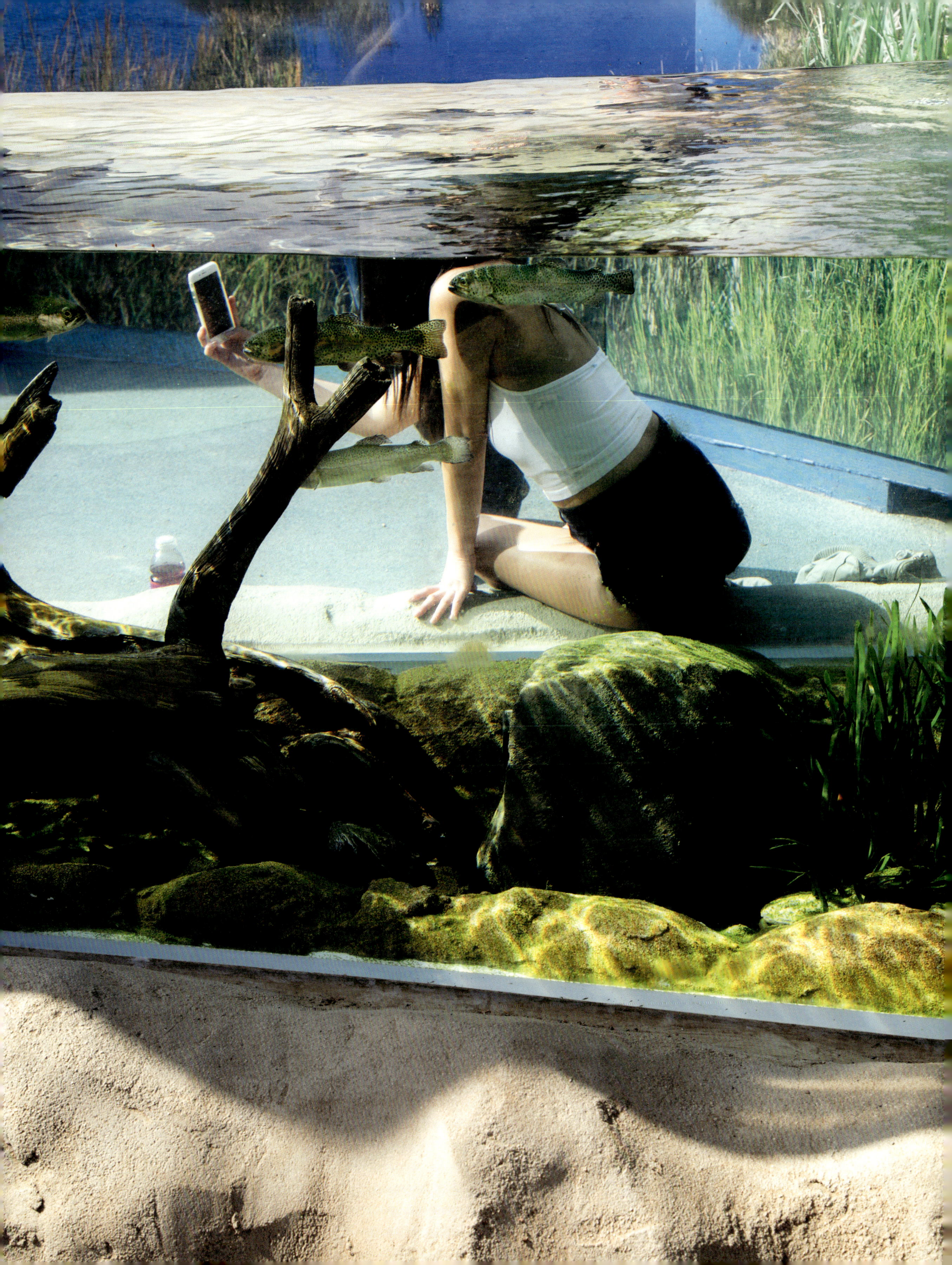

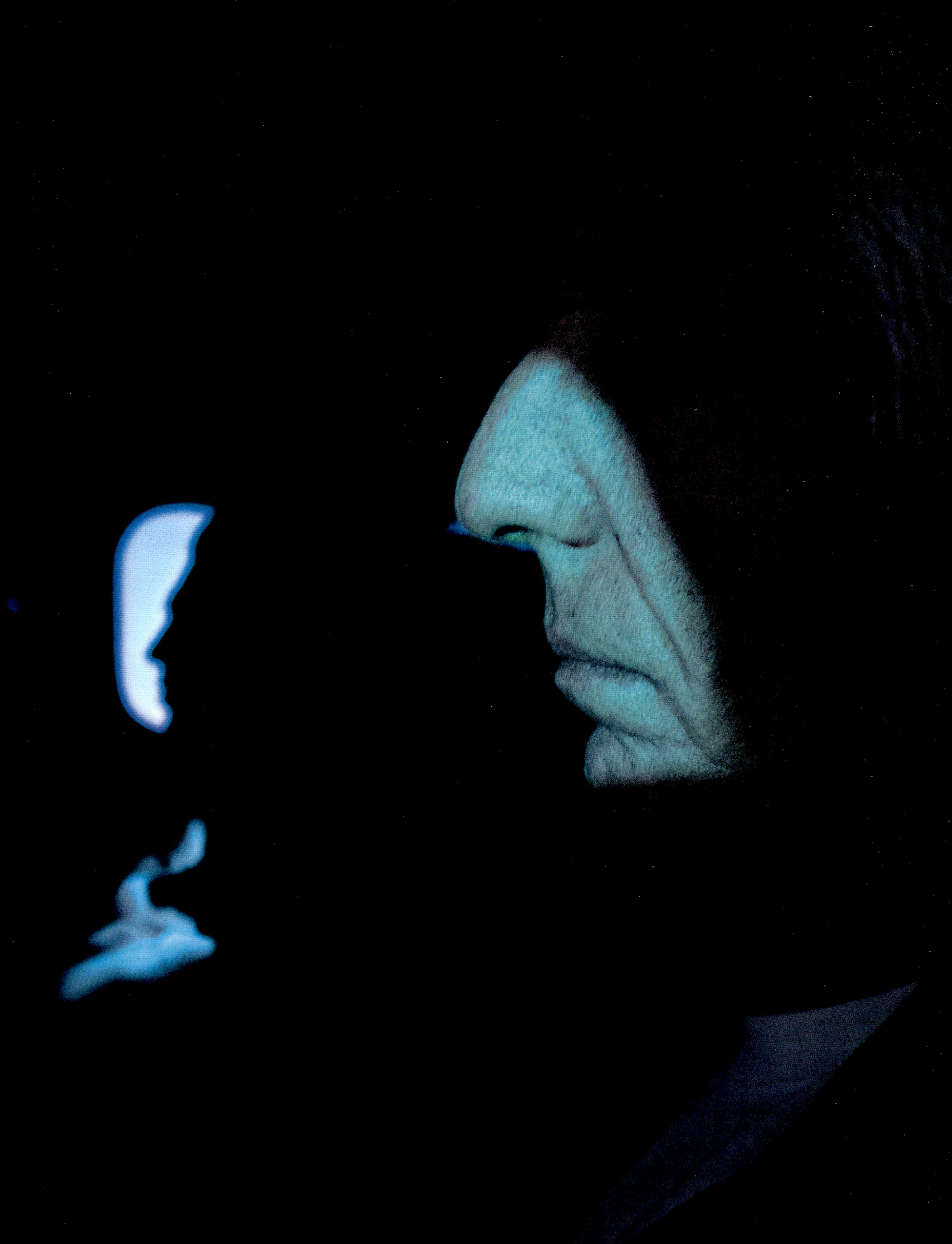

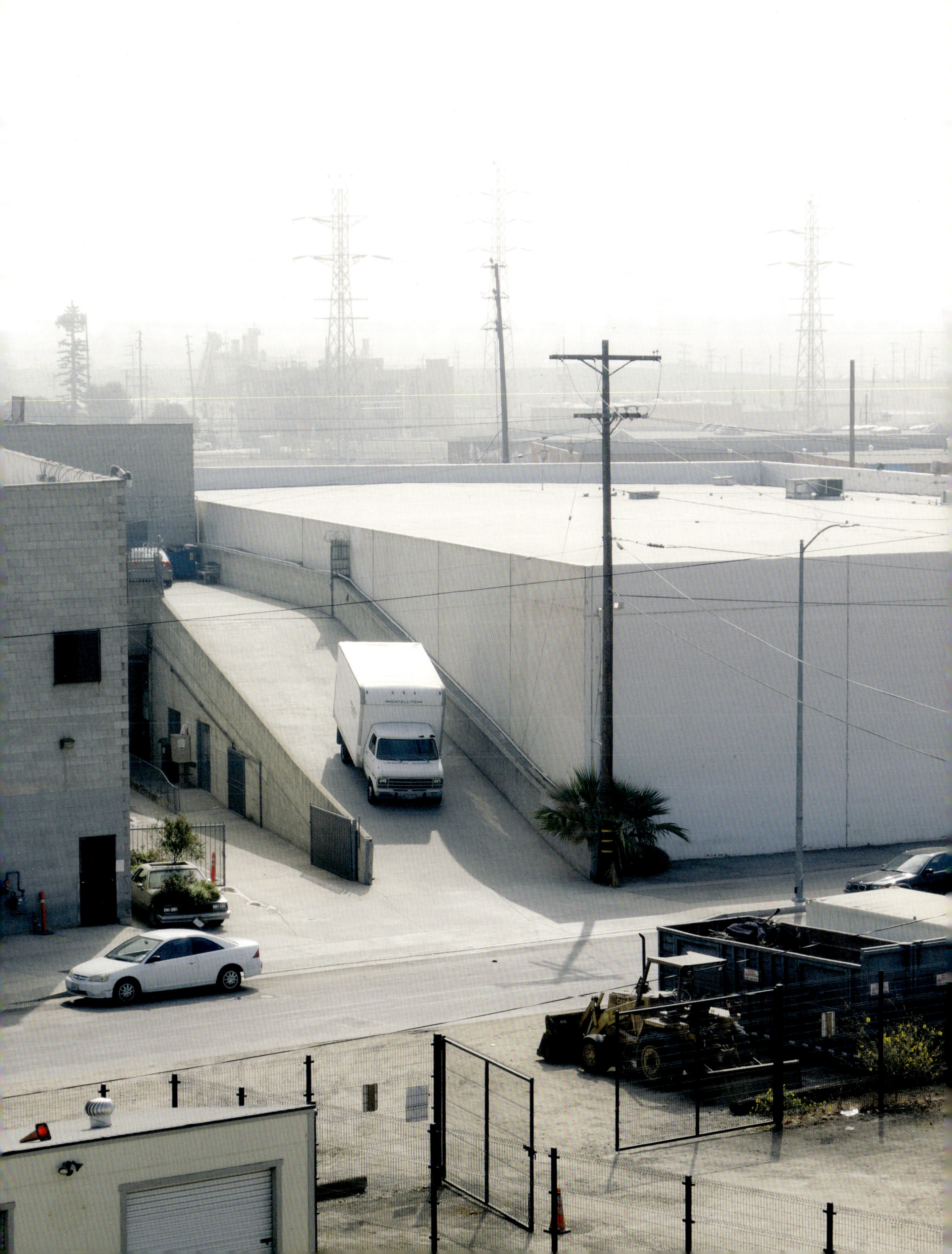

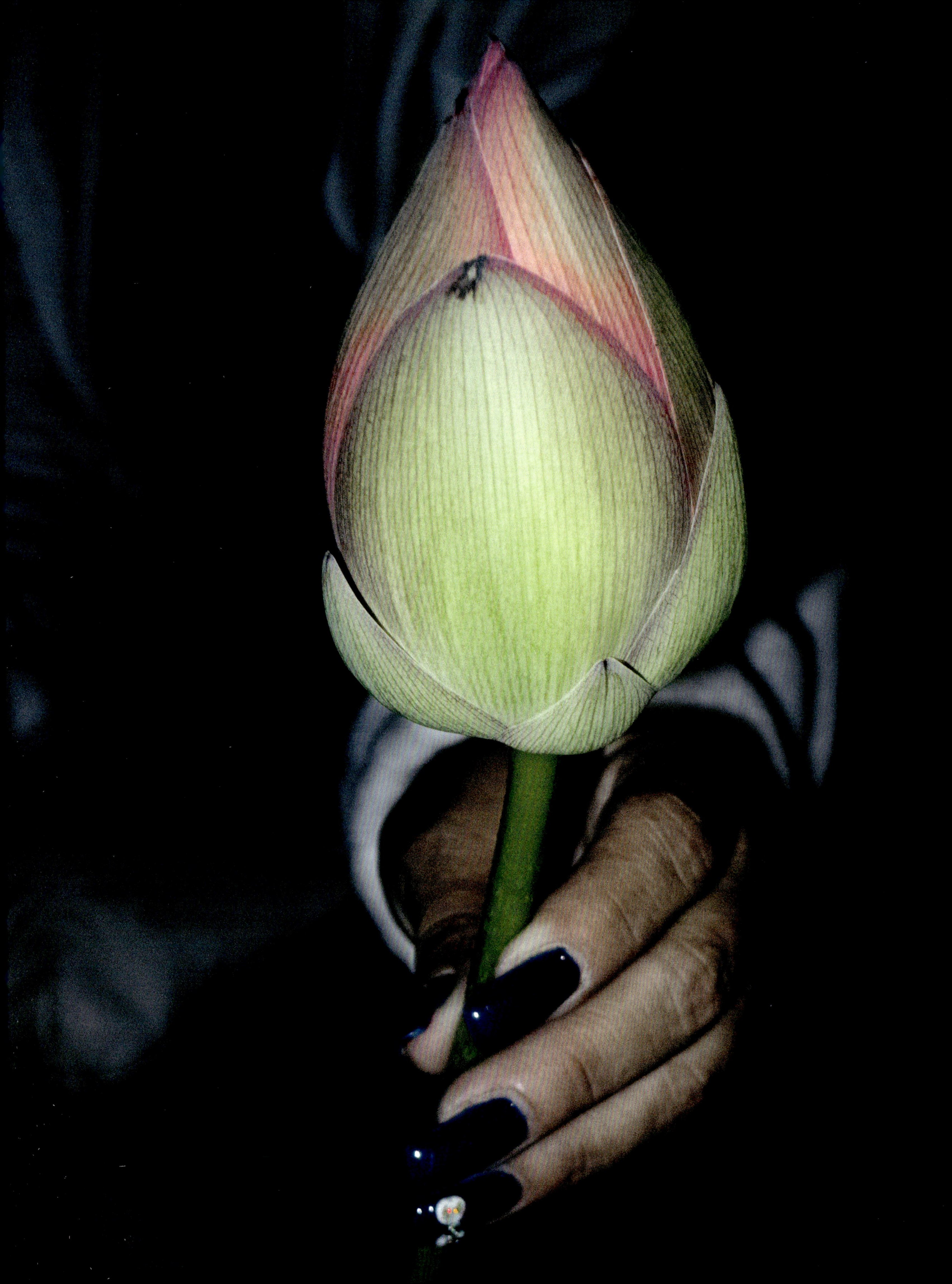

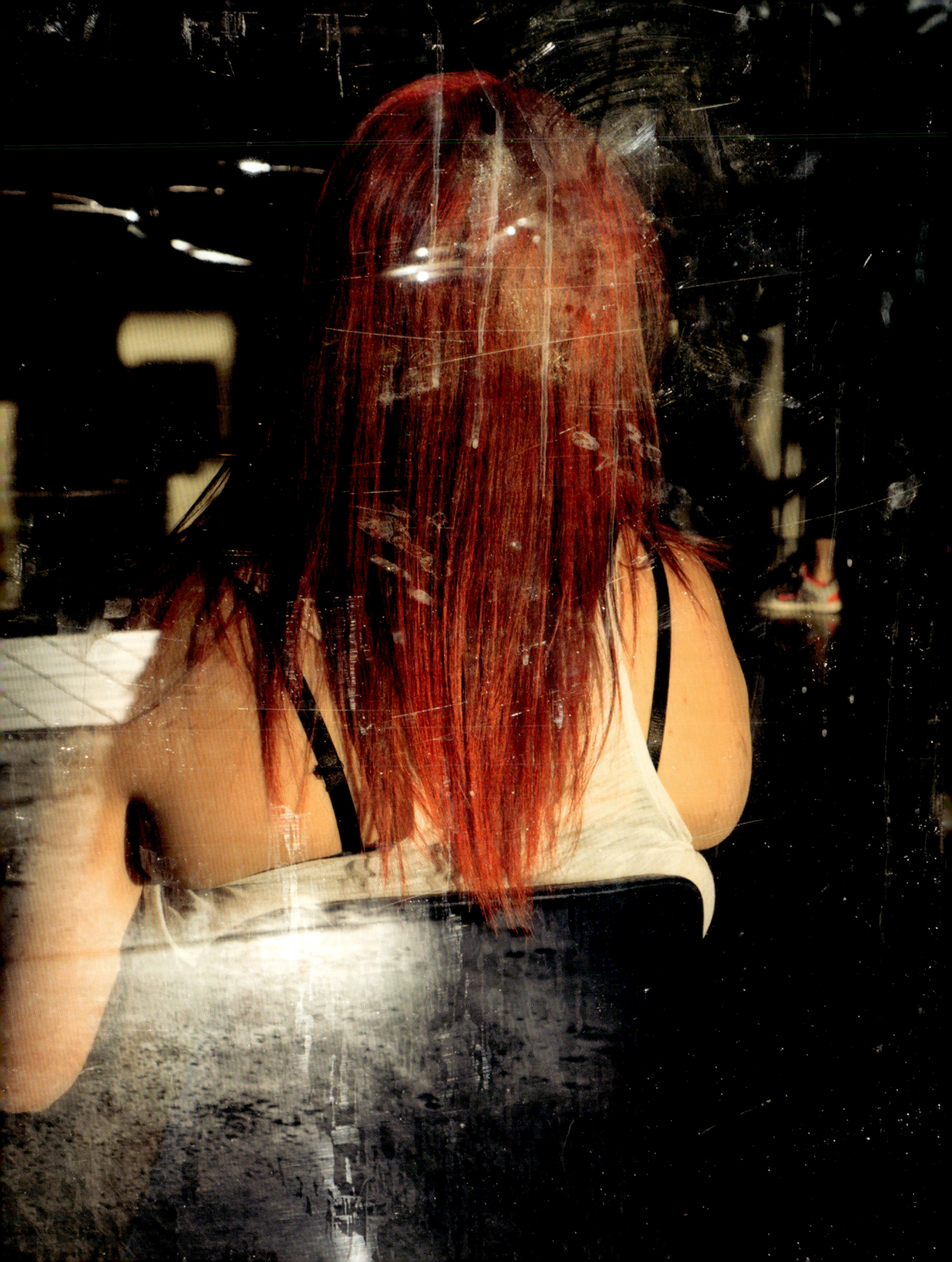

Christina Fernandez

Yxta Maya Murray

Contrary to popular wisdom, Los Angeles does have a center. Its heart is not spatial (hence the misconception), but memorial. Southern California has formed, pearl-like, around the grain of Latinx people and other people of color who claim the city in the names of their ancestors. Latinos and Latinas insist that LA is not Frederick Eaton's irrigated Eden or Hollywood's dream world, but a place whose language and land values, culture and prosperity were created by and with our great dead.

Based in the LA suburb of Norwalk, photographer Christina Fernandez showcases this Los Angeles in her work. Fernandez's early project *Maria's Great Expedition* (1995–96) tells the narrative of an immortal immigrant who journeys from Mexico to Southern California in the nineteenth century. The first image reveals her wearing a muslin gown and a rebozo, and staring off with an expectant look on her face. Maria, ageless, takes on work as a laundress, rides the rails with her hair twirled up in glamorous 1940s spit curls, and lugs orange crates from the back of a truck. The last scene, set in the current day, shows her bent over a stove with a hardened expression that says, I'm still here.

Ruin (1999–2000) is a sequence that reflects on LA's ghosts through the techniques of facial layering. Here, Fernandez superimposes portraits of different women, one from contemporary times, and one that appears salvaged from the practices of Manuel Álvarez Bravo and Tina Modotti. In *Untitled Multiple Exposure #4 (Bravo)* (1999), Fernandez portrays a modern Latina crossing her arms and gazing fixedly off-piste, as if she has just made an important decision; this image is superimposed with that of a shadow-obscured *dama* cloaked in a traditional woven textile.

Beginning in the mid-1990s, Fernandez began to abstract her argument by focusing on city texts, whether industrial signage or marks of protest. In *Manuela Stitched* (1996–2000), she showcases LA's downtown garment district, whose dilapidated buildings are marked with runic names and ironic designations (such as "Fashion Int'l"). In her *Lavanderia* series, from 2002, she narrates the lives of Latinos through the scrims of public laundries' graffiti-frosted shop fronts. *Lavanderia* is a portrait of loss, community, and labor, set in rapidly gentrifying Boyle Heights. Fernandez depicts laundromats whose windows are splashed with white calligraphy that was spray-painted by folks who may soon find themselves forced out of the neighborhood.

As Fernandez explains, "The window is a membrane, because the outside and the inside are delineated by that graffiti. The paint etched into the glass, and was drippy at the same time, so it had the appearance of visual violence in a way, but it's also very beautiful." She adds: "I became interested in the aesthetic because I was living in Boyle Heights in the mid-1990s, and the prices of family homes have just skyrocketed. It's going to become problematic for people. It *has* become problematic for the people."

Yxta Maya Murray is Professor of Law at Loyola Law School, Los Angeles, and the author of the novels *The King's Gold* (2007) and *The Good Girl's Guide to Getting Kidnapped* (2010).

Opposite:
Element #6, from the series *Maria's Great Expedition*, 1995–96

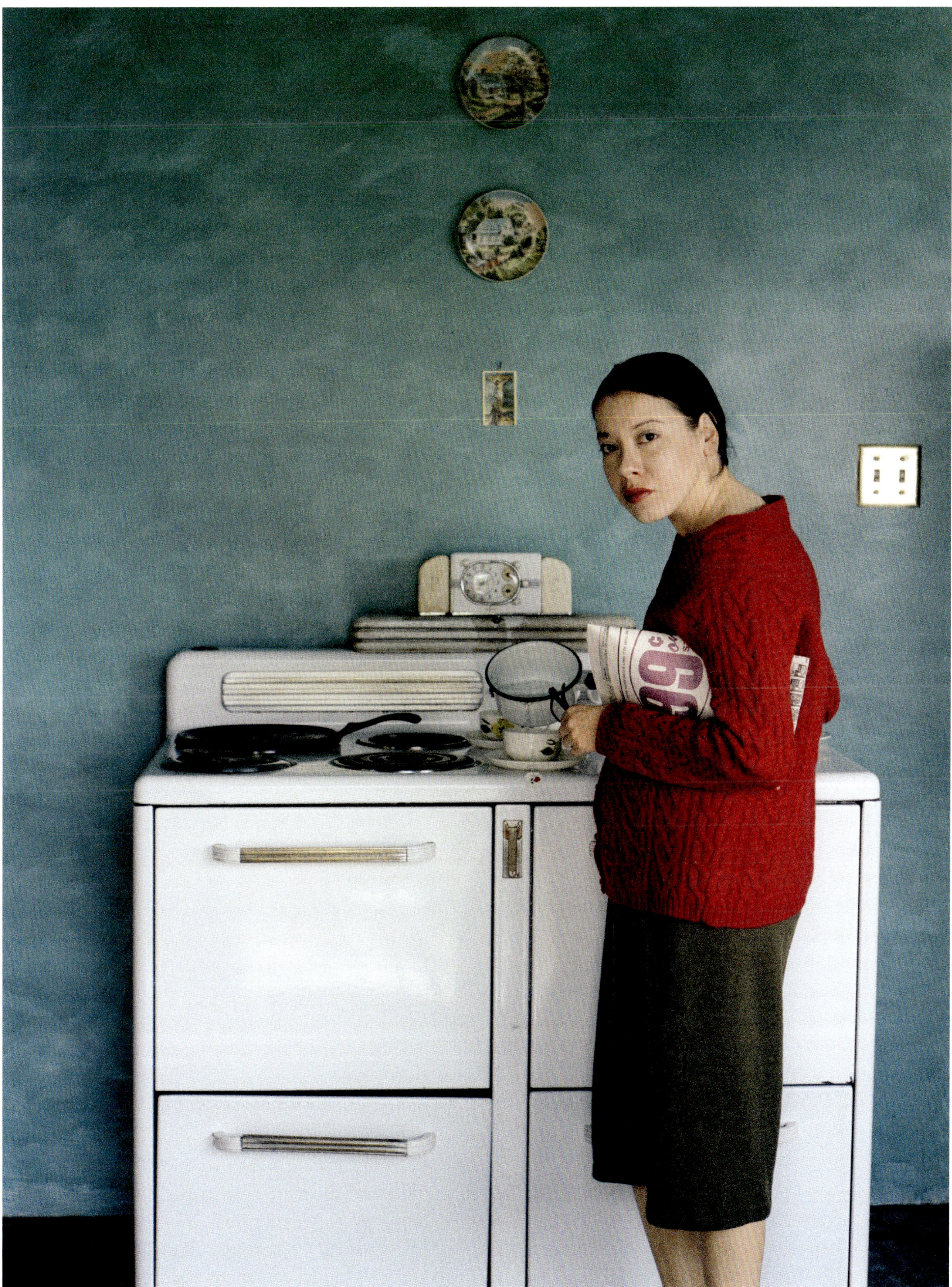

This page:
***Lavanderia #1*, 2002**

Opposite, top:
***Lavanderia #11*, 2003**
Opposite, bottom:
***Lavanderia #8*, 2002**
All photographs courtesy
the artist and Gallery Luisotti,
Santa Monica

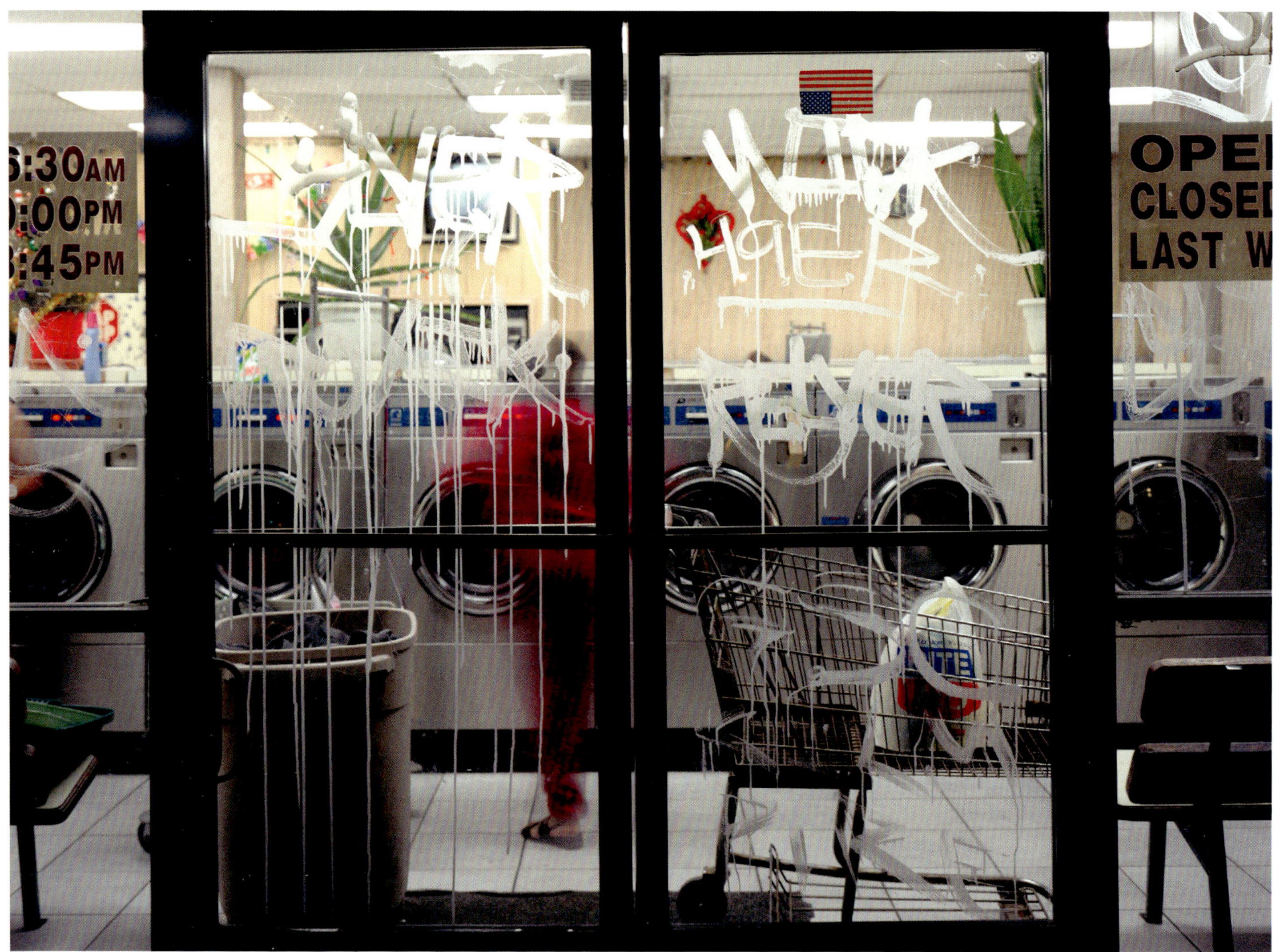

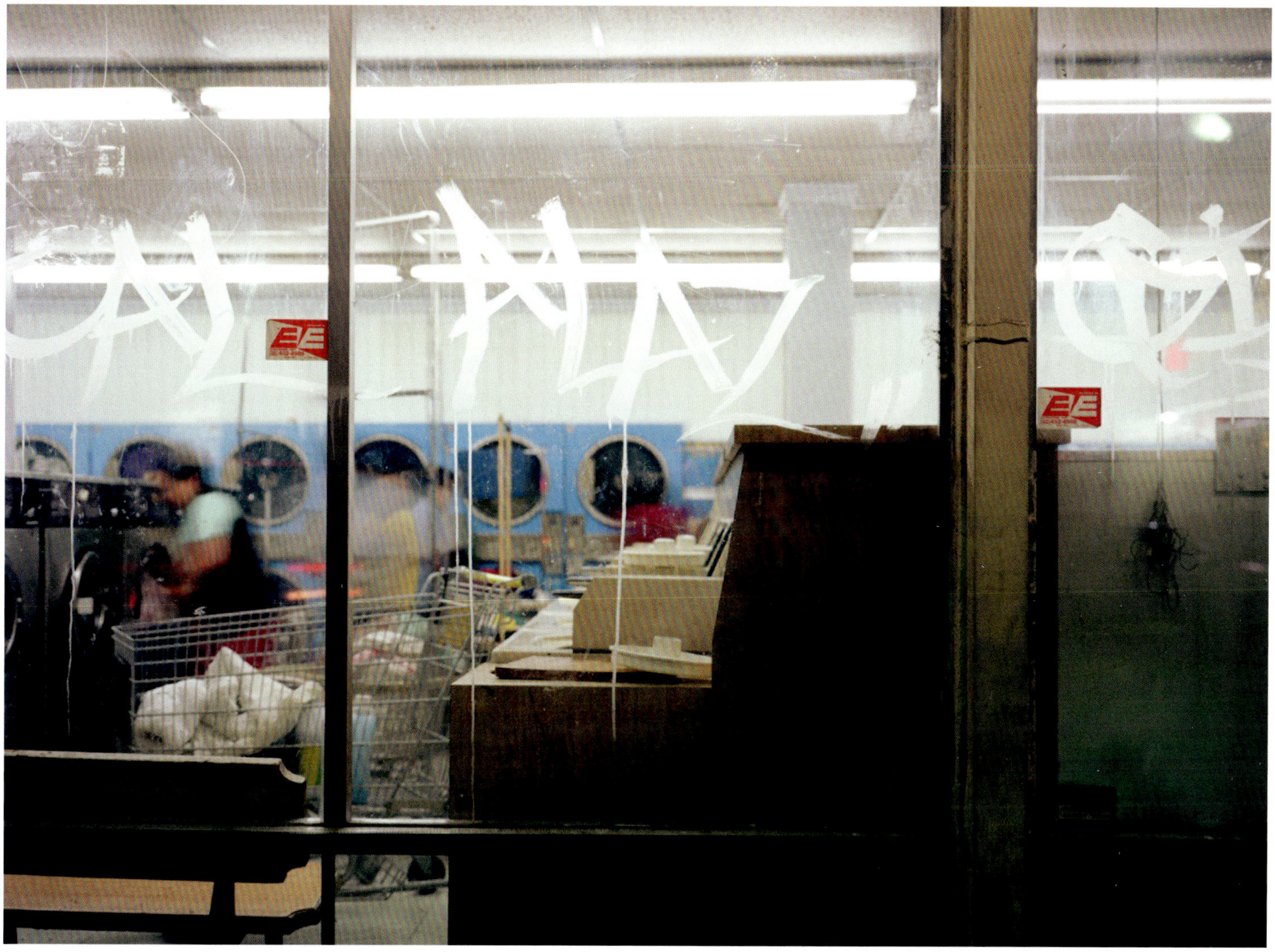

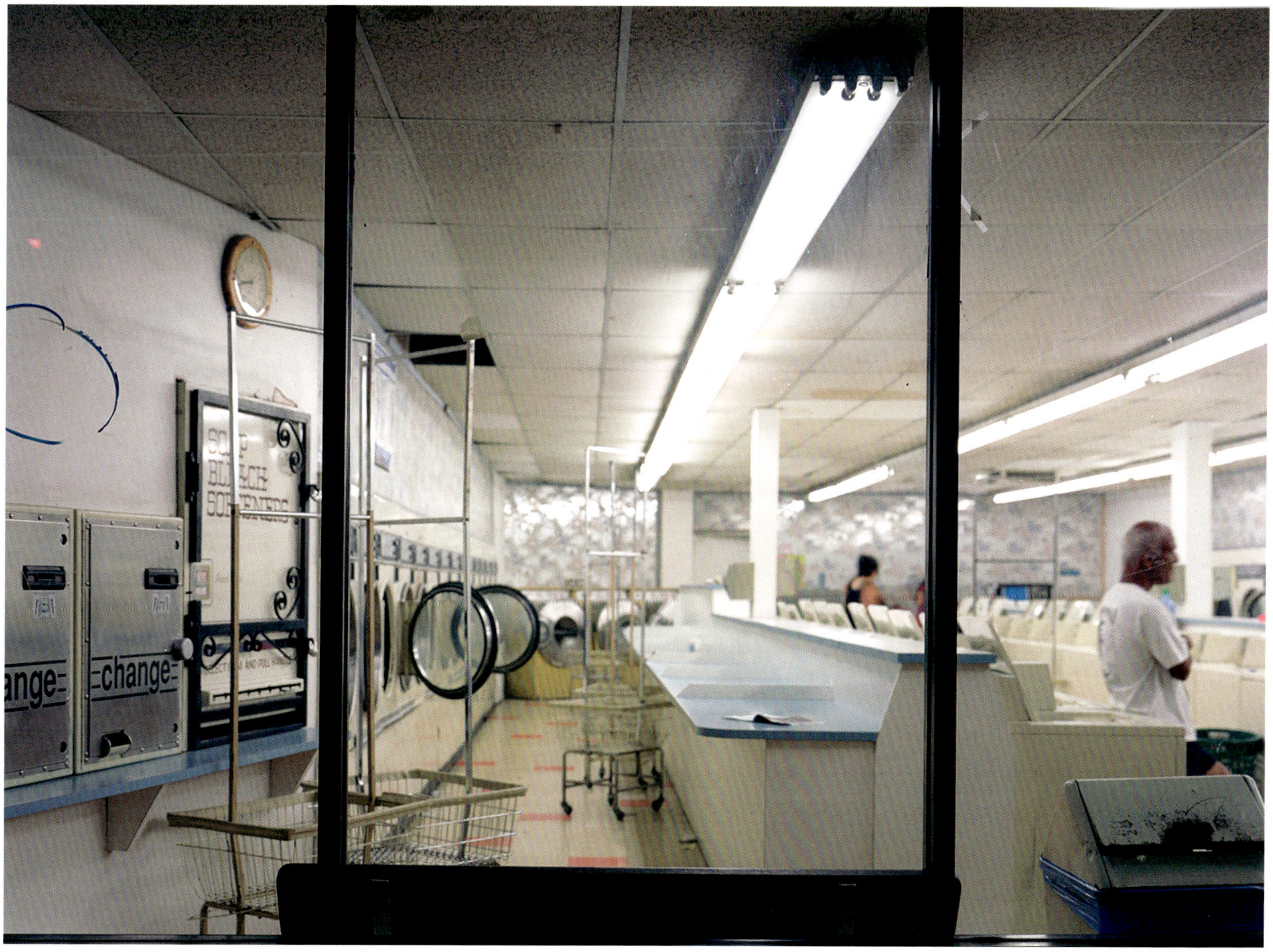

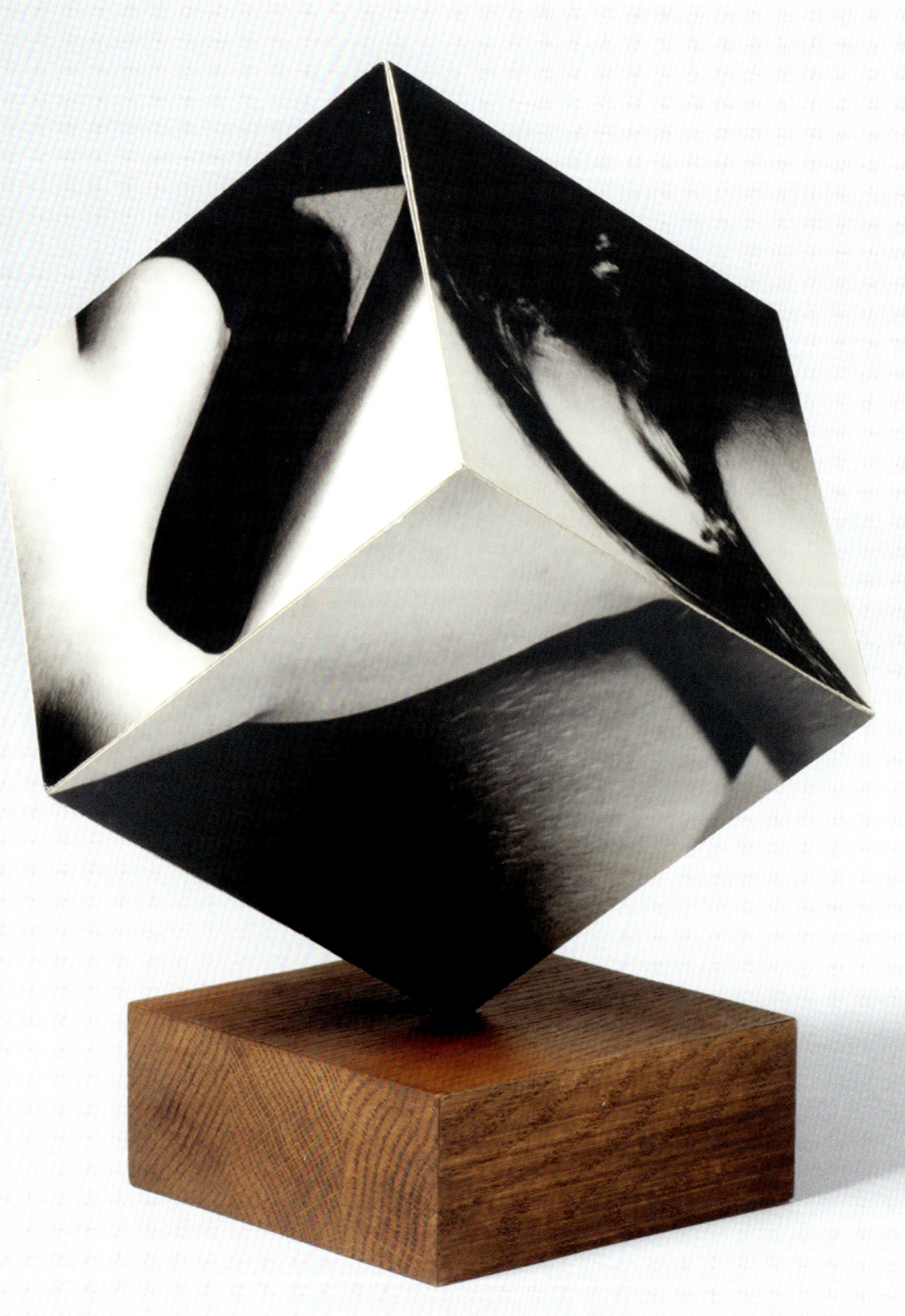

Toward Poetic Vision

Robert Heinecken's ambition for photography

Rebecca Morse

I first met Robert Heinecken, in 1995, at the Center for Creative Photography, located on the campus of the University of Arizona. The center had just acquired Heinecken's personal archive, and he arrived that fall semester to conduct a seminar on his work with the history of photography graduate students. Despite the hundred-degree desert heat and the compressed time frame of a week, the artist's trademark openness and availability were on display as we systematically examined and discussed every one of his 350 works in the archive. Photographs, prints, and 3-D objects, made between 1960 and 1991, revealed an artist who defied tradition and took risks to create multilayered, mass media–rich, color images that were often provocative and always compelling. Never had I been in the presence of an artist assessing his life's work. Without sentimentality, Heinecken shared the experience with us, taking our opinions and questions seriously and, although we were students, treating us like peers—encouraging us to make original assessments because, according to him, it was our responsibility as young scholars to do so. I moved to Los Angeles three years later and over time became acquainted with a vast group of artists who were Heinecken's friends and former students. They repeatedly commented on his generosity as a professor and his ability to encourage young artists to find their own voices through personal artistic expression and experimentation.

Those are perhaps the most defining factors of photography in Los Angeles today—personal expression and experimentation. There is not one photographic style here, but a vast pluralism, along with a dedication to pushing photography in all directions over the boundaries it shares with other media. This position is rooted in the 1960s, when the burgeoning medium gained ground through a network of like-minded artist-professors, led by Heinecken, who launched a strong and steady campaign for innovative photography. They did so by way of teaching, building collections, and organizing exhibitions throughout the region in exhibition spaces affiliated with higher education—and by producing accompanying catalogs that would substantiate their efforts. Instead of the institutionalized art museum, the commercial gallery, the advertising-supported art magazine, or the capricious collector, higher education emerged as the support network for photography in Los Angeles. Today, the

Page 72:
Robert Heinecken, *Figure Cube*, 1965
© the Robert Heinecken Trust and courtesy Center for Creative Photography, University of Arizona

This page:
Lewis Baltz, *Newport Beach, Showing Actual Damage*, 1973, from the series *Prototype Works*. From the exhibition *24 from L.A.*, 1973
© The Lewis Baltz Trust and courtesy Gallery Luisotti, Santa Monica

Opposite:
Leland Rice, *Untitled*, 1969. From the exhibition *California Photographers, 1970*
© the artist and courtesy the San Francisco Museum of Modern Art

most pioneering and influential artists work at the helm of these same educational institutions advancing the inherent principles of open investigation.

In 1966, as assistant professor of art at UCLA, Heinecken organized his first exhibition, *Photographic Imagery/UCLA*, held at San Diego State College's gallery. The exhibition, consisting of his students' work, was on view for just eleven days. The accompanying five-page catalog serves as a manifesto on photography in 1960s Los Angeles. In it, Heinecken lays out the tenets of UCLA's program: photography was taught alongside, and on equal footing with, painting, drawing, sculpture, and printmaking as part of the pictorial arts. It was neither "informational" nor in the service of other media, but a poetic gesture for the purpose of "personal artistic expression." The timing of this show, and the accompanying public statement, is significant—it coincided with the graduation of the first student, Kenneth McGowan, to complete thesis work in photography at UCLA.

Instead of the museum, the commercial gallery, or the art magazine, higher education emerged as the support network for photography in Los Angeles.

Photographic Imagery/1968 soon followed at San Diego State College, as the second exhibition in this series devoted to photography in Los Angeles. Organized by gallery director Allan Miller, the show included three-dimensional, camera-less, layered work by Heinecken and Miller, along with work by Carl Cheng, Darryl Curran, Pat O'Neill, and others, all of whom were local professors. The artists engaged with photography via specialties that lay outside the medium—from optical physics, motion pictures, and animated films to sculpture and graphic design. This reflected both the diversity of personal approaches and photography's extraordinary adaptability. "It threw the doors open to creativity," said Curran, and this "creative photography" was well received by the small, but passionate, photography enthusiasts who were mostly students and their instructors.

Heinecken was adamant that young artists engage with photographs in person rather than in reproduction. In the fall of 1968, he organized an exhibition for UCLA's Dickson Art Center that would become the nucleus of the university's study collection. *Contemporary Photographs*, a survey of twenty-two artists' work, was aimed at "the serious student of the medium"

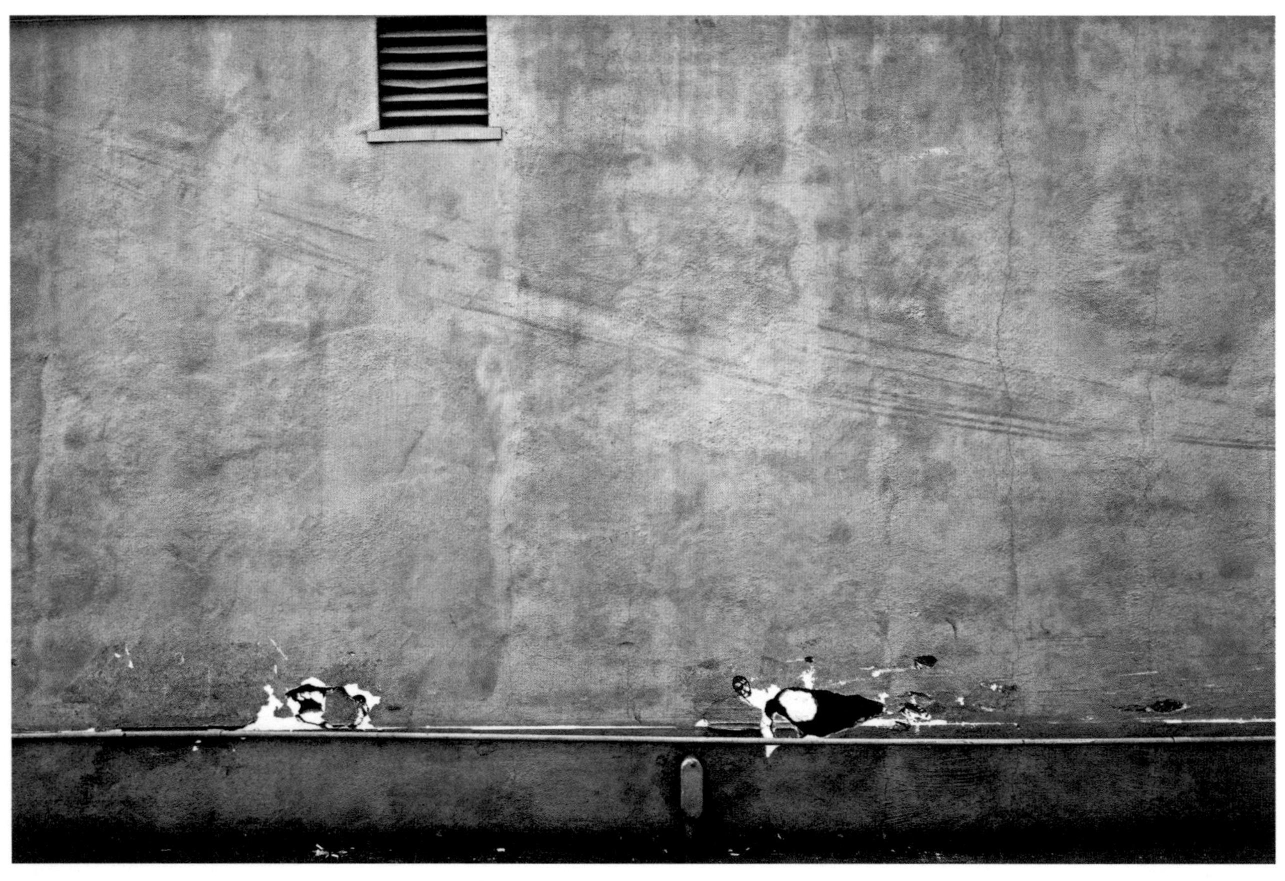

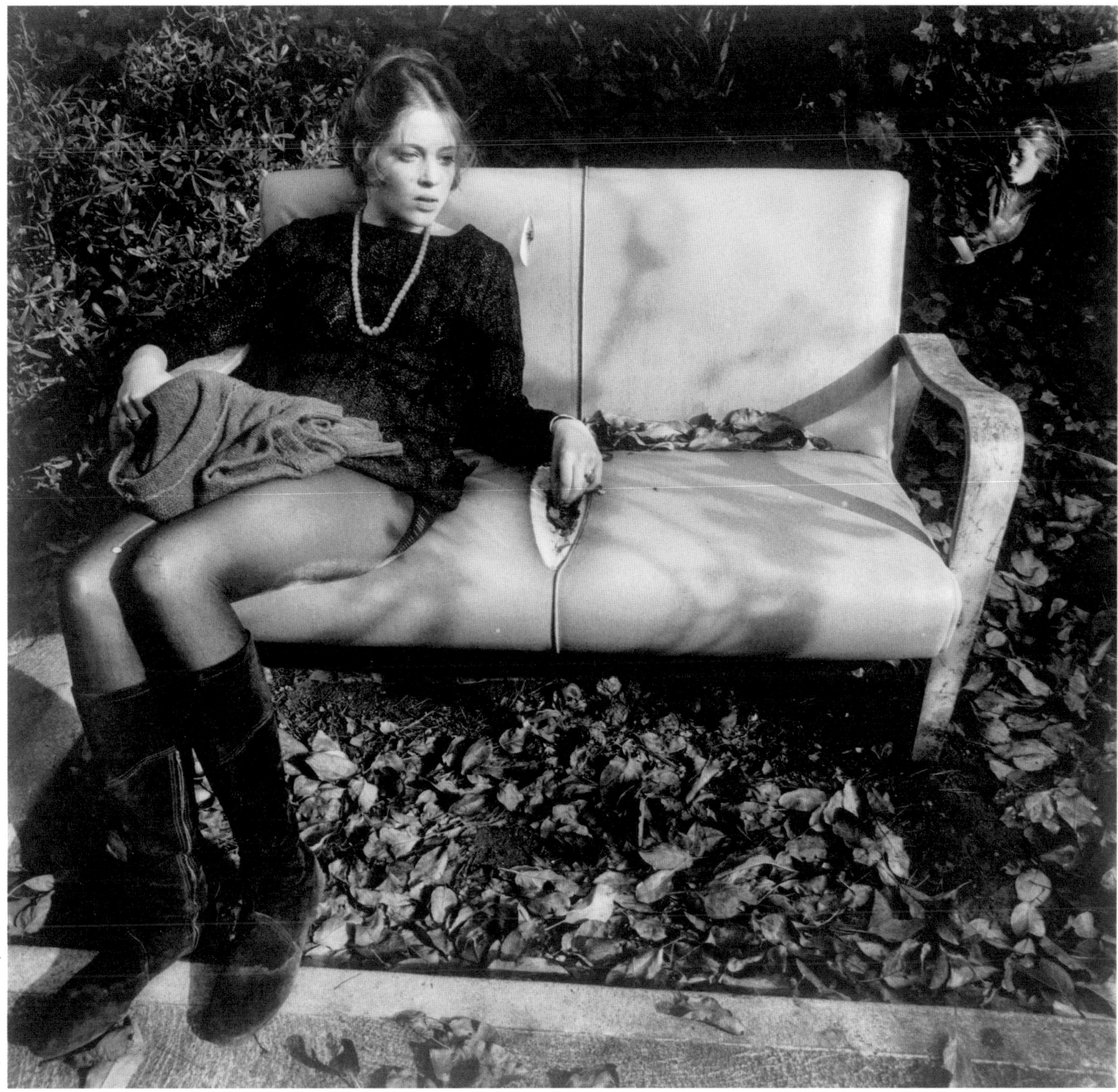

so that they could "see and experience the fine photograph in its primary state as an *object about*; rather than in reproduced form as a *picture of*." Photographs of photographs, disorienting angles, nonobjective imagery, and layered figures dominated this exhibition, which included anything but straight photography. Many of the artists worked in California, and more than 70 percent of them taught in higher education—a detail that Heinecken readily acknowledged, crediting academia with supporting and fostering their creative practices. The work of well-known artists such as Nathan Lyons and Jerry Uelsmann was included alongside that of less familiar figures such as Jerome Liebling and Todd Walker.

A curator who would have a profound impact on photography in Los Angeles—Fred R. Parker—organized *California Photographers, 1970* at the Memorial Union Art Gallery on the campus of the University of California, Davis. He began working on the show while he was the gallery's director and transitioned to the position of exhibitions coordinator and curator of photography at the Pasadena Art Museum, where the show traveled to that year. His catalog essay asserts that a strong overview of contemporary California photography had not yet been compiled. Parker acknowledged that, for many, the assumption was that the work of Ansel Adams, Edward Weston, and Dorothea Lange "would continue to be the most honest, potent and exemplary for further generations of California photographers." However, Parker's show revealed his conclusion that contemporary photography in California was considerably more experimental and "every phase of technical or visual manipulation that was held suspect, if not in total disrepute a few decades ago, is now freely being used." Photomontage (Leland Rice), photolithograph (Heinecken), sun print (Helena Hofmanis), dry photocopy (Roger Cinnamond), gum print (Gayle Smalley), photo-silk screen on fabric (Barbara Kasten), hand-colored photograph in a plastic bubble (Michael Stone), Verifax (Robert Fichter), and film overlay (Allan Miller) dominated the exhibition.

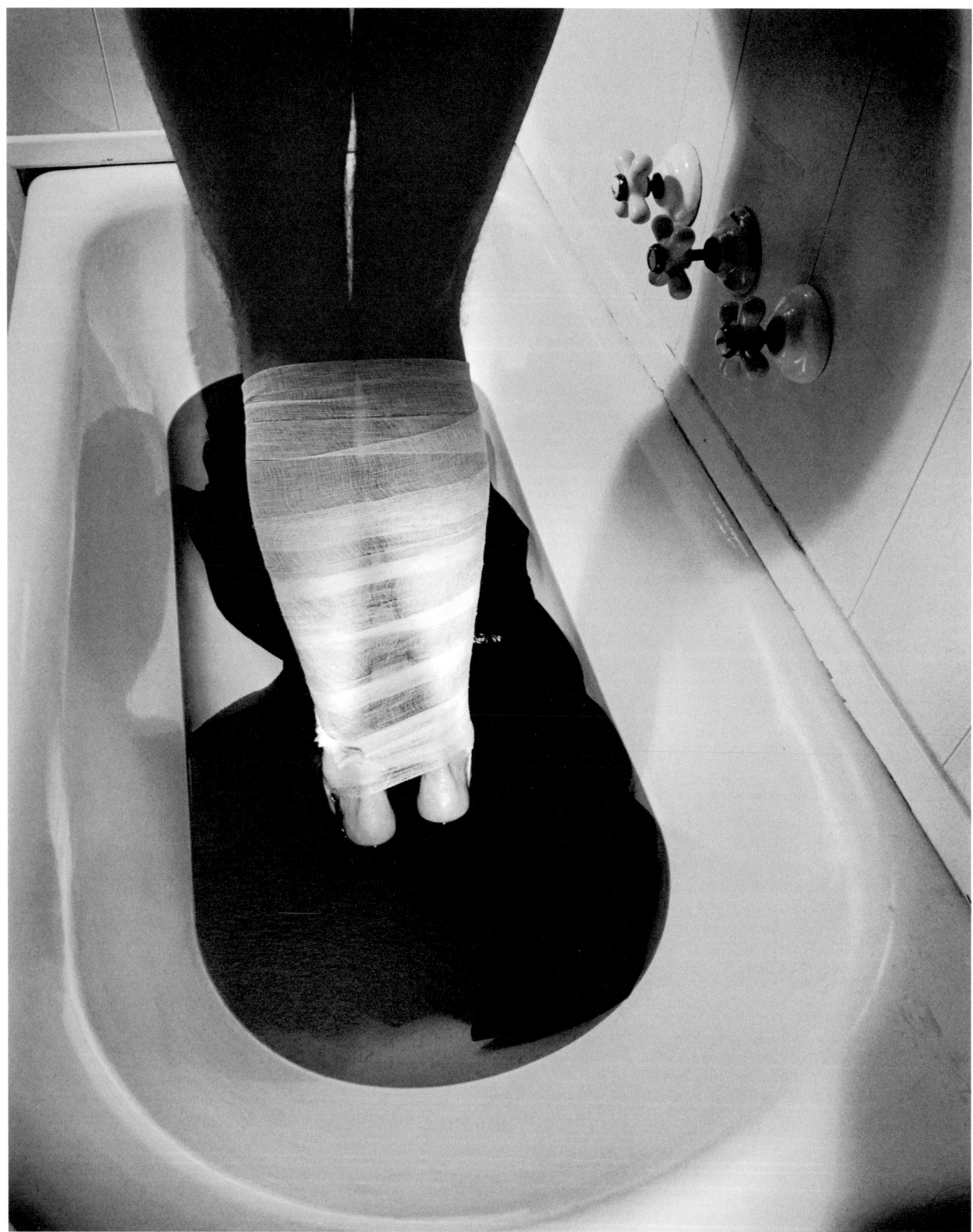

Opposite:
Jo Ann Callis, *Untitled*, 1976. From the exhibition *Exposing: Photographic Definitions*, 1976

This page:
Barbara Kasten, *Untitled*, 1969. From the exhibition *California Photographers, 1970*
Courtesy the artist; Bortolami, New York; Galerie Kadel Willborn, Düsseldorf; and Thomas Dane Gallery, London

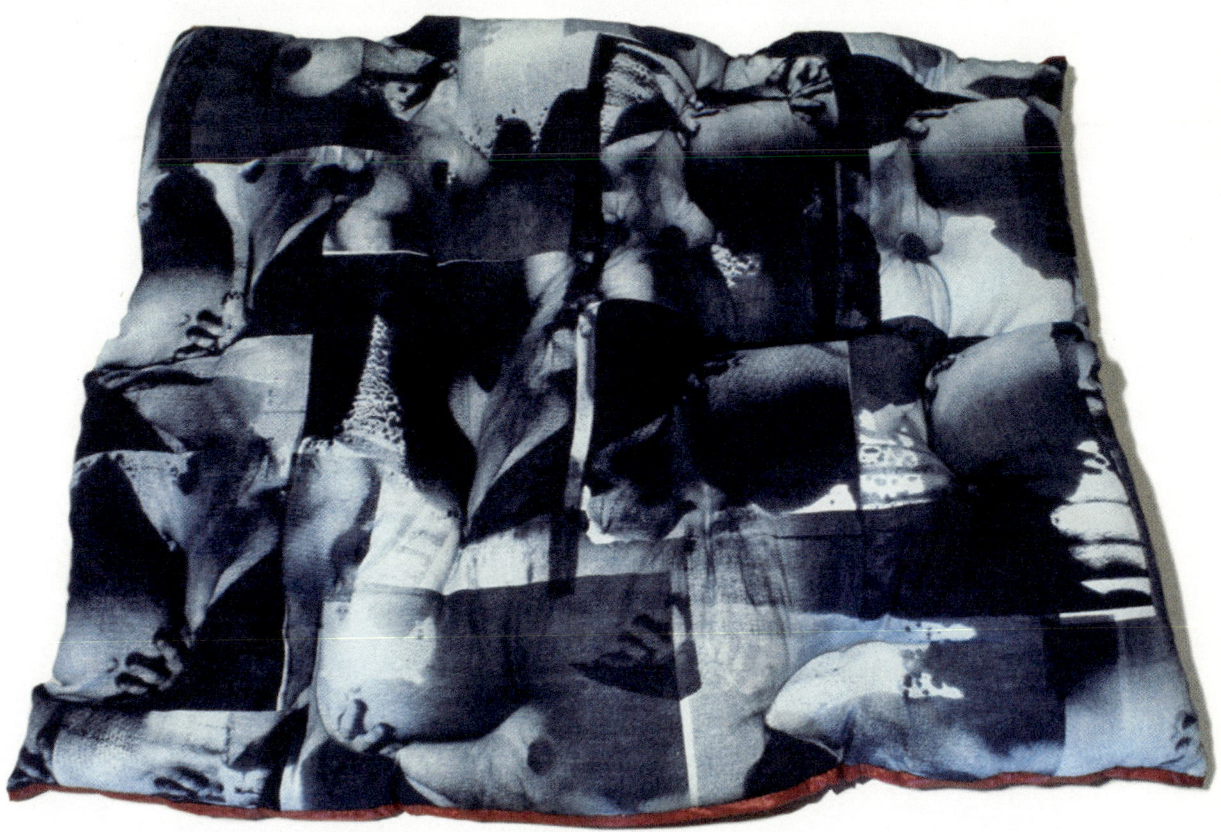

Parker followed, in 1971, with *The Crowded Vacancy: Three Los Angeles Photographers* for the Memorial Union Art Gallery, which traveled to the Pasadena Art Museum. Lewis Baltz, Anthony Hernandez, and Terry Wild were the three artists and each a product of the Los Angeles higher education system. The exhibition's catalog essay is beautifully concise—it includes three statistics for Los Angeles County in 1970: 7,032,075 people; 2,575,789 dwellings; 4,668,761 automobiles. The work was not three-dimensional or particularly experimental in process, but instead it heralded a new perspective on the urban landscape that would come to be known four years later as New Topographics. Baltz, who was included in the 1975 George Eastman House show *New Topographics: Photographs of a Man-Altered Landscape* that coined the term, reveals, along with Wild, the hard lines that make up the architecture of the sprawling suburban West. Hernandez, among the few street photographers in Los Angeles, takes that deadpan black-and-white aesthetic to beaches, public fishing areas, and corporate interiors.

In 1973, the San Francisco Museum of Modern Art invited Darryl Curran to curate *24 from L.A.*, which predated the establishment of the museum's photography department by seven years. The institution found an outside expert in Curran, who was an artist, a university professor, and one of Heinecken's former students. The human figure dominated the exhibition through image transfer, shadow, Sabatier effect, and collage. Included was work by Robert Mautner, a student of Curran's at California State University, Fullerton. Three years later, Mautner curated *Exposing: Photographic Definitions* for the Los Angeles Institute of Contemporary Art, which was aimed at a broad audience and funded by the National Endowment for the Arts. Mautner affirmed that the concentration of local photography programs taught by "the most innovative and influential artists working in the medium" made Southern California the epicenter for experimental photography. Images by professors and their graduate students were installed together, including the psychological figurative works of Edmund Teske and Jo Ann Callis, the aluminum photoetchings of Jerry McMillan, the prints on cotton and constructions of Kay Shuper and Susan Haller, the small domestic façades of Judy Fiskin, the interior doors of Steve Kahn, and the deserted, painted interiors of John Divola.

The first exhibition about Los Angeles photography to travel outside of California was *Untitled 11: Emerging Los Angeles Photographers*, which was organized by artist Rodney Stuart and began at Northern California's Friends of Photography in 1977. Stuart states that he "had virtually no impression of what was happening in Los Angeles" so he contacted Heinecken, who formed an advisory committee of five local art professors for the show. In Heinecken's accompanying catalog essay, he shifts from imploring the viewer to consider photographic images poetic, as he did in 1966, to embodying the position of the artist, stating, "I have the feeling that Los Angeles, unlike other locales, epitomizes the attitude that says 'This is art because I say it is; I am art because I say I am.'"

Rebecca Morse is Curator of Photography at the Los Angeles County Museum of Art.

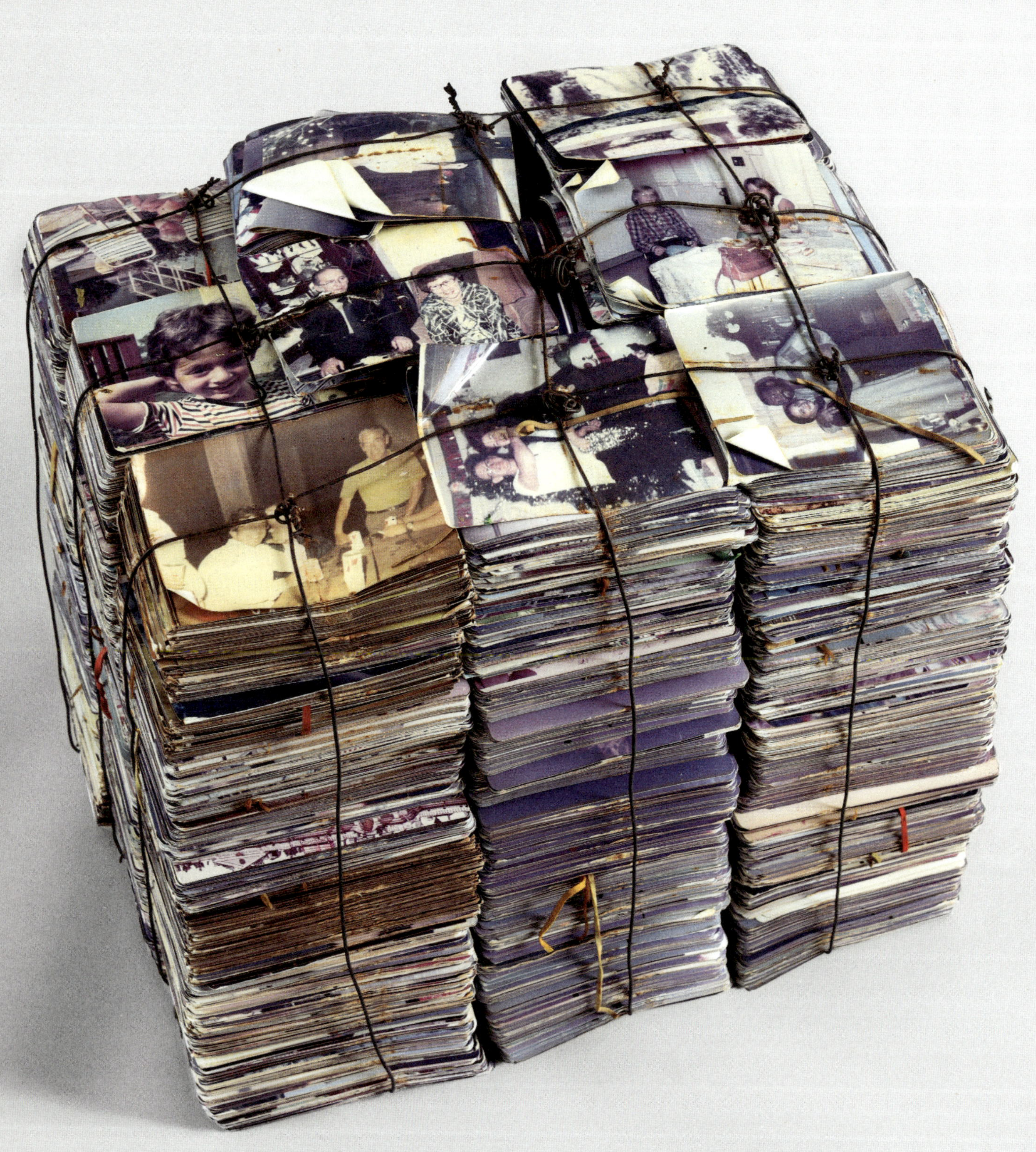

How one groundbreaking exhibition defined experimental photography in Southern California.

The Genuine in a World of Copies

Erin O'Toole

In the 1970s, the desire to integrate photography into a broader art context was still a minority position. Two decades later, however, when Charles Desmarais was director of the Laguna Art Museum, photography had become mainstream, and the medium had been all but fully embraced by the contemporary art world. Desmarais welcomed this shift. But, as he told me recently, he regretted that while Cindy Sherman, Richard Prince, Barbara Kruger, and other members of the so-called Pictures Generation had become art world darlings, many of the photographers and artists he knew and admired in Southern California who used photography in their work had been "left behind." With *Proof: Los Angeles Art and the Photograph 1960–1980*, an exhibition he organized for the Laguna Art Museum in 1992, Desmarais made a case for Los Angeles as an important, but overlooked, center for the convergence of photography and contemporary art, and argued that figures such

George Blakely, *A Cubic Foot of Photographs*, 1978. Photograph by Chris Bliss, 2018
Courtesy the artist and the Laguna Art Museum

This page:
Wallace Berman,
***Untitled*, ca. 1968**
Courtesy the Estate of Wallace Berman and Kohn Gallery, Los Angeles

Opposite:
Steve H. Kahn,
***Door/Window #3*, 1978**
© Steve H. Kahn Trust and courtesy Casemore Kirkeby Gallery, San Francisco

as photographer and educator Robert Heinecken, along with artists Ed Ruscha, John Baldessari, and Wallace Berman, had anticipated, in some cases by several decades, many of the concerns that would later come to define postmodernism and the work of the Pictures Generation group.

Desmarais, who has held leadership positions at various museums and other art institutions across the country over his long career and is now the art critic for the *San Francisco Chronicle*, got his start in the photography world. His first job before attending graduate school was at Friends of Photography, in Carmel, California, where he had initially gone to attend a summer workshop and meet Ansel Adams. After getting to know Heinecken, whom he met at the job around 1971 and whose ideas about the medium, as he put it, "turned my head around," Desmarais increasingly sought ways to, as he termed it, "use what I knew and the experience I had to relate it to a larger art world that I thought photography could be, and should be, a part of."

A project like *Proof* was an intervention, in part because the New York–centric art world had long considered Southern California to be an artistic backwater.

A recuperative project like *Proof* was, in the 1990s, an intervention, at least in part because the New York–centric art world had long considered Southern California to be an artistic backwater and had been, until relatively recently, reluctant to embrace LA artists. Given the vibrancy of the art scene in LA today, it might be difficult for younger readers to believe, but with few

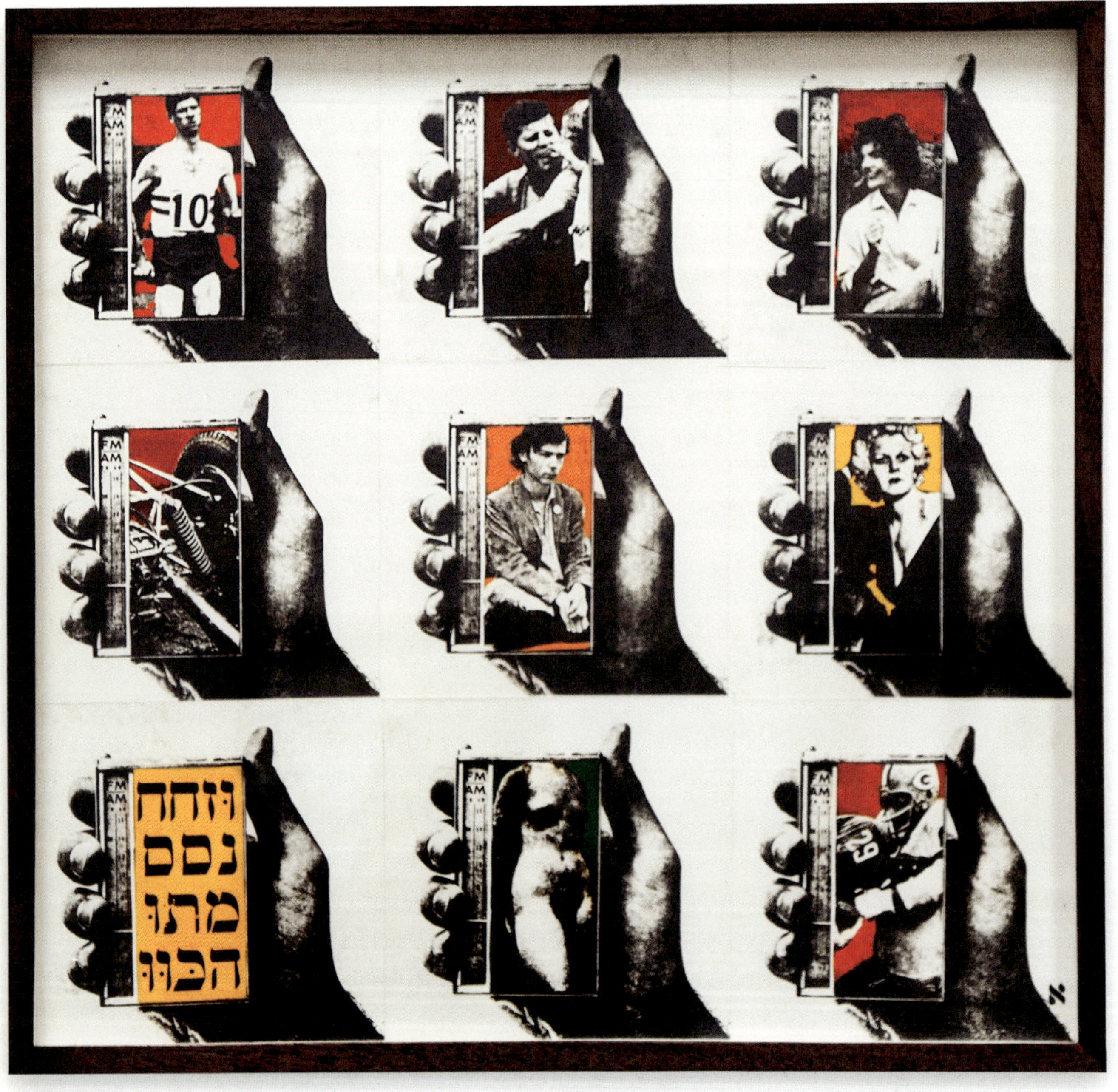

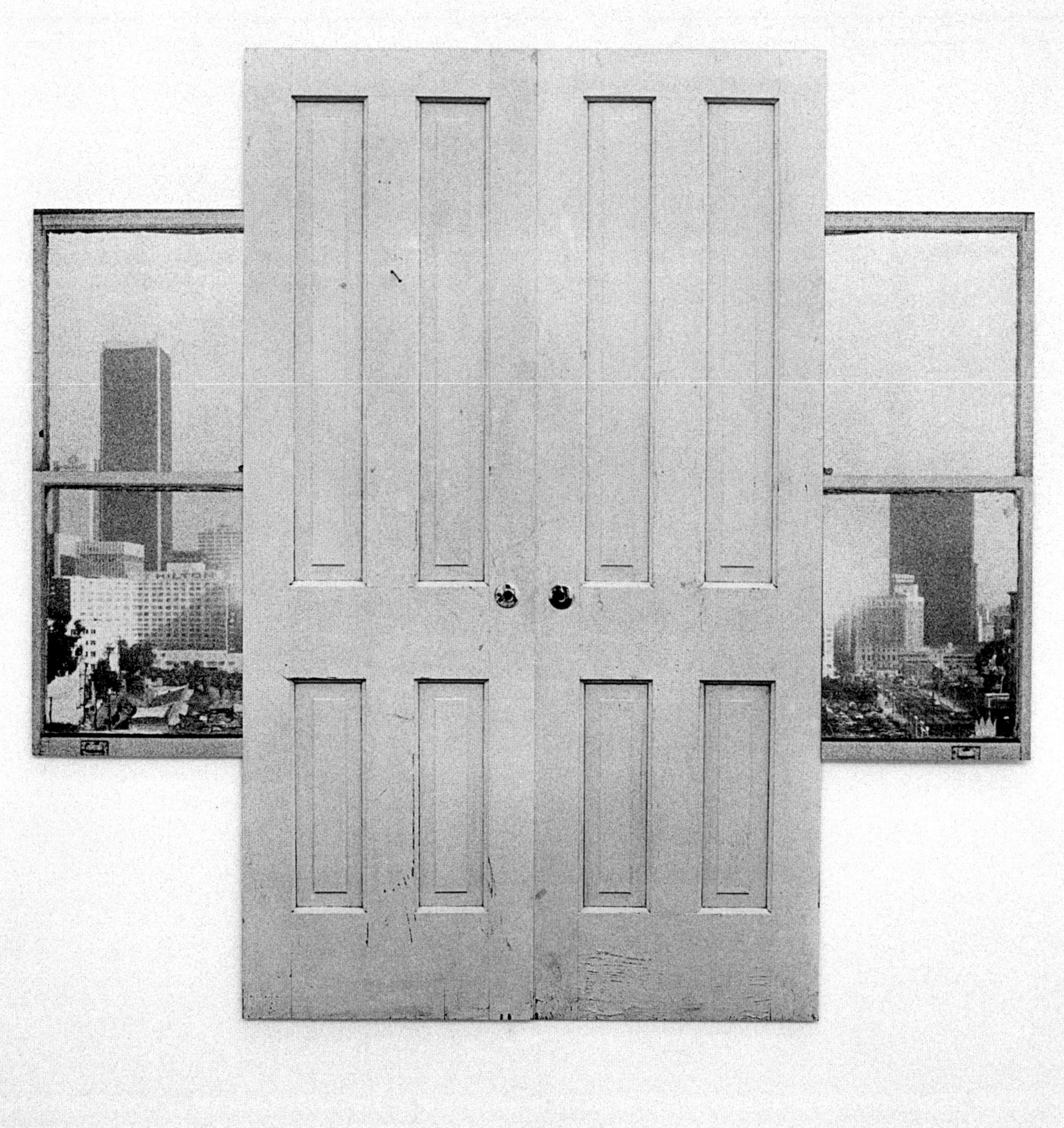

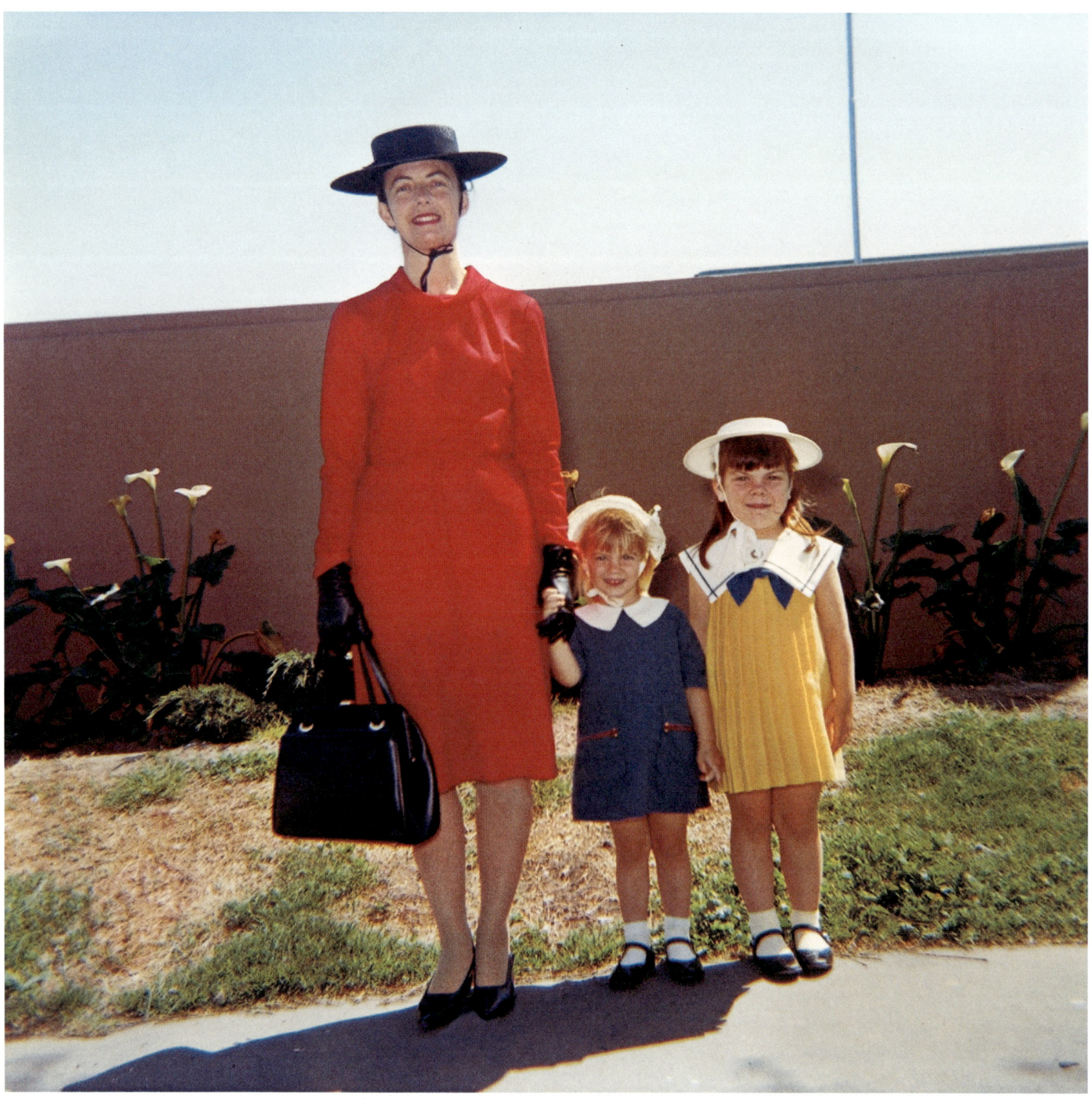

Allan Sekula, *Meditations on a Triptych* (detail), 1973/78
Courtesy Allan Sekula Studio

museums, galleries, or collectors, and negligible artistic heritage to speak of, LA had seemingly little to offer aspiring artists in the period covered by the exhibition, aside from ample sunshine and large, inexpensive spaces available for studios. For many who worked there, however, the very lack of institutional infrastructure and attention from the New York art world was what made LA so appealing. The sense of freedom and possibility was energizing and generative for those with the right mindset, and, as *Proof* demonstrated, the conditions were ripe for experimentation, especially with photography.

Eleanor Antin, whose work was included in *Proof*, told Desmarais, in an interview conducted for the exhibition, that in Southern California there was "an openness not found on the East Coast and a generosity of spirit. New York was always formulating the correct ways to work and think while back here we were always eager to be surprised and engage in new ways."

Freedom from the "correct" way of working could be especially fruitful for photographers, Jack Butler, another artist in the show, noted. "Individuals just worked on their work without concern for acceptance by a 'ruling' authority, i.e., John Szarkowski in New York," he said, adding, "the dogmatic prejudice of straight photography towards alternative methods of working with the photographic image did not exist here." Crucially, there also wasn't the same sort of segregation between photographers and artists working in other media as there was in places like New York or San Francisco. With fewer local elders to look to, many of the photographers included in *Proof* found inspiration in the work of painters and sculptors instead. A boundary-defying intermixing of photography with printmaking, sculpture, and painting was the happy result.

The forty-five artists included in *Proof* had practices that ranged widely, from the more conceptual, like Douglas Huebler, Allen Ruppersberg, or John Baldessari, to those with roots in California funk and assemblage, like Wallace Berman, George Herms, Llyn Foulkes, and Edward Kienholz. A large percentage of the younger artists in the show, such as John Divola, Ellen Brooks, Darryl Curran, Michael Stone, and Carl Cheng, had studied with Heinecken at the University of California, Los Angeles, and had embraced his unconventional belief that photographs are not just images, but objects. While they didn't constitute a cohesive movement of any kind, the artists in the show were united by an interest, Desmarais contends, to varying degrees and for different lengths of time, in "an investigation of the photograph's essence," of its dual nature as evidence and interpretation. "Challenging its authority as a repository of fact," he writes, these artists used photography "... to lie, or to detect lies, or to rethink the conventional distinction between lie and truth." Like the Pictures Generation artists, they also drew from mass media sources, repurposed found imagery, and incorporated text into their works, using photography, as Desmarais termed it, "as a basic tool for examining our culture's self-image and for searching out the genuine in a world of copies."

Reviewing the catalog, one is struck by the variety of forms and subject matter, as well as the humor, the lively energy, and the insouciance of much of the work. The exhibition contained everything from a Kienholz sculpture made from a salvaged car door, where a silk-screened print from a photograph, rather than glass, fills the window frame; a bundle of snapshots tied together with string like a stack of newspapers (George Blakely's *A Cubic Foot of Photographs*, 1978); abstracted image fragments of female body parts sourced from porn and printed on maxi pads (Suda House's *Stay Free Series*, 1976); a classic Berman Verifax collage featuring pictures of John and Jackie Kennedy (*Untitled*, ca. 1968); a text-heavy study of three snapshots, each of which includes the same woman wearing a bright red dress (Allan Sekula's *Meditations on a Triptych*, 1973/78); a forbidding simulacrum of a door and two windows with grainy views of a grim LA cityscape (Steve Kahn's *Door/Window #3*, 1978); and, not surprisingly, a selection of books by Ruscha.

By reframing the story of postwar art in LA around the photograph, Desmarais surprised even those already well versed in the history of art in Southern California. In his review of *Proof* for the *Los Angeles Times*, published November 12, 1992, Christopher Knight, an art critic and one of the most astute chroniclers of the region's art, described the experience of visiting the exhibition as a classic *aha!* moment: "Once in a while, an analytical museum exhibition comes along at which you find yourself exclaiming, 'Of course. It's so obvious. Why hasn't anyone thought of this before?' With straightforwardness and concision, it manages to uncover what was hitherto hidden—right before your very eyes."

Suda House, *Stay Free Series*, Los Angeles, 1976. 3M color-in-color transfer on 28 sanitary napkins

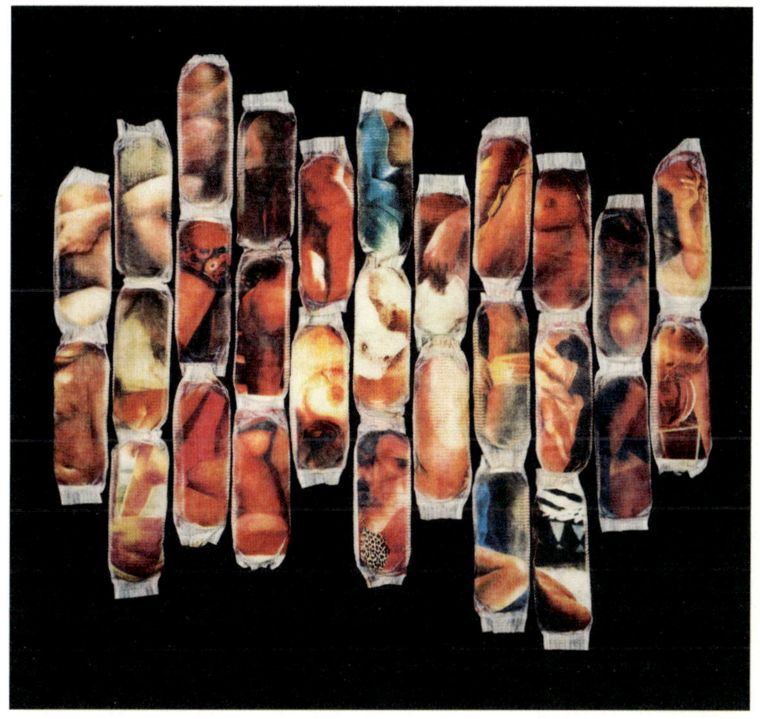

Erin O'Toole is the Baker Street Foundation Associate Curator of Photography at the San Francisco Museum of Modern Art.

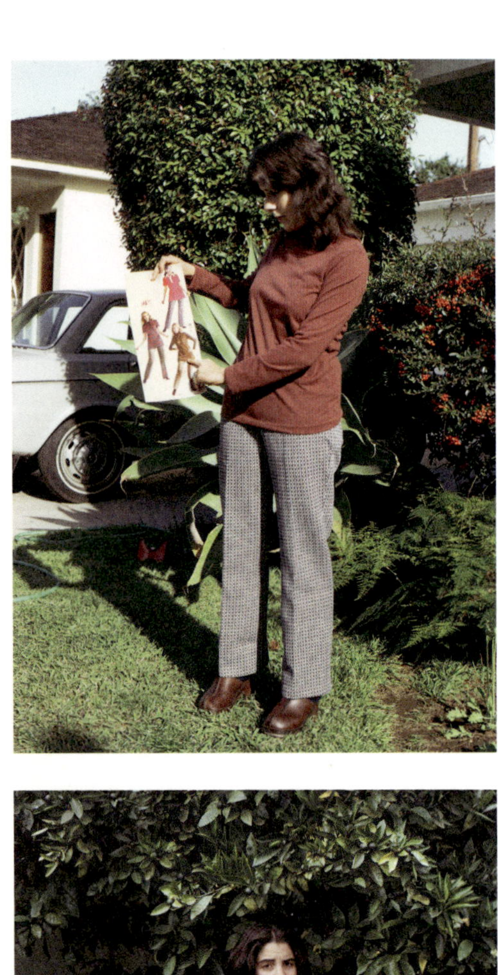
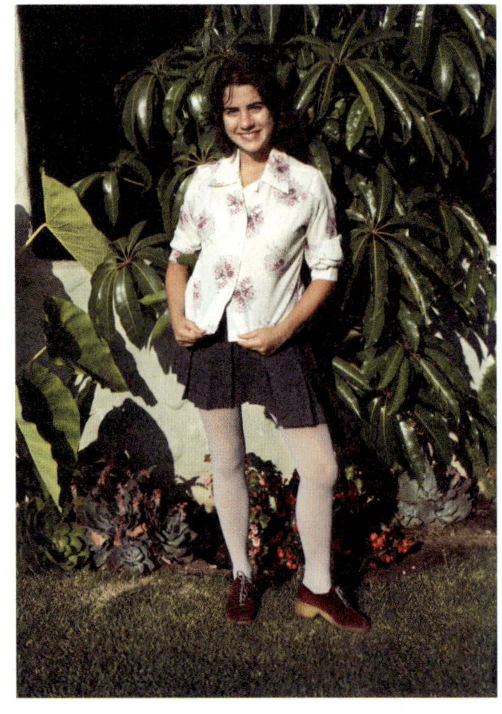
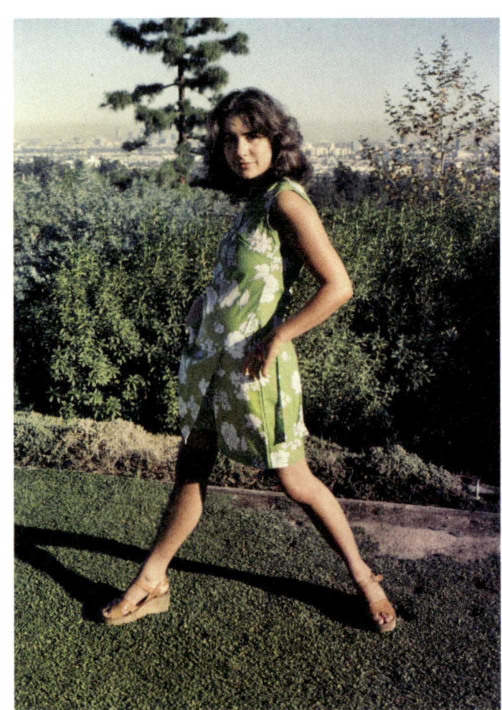
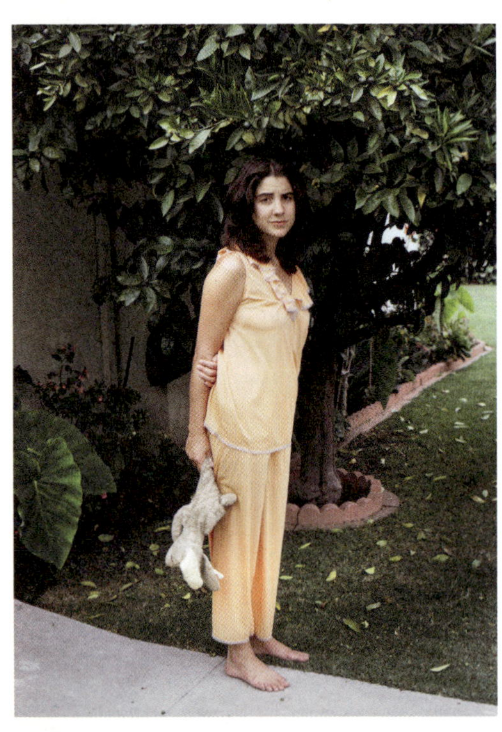
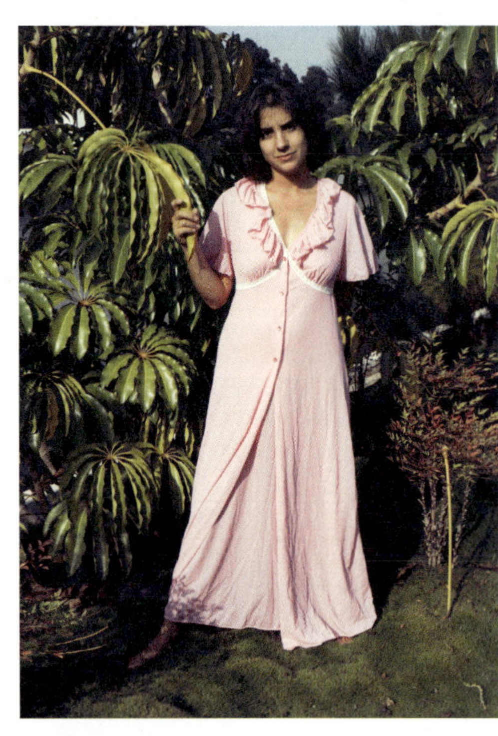
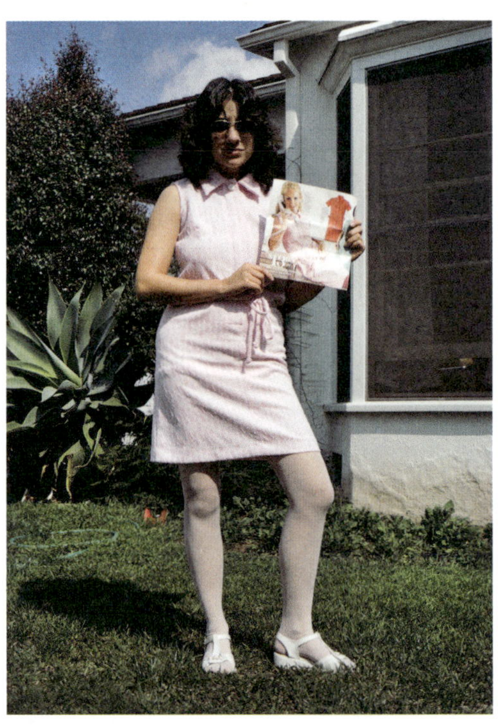
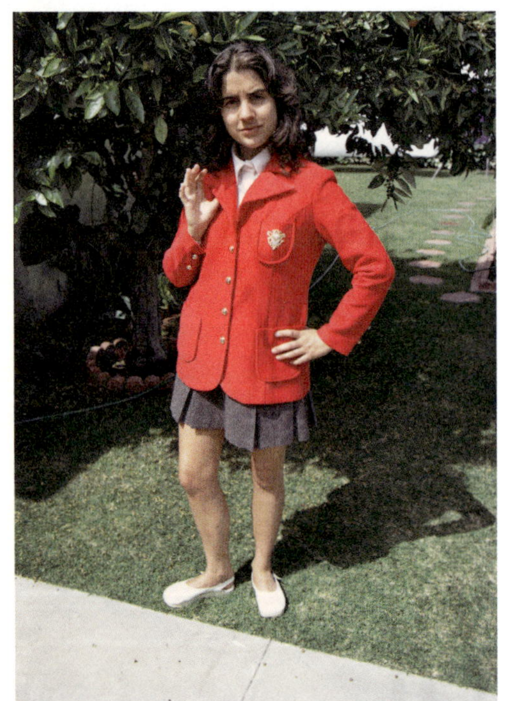
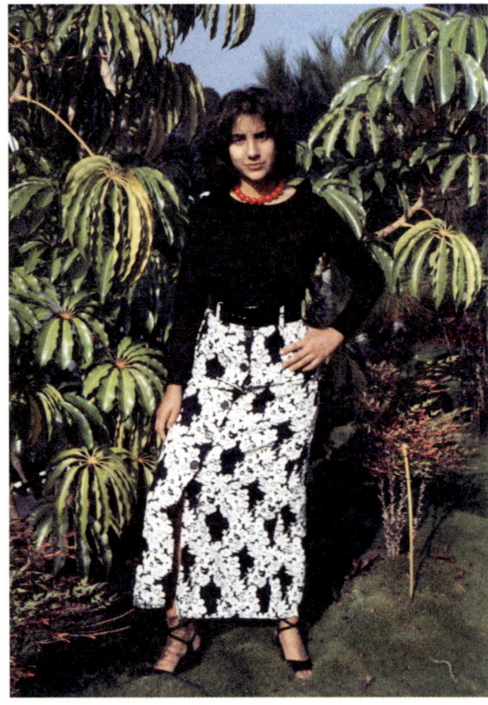
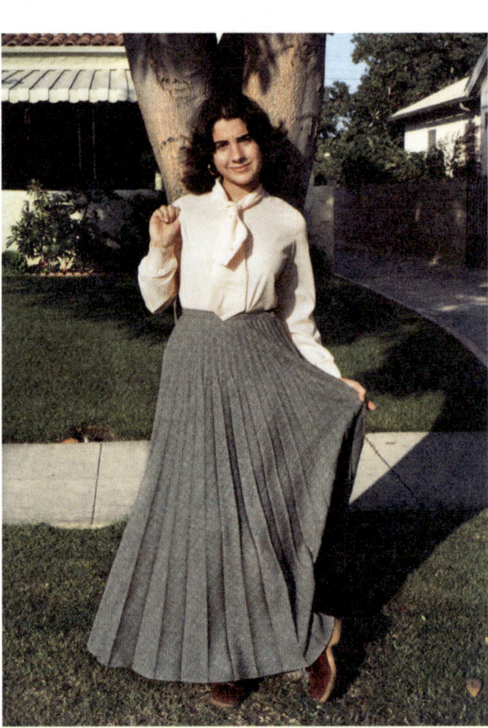

Ilene Segalove's Modern America

A Conversation with Charlotte Cotton

"There was an obvious, loud blur between artifice and reality," Ilene Segalove says of growing up in Los Angeles. "*The Graduate* was filmed across the street from my house in Beverly Hills. Dustin Hoffman's stand-in kept asking me out on dates. My mom told me I should wait for the 'real' Dustin Hoffman, and then say, 'Yes.' That never happened."

Maybe not, but such slippages between reality and illusion would shape Segalove's development as an artist. After studying with John Baldessari at CalArts, she worked in his studio, an experience that cemented the idea that in art anything is permissible. An early adopter of video art before the form even had a name, Segalove used playfulness and wit to create a distinctive body of work throughout the 1970s, often casting her own mother as lead protagonist. In *The Mom Tapes* (1974–78), Segalove, influenced by protoforms of reality television like the 1973 PBS series *An American Family*, adopted a mock-documentary approach, interviewing and following her mother around her spacious home. Other photo-based works from this time were influenced by feminist discourse and offer humorous commentary on the everyday. Segalove, who now lives in Santa Barbara, recently spoke with curator Charlotte Cotton about this period and growing up in LA's celebrity culture.

Page 84:
New Process Mail Order Wear, Then Send Back Polyester Clothes, 1973

This page, top and bottom: Stills from *The Mom Tapes*, 1974–78. Single-channel digital video, transferred from U-Matic video tape, 26:52 minutes, black-and-white and color, sound

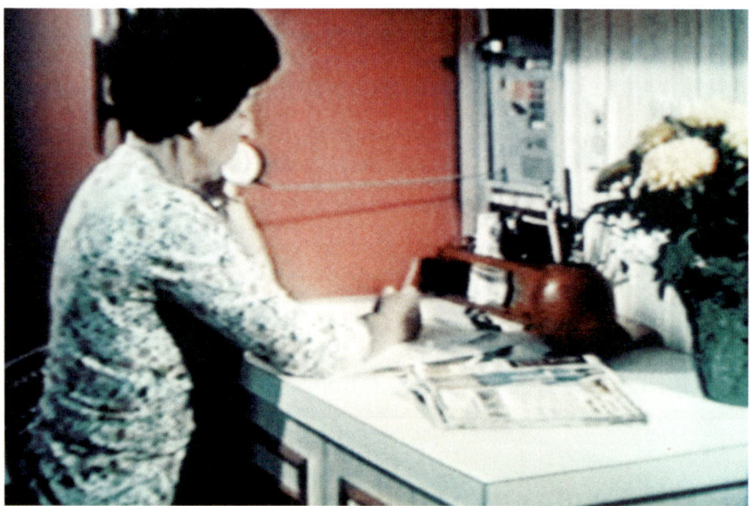

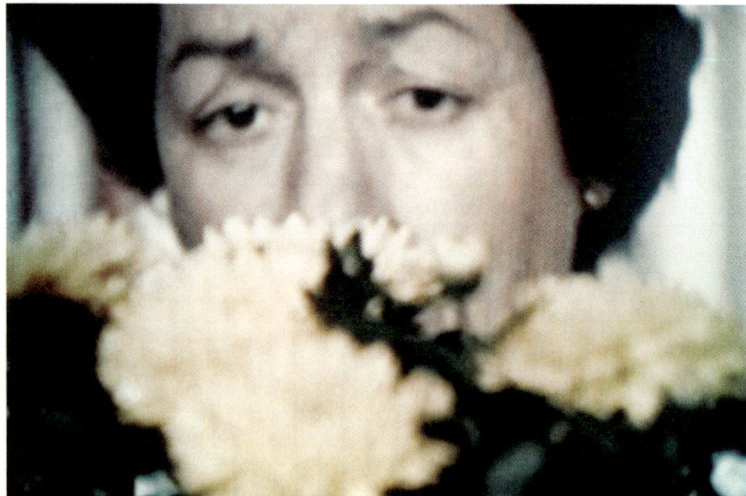

Charlotte Cotton: **Ilene, tell me about growing up in LA.**

Ilene Segalove: I grew up in Culver City, then we moved to Beverly Hills when it was just a little, tiny town. It influenced my point of view completely. Everybody was just a human being, and my mother did not make a big deal about celebrities. My best friend was Rita Hayworth's daughter Yasmin. I'd go over to Rita's house as a young girl of eleven years old, and I'd see Rita lying on the bed, often drunk and disheveled, and then, within about an hour and a half, she would become movie starlet Rita Hayworth going out on the town with a prince.

I was definitely fascinated by what was real and what wasn't. When Disneyland opened, I was part of a group of kids who got to go behind the scenes. There was a ride called Rocket to the Moon, and they showed us how they rigged the seats to shake and exposed the trick. That tainted me, but it also made me kind of insightful about the fine line between reality and illusion.

CC: **What did your parents do?**

IS: My father was a scientist, and my mother was a woman out of time. She was a very feisty, irreverent person who questioned authority and was pretty funny. She lived to be 101 and drove me crazy my whole life. She was great, because she just said to me, "Be an individual. Be original. Don't be a knockoff." She encouraged that.

CC: **Did she have any outlets to express herself?**

IS: She had a lot of friends, and she was like their pseudopsychiatrist. She had been a social worker and had a master's degree in psychiatric social work. But she was a full-time Jewish mother. She could have run a small country, but like a lot of women born in the 1910s, she had a hard time finding a place outside of the home.

My mother was a big part of my artwork. We did a lot of performances, and we worked on *The Mom Tapes* for what seemed like decades. I figured that if I couldn't always deal with her, at least I could direct her! For *Mother's Treasures* (1974), I posed Mom with a dozen of my art projects from elementary and junior high school. She was so proud of even the worst stuff and chastised me for not dating the work! The groundbreaking *An American Family* reality TV show was broadcast around that time on public television. This was the "first" reality TV show, about the Loud family in Santa Barbara, and I was really moved by it. I got why it had impact and understood why it was so profound. Ironically, my mom is in one of the works in the collection of the Metropolitan Museum of Art and they often screen her talking and walking around her house. She's going to outlive you and me.

CC: **Did contemporary art figure in your upbringing?**

IS: I first saw an Andy Warhol soup can painting at a bazaar held at my family's Reform synagogue Temple Emanuel in Beverly Hills. It was not so much that it was a soup can, but that it got into an art show and had clout that impressed me. I remember going to an exhibition at LACMA with my dad that included works by Kazimir Malevich. My dad was so disgusted with it; he went home and made an exact knockoff of it. I just said to him, "It's not the work, Dad; it's the fact that Malevich got in. Like, there's some reason he's there; it's not just the painting." I had a feeling there was something important going on in art.

CC: **When did you meet living artists?**

IS: When I was in college at the University of California, Santa Barbara, I met Billy Adler and John Margolies, and we worked

This page:
***Mother's Treasures*, 1974**
Clockwise from right:
"It's upside down. You did this when you were nine. I framed it. It is so beautiful. I wish you would have put your name and a date on it."; "A study in black and white. You seem to be brave with shapes. I like the movement and I can hear the song he's singing."; "It looks like you. I like the colors and the whole perspective. I see her confusion."; "These were done when you were four. You drew me very pretty, and there is Daddy. You printed your name finally."; "This was a class assignment. I think you won an award. You can collage so well."

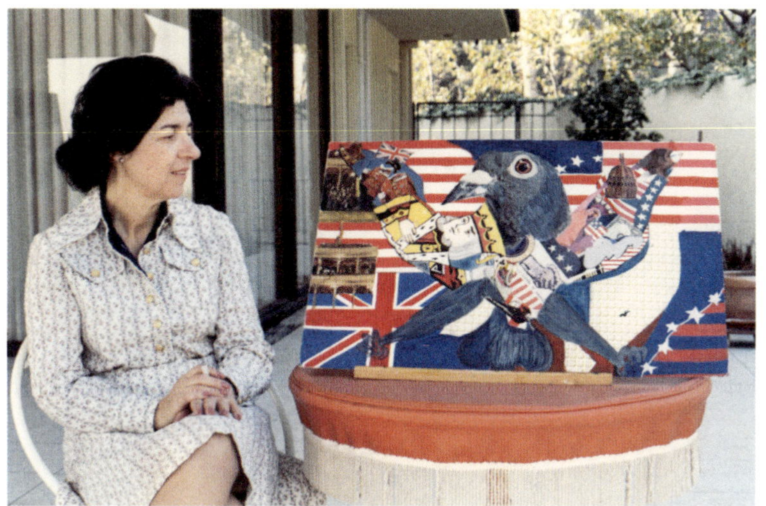

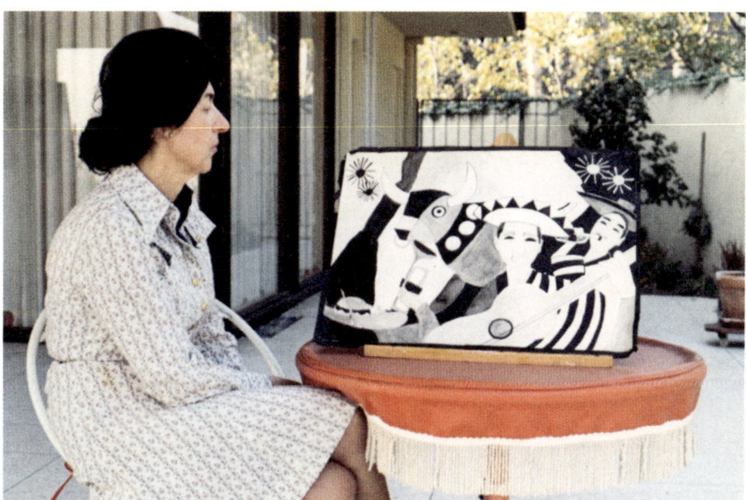

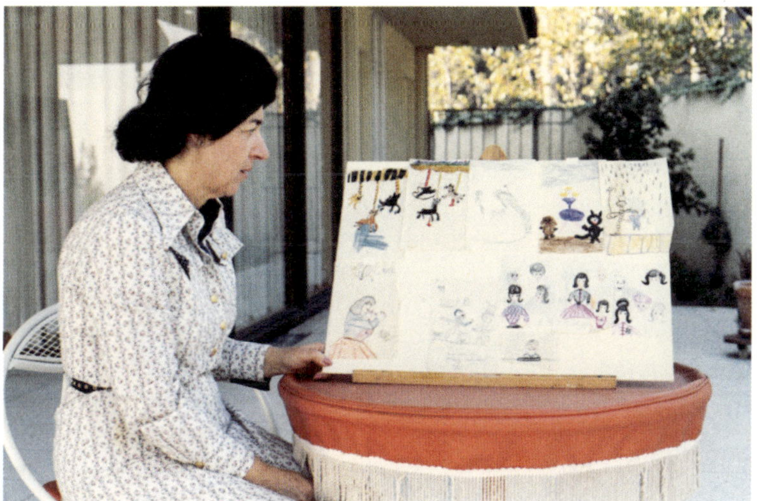

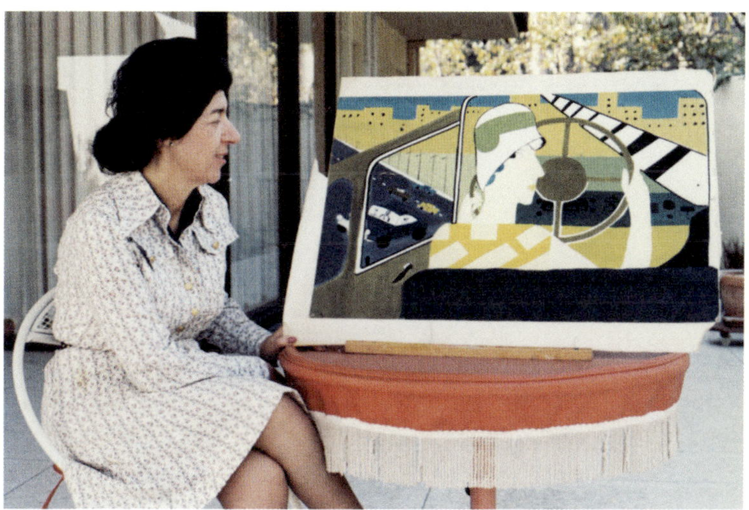

For *Mother's Treasures*, I posed Mom with a dozen of my art projects from elementary and junior high school.

together as a group called Telethon, making video, still photography, and slide shows. They were very, very influential on me; they really mined personal narrative. I remember seeing a wonderful series of photo pieces they made documenting the coffee cups at coffee shops around LA, and I thought, Okay. I got it. I have all the material in the world. I have a mother. I am a woman. And I have a life. That's all I need to make some art.

For my undergraduate show in 1972, I "installed" a fake swimming pool on the roof of the college art gallery. I was playing with the rarefied gallery space of art and the outside, recreational space, playing with what's real and what's art. You can see that I used everyday experiences in my work. With *New Process Mail Order Wear, Then Send Back Polyester Clothes* (1973), I was sent an advertisement promoting no-iron clothes with a magical,

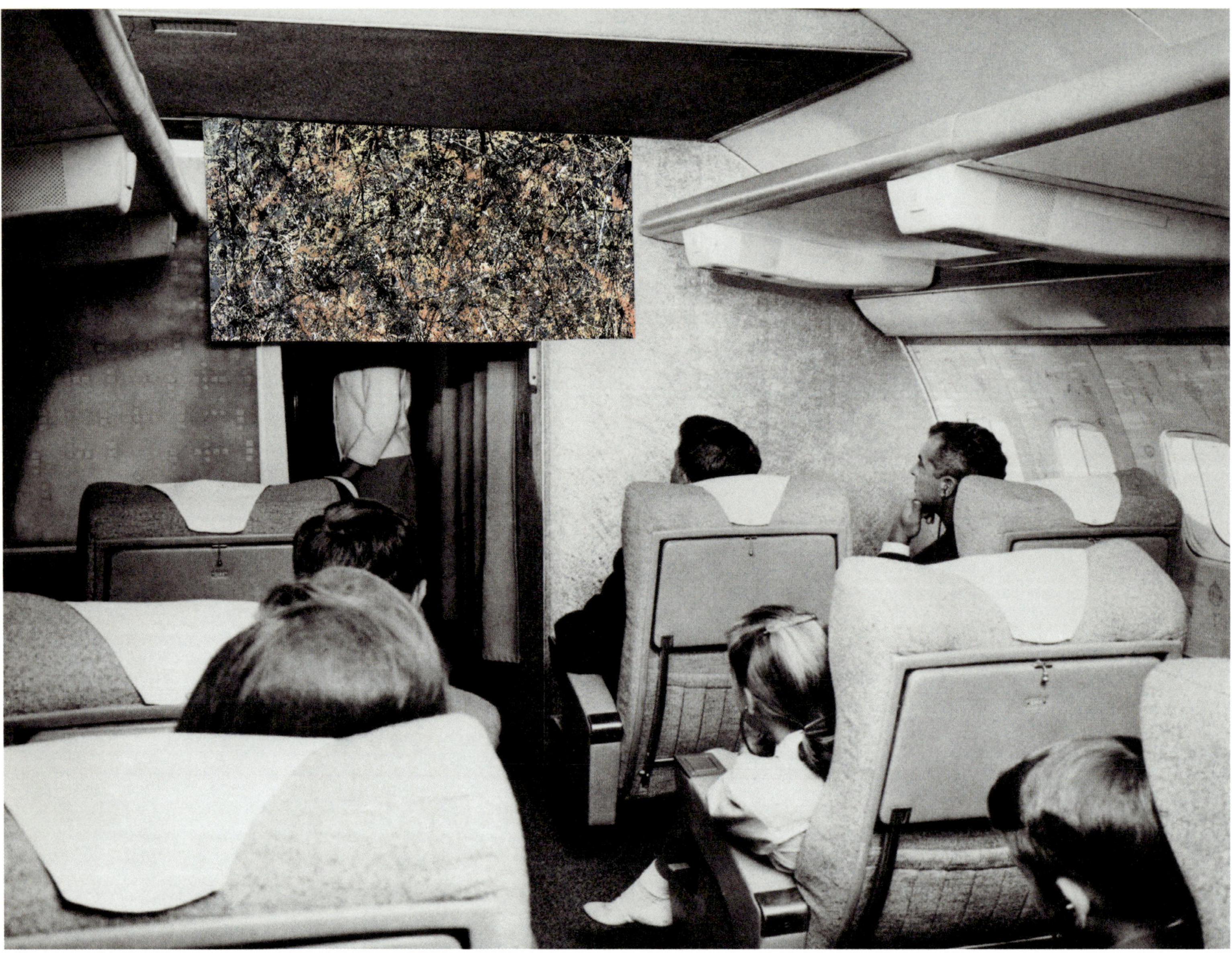

new polyester material. I'd order, wear, pose, shoot, return. They were mostly hideous and felt creepy; the material crawled on my skin. I was exploring how marketing was determining what women want and how we should look, and the difference between illusion and reality.

CC: **And that playing with—and playful confusion between—illusion and reality seems also to have been very much part of the way that you work with conceptual practice and the channels of popular media, especially in terms of your video work and its relationship to TV.**

IS: When I began making *The Mom Tapes*, in 1974, I showed them at Loyola, and a TV director for *General Hospital*—a classic television soap opera—watched it, and his comment was, "You should get someone else to play your mom and someone else to do her voice." I played the same tape in John Baldessari's class at CalArts, and everyone was like, "Wow, that's great." I thought, What do I do?

CC: **You worked at Baldessari's studio? How did you connect with him?**

IS: I went to graduate school at Loyola Marymount University in LA because they had a film and TV department, and I thought that would be interesting. I knew a lot of people in Hollywood and thought maybe I could do that. So, by night, I got my master's. By day, I audited at CalArts and just moseyed into a class by Baldessari, and we became friends. I just loved the way he thought. I got his love of text, movies, mundane content ... everything was permissible. But he was rigorous. It was like, "Don't fuck around. Pull it out of the hat."

CC: **Were you making any distinctions between what would become photographs and what would become video?**

IS: I was pretty clear. The concept was the driving force. I really liked going back and forth between photography, video, and text-driven work. The early days of video were fun because it didn't fully exist yet as an art medium. When I was more focused on making video, I taught at Otis College of Art and Design. There wasn't a video department; there was nothing. I had to bring in my own equipment to teach a class. It was before things were named and given titles, and before there were departments. I taught a class called Intermedia, which was the only name they had at the time for "something else." It was a really fun nowheresland. I really like being places before things get defined.

CC: **I really identify with what you are saying, Ilene. One of the reasons that I adore being in Los Angeles more than other places is that I think of the art schools as holding the critical mass of creative practice here. It is also set within the climate of Hollywood, where everyone is freelance and there are lots of people getting up every day and having a practice, and that's not a shameful thing. The reality is that most people**

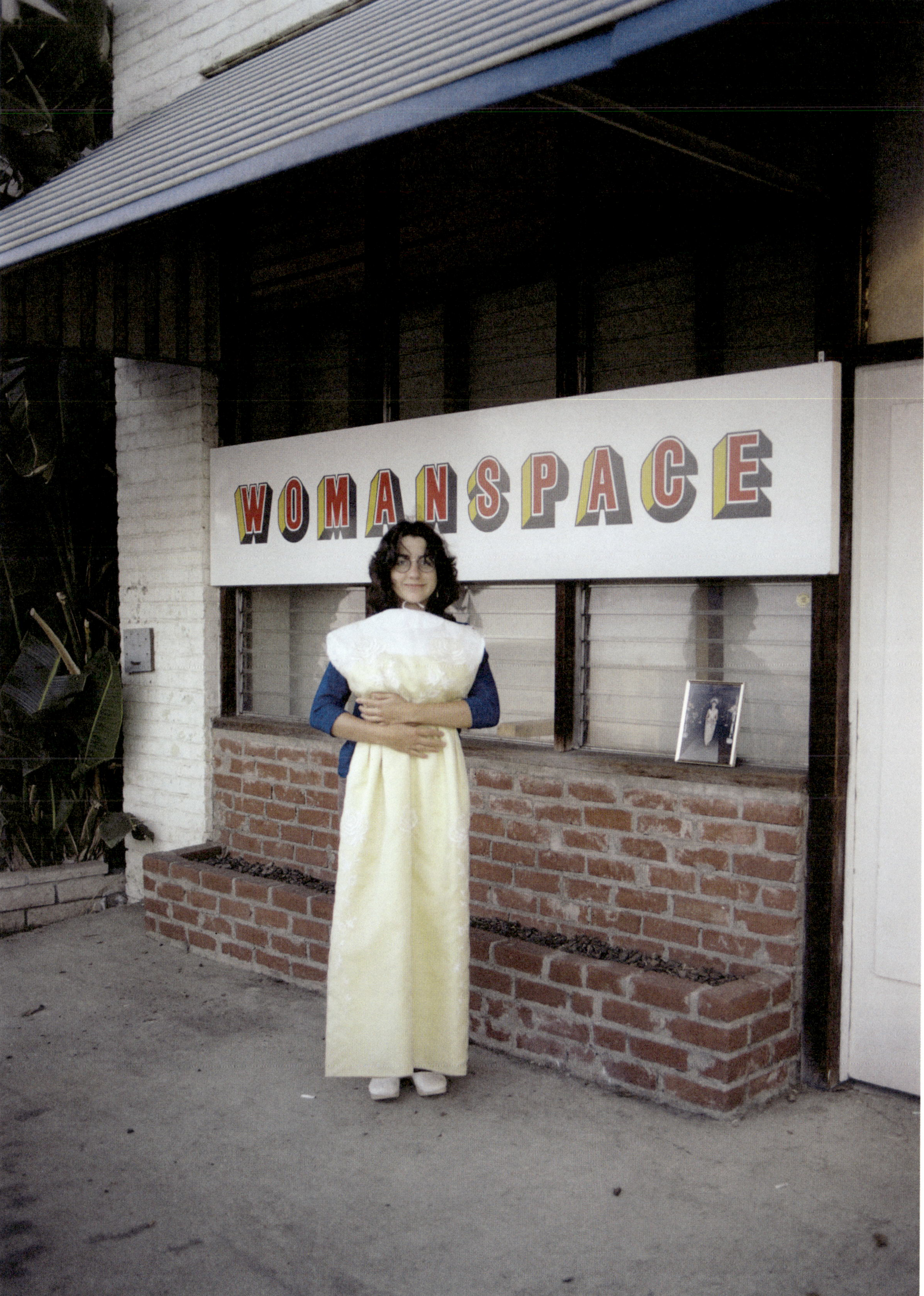
WOMANSPACE

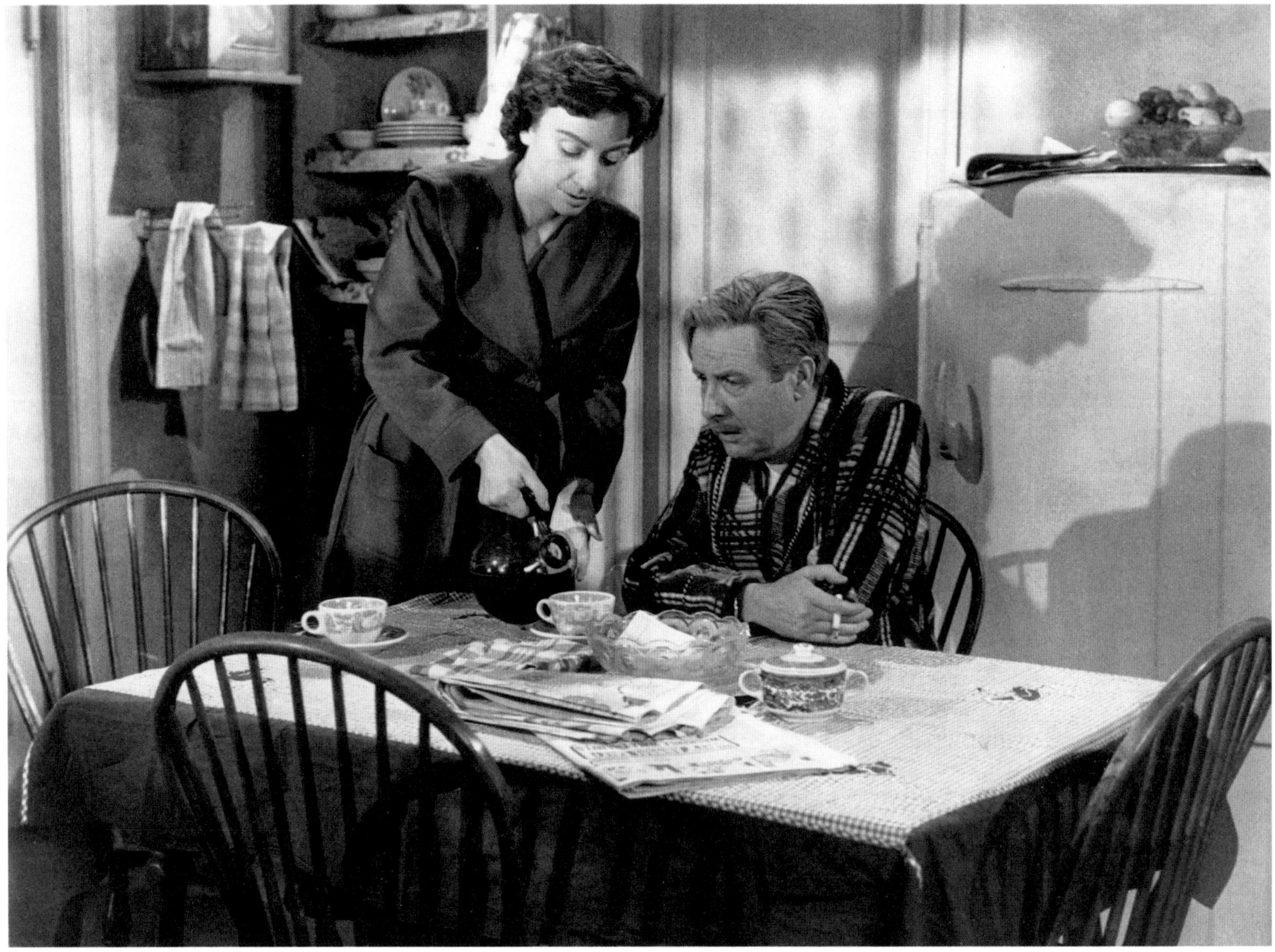

Page 88:
Today's Program: Jackson Pollock, Lavender Mist, 1950, 1974

Previous page:
Ilene Segalove preparing for an installation piece titled *Maid of Honor. Made of Honor.*, Womanspace Gallery, Los Angeles, 1973

don't think for very long that they're going to be the one in ten million who is going to earn ridiculous amounts of money and become totally famous for what they do, but you'd rather be here than in another city where you'd be constantly justifying making this your daily life. I think LA does allow you to explore the in-between. I think it also gives you the strength to change creative direction. This leads me to my next question for you: What were the significant turning points for your creative practice after the heady conceptual art days?

I have all the material in the world. I have a mother. I am a woman. And I have a life. That's all I need to make some art.

IS: Well, I don't know if this is a significant one, but it changed me. I had been making video works from 1972 to 1986, and was pretty well identified as a video artist. A producer from National Public Radio, Steve Proffitt, was in LA making profiles on artists, and I was one of the people he chose. In postproduction, he needed some of my tapes to use as audio tracks to illustrate a story. When I listened to his NPR piece, I realized that my work held up perfectly without the visuals! The videos were great without the pictures! I was like, Wait a minute. That's where all the money went, to make the images, to create the sets, and to create the costumes.

That was 1986, and I decided I didn't want to make any more videotapes and I wanted to do radio. I had never been a radio buff and had no idea how you did it. But this was pre–*This American Life*, so people weren't used to highly produced narratives at all. I slid in and became a regular—"Ilene Segalove comments on growing up in modern America." Steve and I produced a number of my personal stories, and NPR just aired them without much editing. It was like

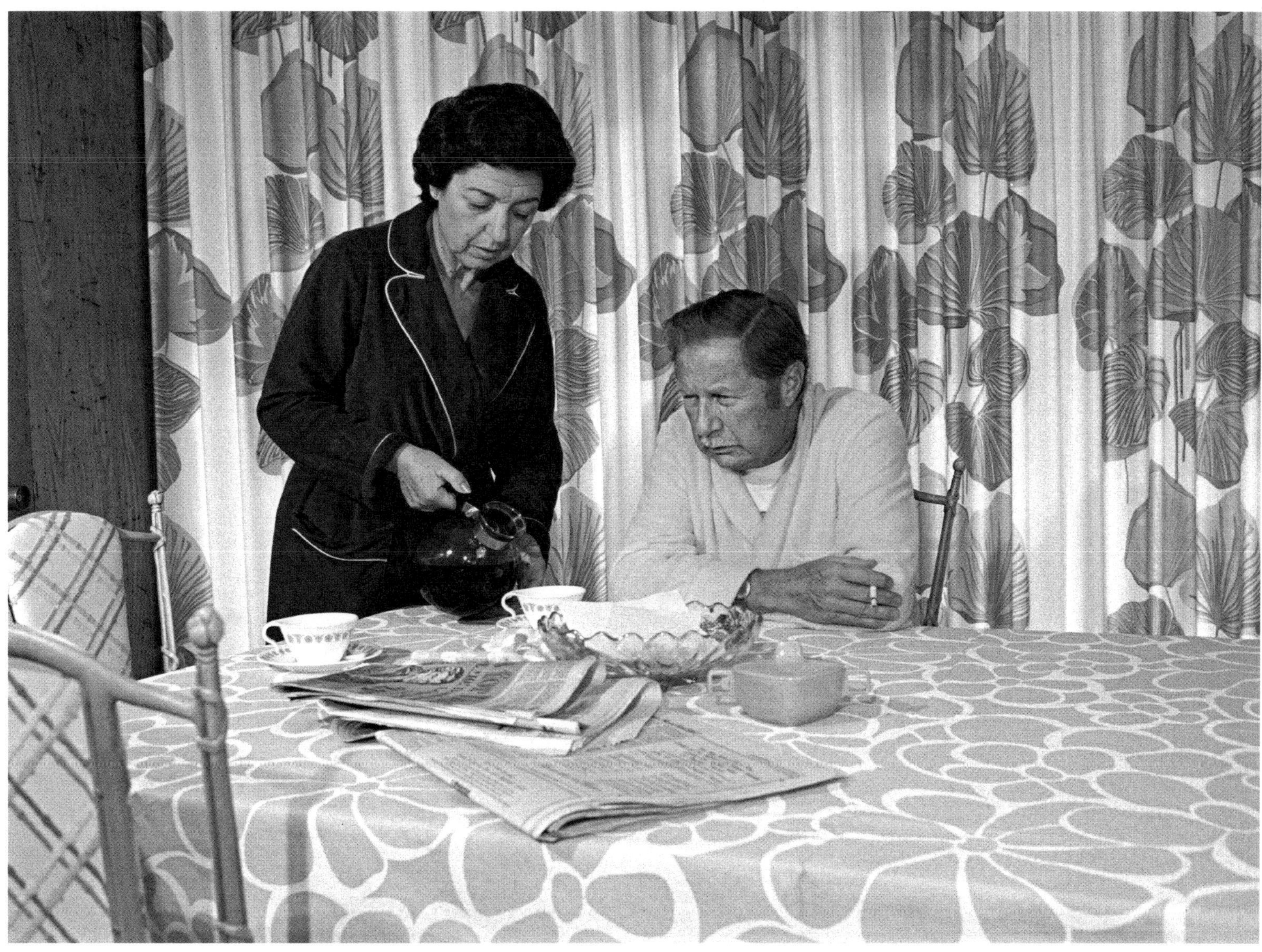

magic. I made about thirty hours of programming; it was so much fun and easy and genuine and direct. It's like shooting a great photograph with your iPhone compared to all the effort of producing a visual piece. All I did was hang out with strangers and interview them. I could cut the tape reel to reel with a razor blade and tape it together. I could do everything at home; I didn't have to go down to a postproduction studio. So, in a way, it was like being a real artist, creating independent work, but with the added beauty that it had a platform that was friendly. People would randomly press a button in their cars and comment: "Oh, I heard you. I was driving down the road."

CC: **I might be projecting here, but that seems to be your through line—a conceptual practice that roves into the areas where you are curious and have fun collaborating?**

IS: Well, when I started making radio it was a big turning point because it meant I was giving up some of my identity. If you give up your persona as an artist and your signature way of working, you may fall by the wayside—and I decided I'd fall by the art wayside. I really got into the idea of publishing blank journal books, which catapulted me into a quirkier version of asking personal questions to a wider audience that were nonthreatening but valuable to a lot of people. With Paul Bob Velick, I created *List Your Self*, which sold almost 500,000 copies and hopefully gave many people the excuse to narrate themselves. Being an author actually gave me more respect and adulation than I've had doing anything else. It's really funny.... It's so funny.

This spread:
***If You Live Near Hollywood You Can't Help But Look Like Some 8 × 10 Glossy*, 1976**
Left: A gripping scene from the powerful drama *The Violators*, starring Irene Blackburn and Arthur O'Connell; Right: My parents having breakfast in their home near Hollywood

All works courtesy the artist

Charlotte Cotton is a writer and curator based in Los Angeles. She is the editor of the Aperture books *Public, Private, Secret: On Photography and the Configuration of the Self* (2018) and *Photography is Magic* (2015).

Jennifer Piejko

Sophie Tianxin Chen

Wary cartographies comprise Los Angeles. The city's relentless sprawl—spreading itself thin over five hundred square miles—evades any attempt to cultivate a singular identity. The area we consider LA is cut into eighty-eight little cities (Culver City, Inglewood) often patched together to approximate neighborhoods and informal districts (the Westside, East LA). Greater Hollywood is at the center, both in geography and mission, the metonymic scene hosting the storied studios, the Walk of Fame, and the iconic sign at the foot of the Hollywood Hills. Just over it, though, North Hollywood, in the San Fernando Valley, has become infamous for a parallel path to notoriety: since the 1970s, the Valley has been the hub for pornography production and distribution. The area's low-lying, nondescript seediness and latent unease have fascinated establishment Hollywood (Paul Thomas Anderson's *Boogie Nights*), portraitists (Larry Sultan's *The Valley* series, shot on location a few blocks from where he grew up), and hustlers of every stripe.

"The 818" (area code shorthand for the Valley) is also home to another singularly postwar, American climate: suburbia. Taiwanese American photographer Sophie Tianxin Chen found herself at these crossroads of normative domesticity and acute malaise when, after finishing her MFA at UCLA, a campus-village located in LA's Westwood neighborhood, she relocated to the Valley, landing in Burbank. Describing her new residence as an "armpit town," she began to identify it by its "mediocrity in every way ... middle-class family houses, old-fashioned diners with elderly customers, front yard decorations for every holiday."

Having a child and becoming a caretaker while maintaining a studio practice at home only distilled these feelings of isolation. Chen longed to puncture the heaving, long stretches of dullness, much like Sultan's pornographic film subjects who wait hours in rented tract houses for a single moment of action in front of the camera. "I kept hoping for a stranger's phone call telling me my dogs had gotten loose to happen," she said. "My six-week-old fell off the bed and was taken to the hospital by an ambulance. These disastrous events brought me moments of relief."

Chen used what was in front of her, staging mise-en-scènes of the unremarkable for her large-format camera: rag dolls scattered over sandstone, bleached by the sun; bananas rendered in wholly nonsensical colors; a diaphanous cascade of plastic hangers suspended from the ceiling. Giving birth had her ceding a certain amount of control: "I am now less polite or shy in my work; it's become more raw and careless." The forfeiture has allowed for a self-objectification as well, stretching out her body for maximum unsentimental exposure to her own camera's roving lens. Like the town's X-rated permeations, Chen's late-afternoon delights feed into our voyeuristic appetites for pleasure, drama, and perversion. If watching alone isn't enough to satisfy you, then build a scene that will.

Jennifer Piejko is a writer and editor based in Los Angeles.

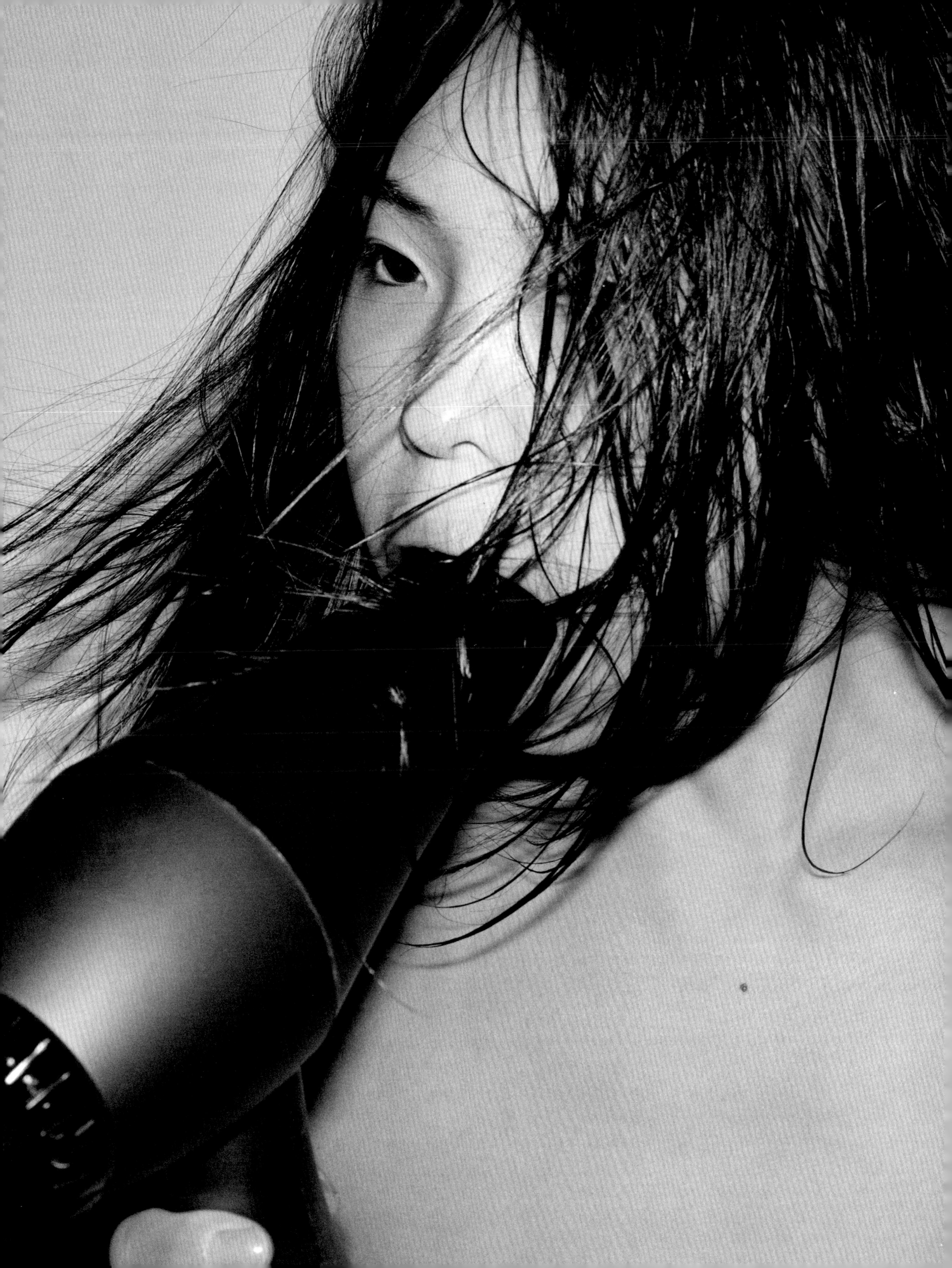

Previous page:
Untitled, 2018

This page:
Dog Day, 2016

Opposite:
Good Job, 2015

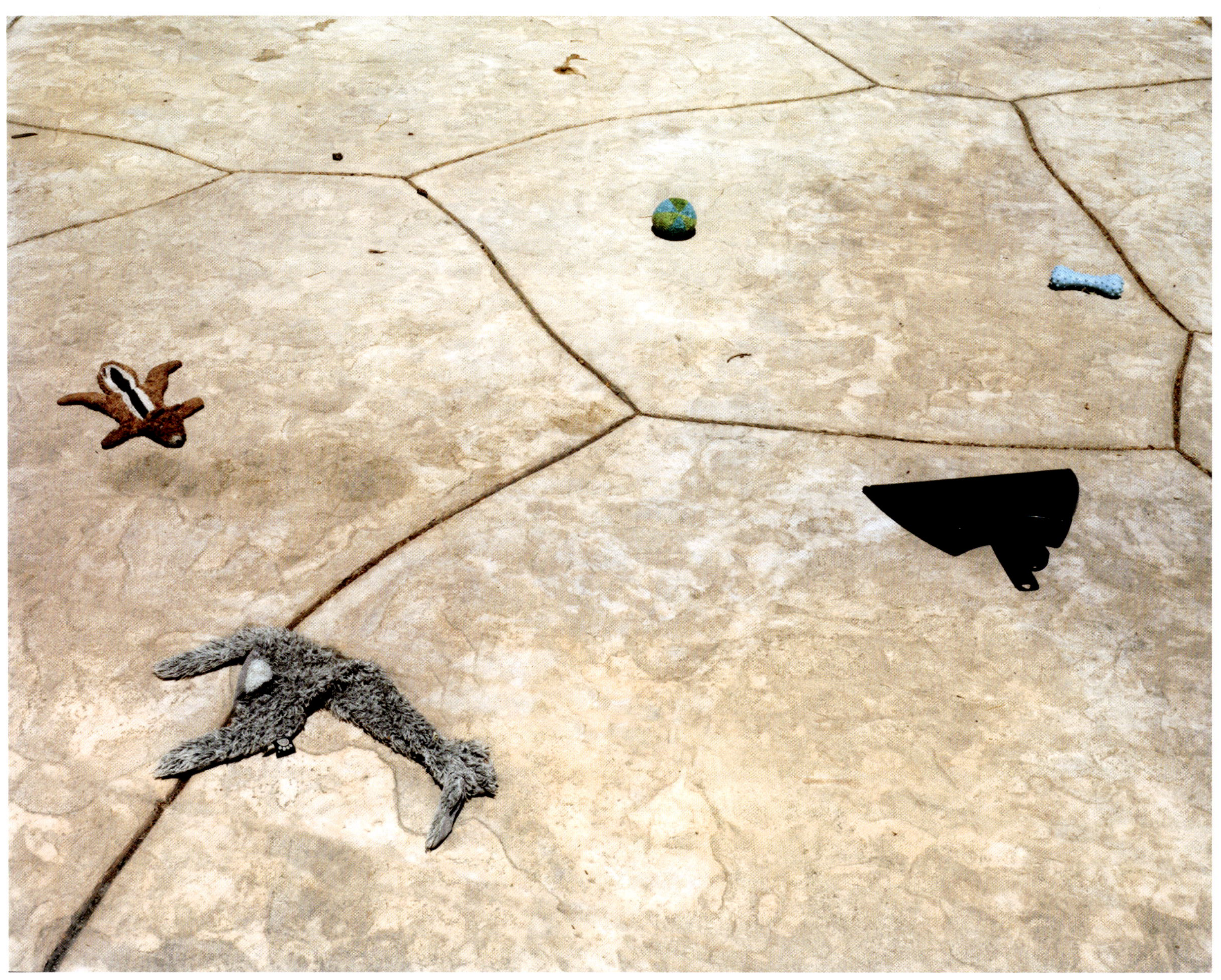

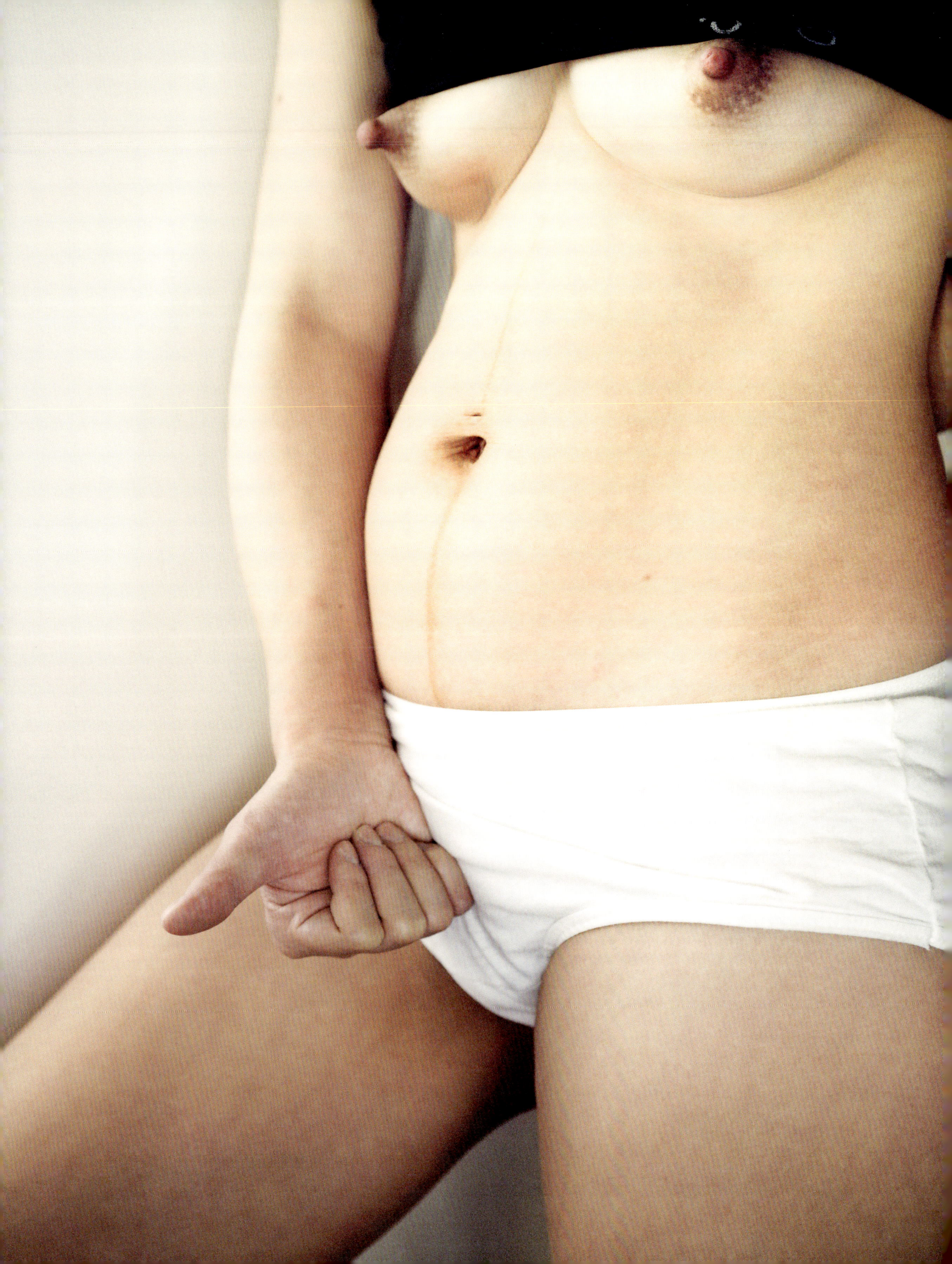

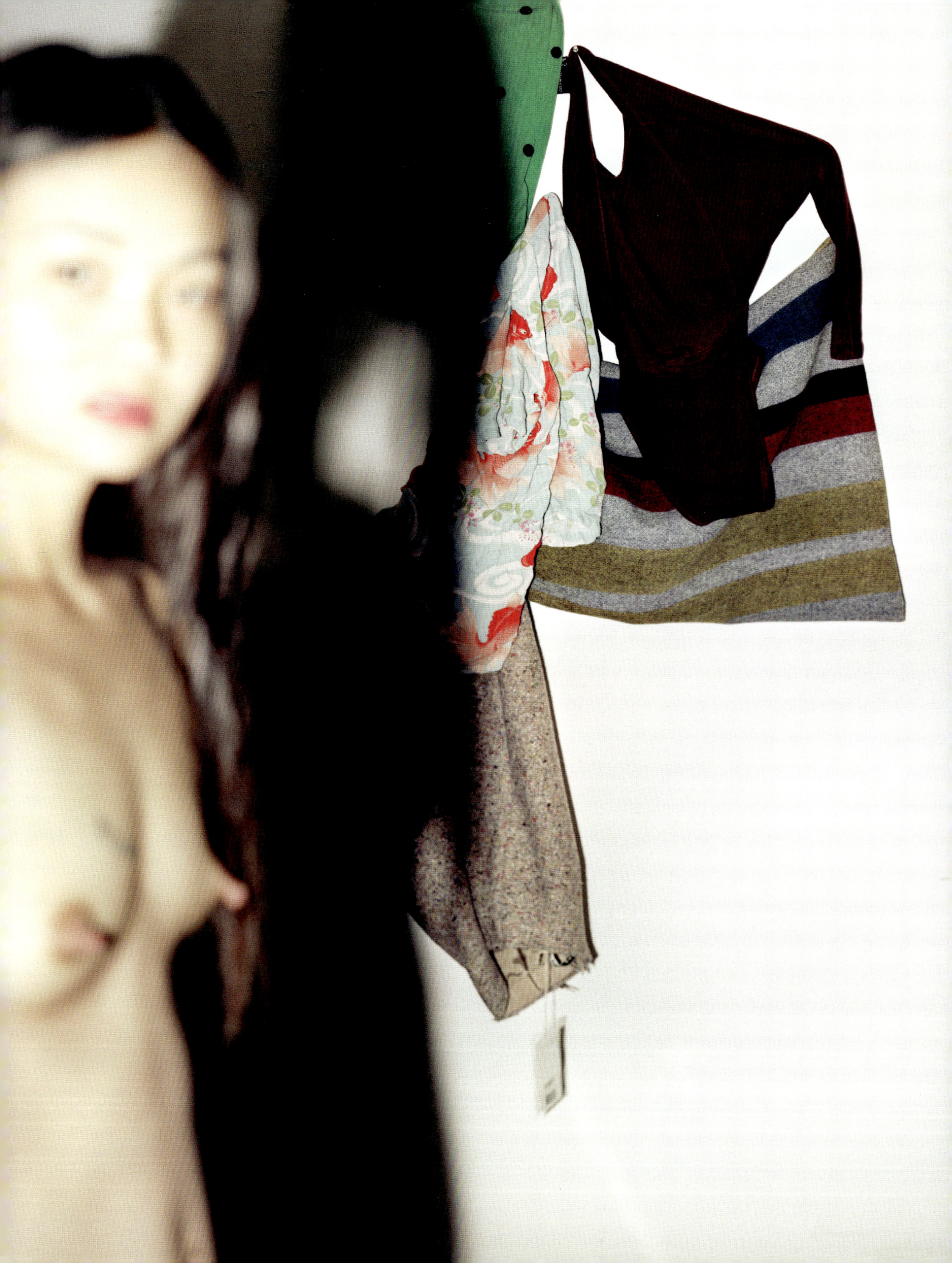

Opposite:
***Untitled*, 2017**

This page:
***Man Working*, 2017**

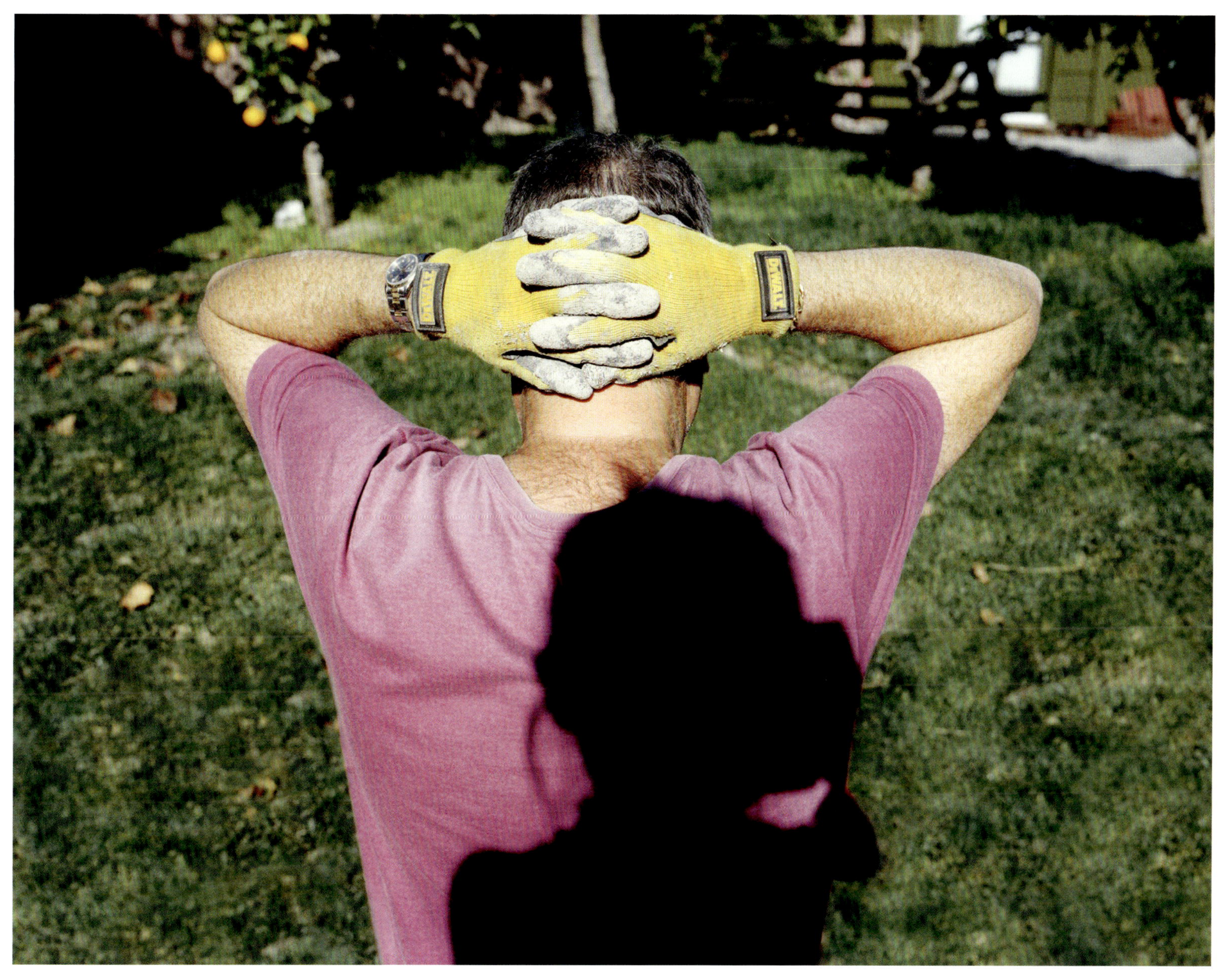

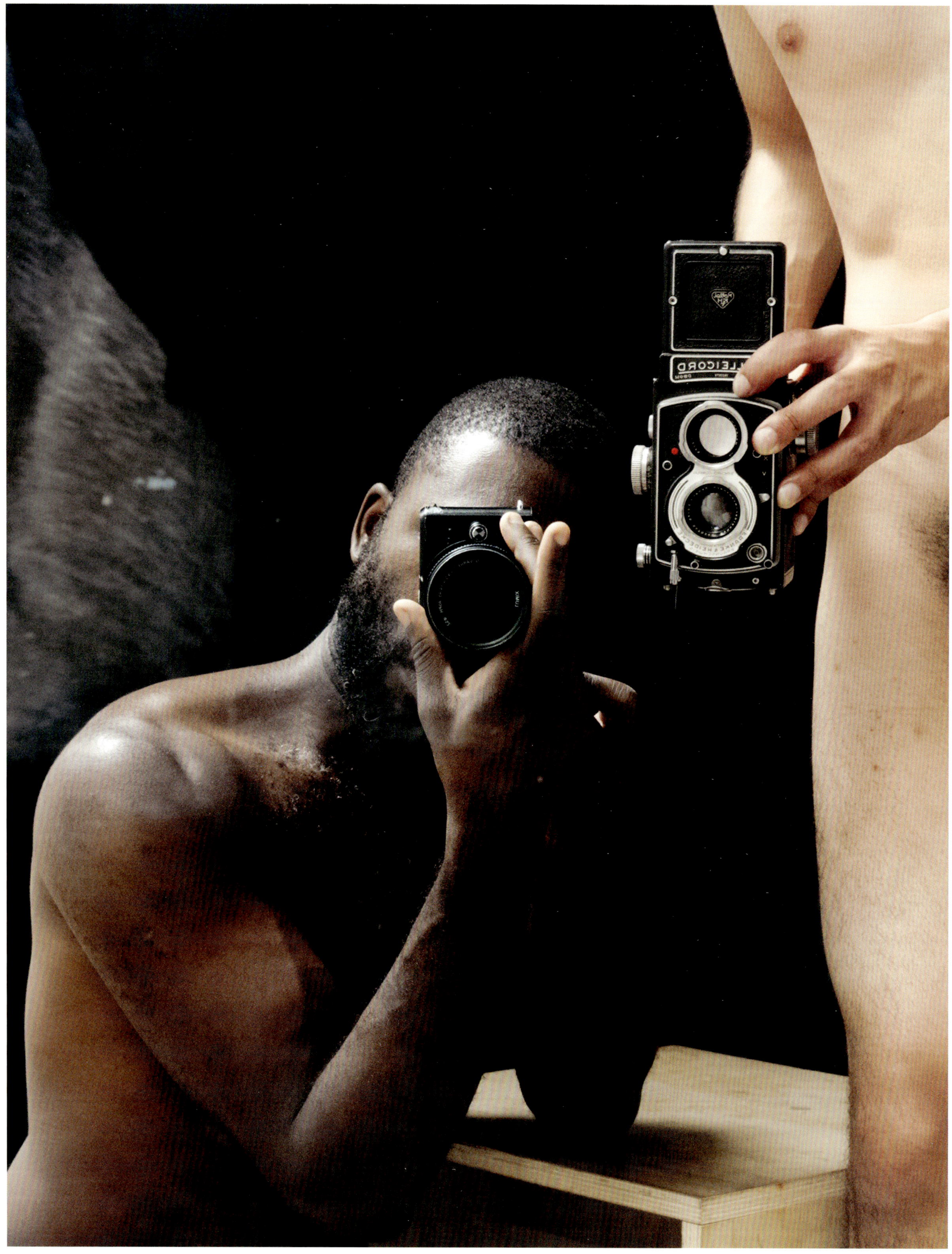

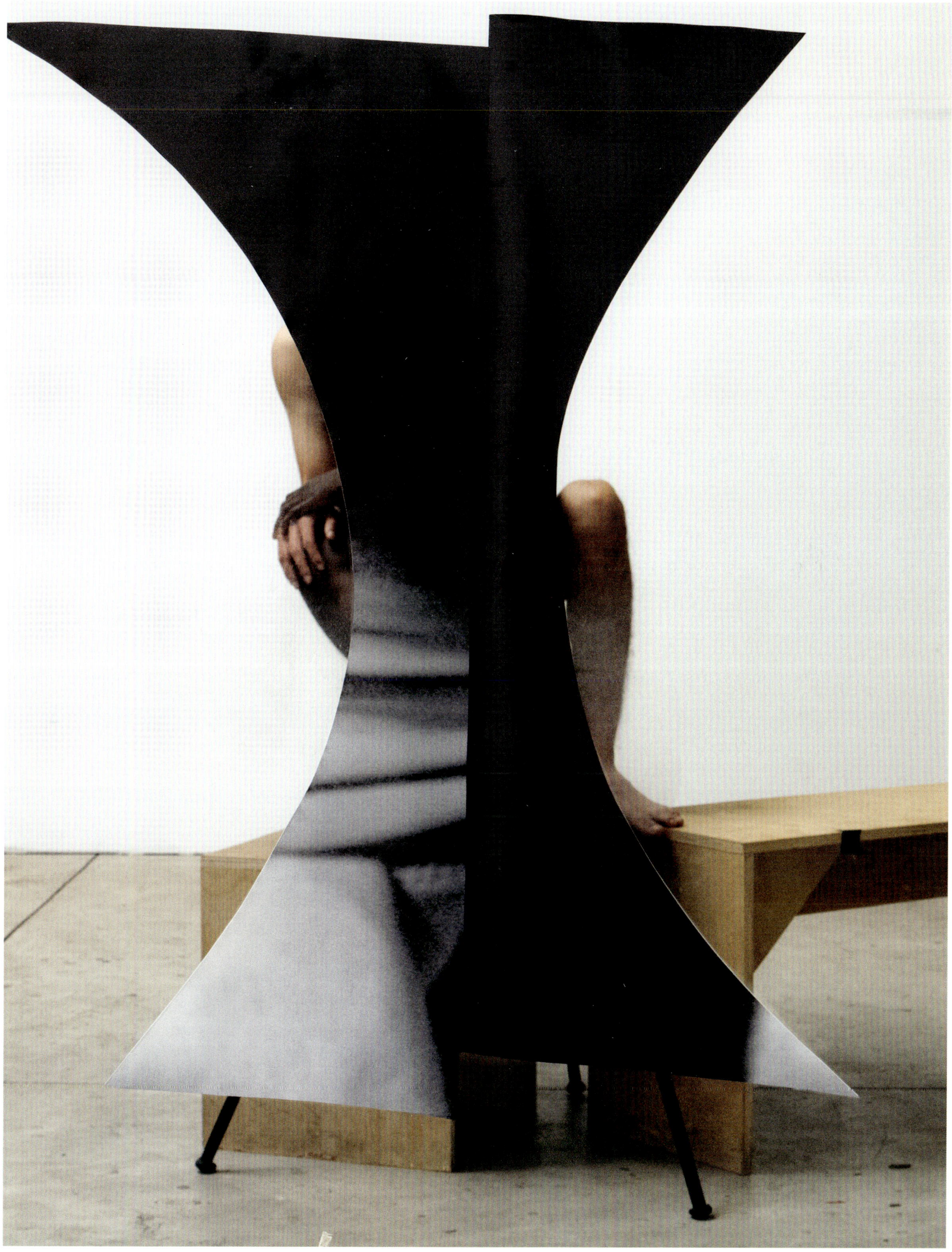

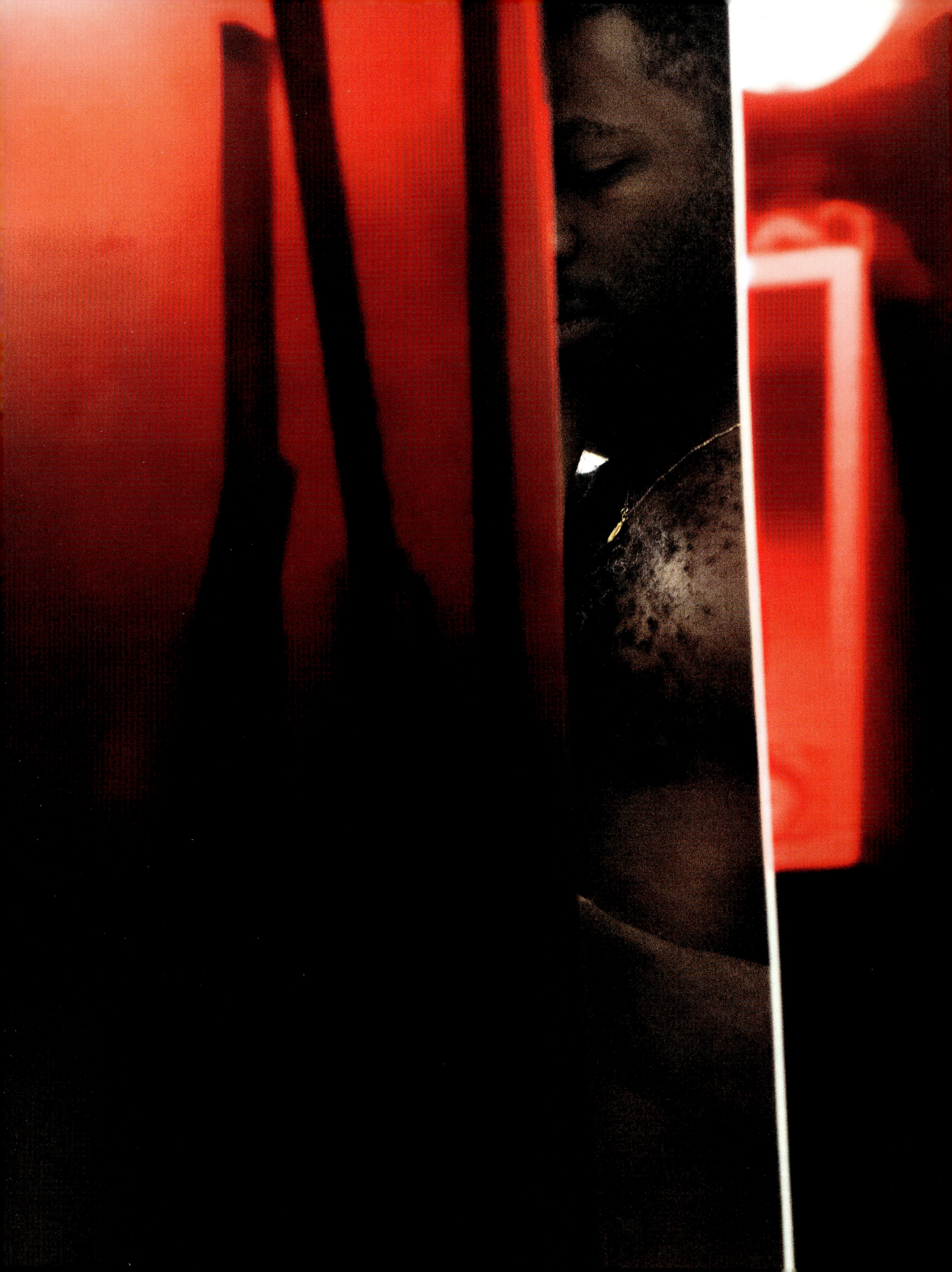

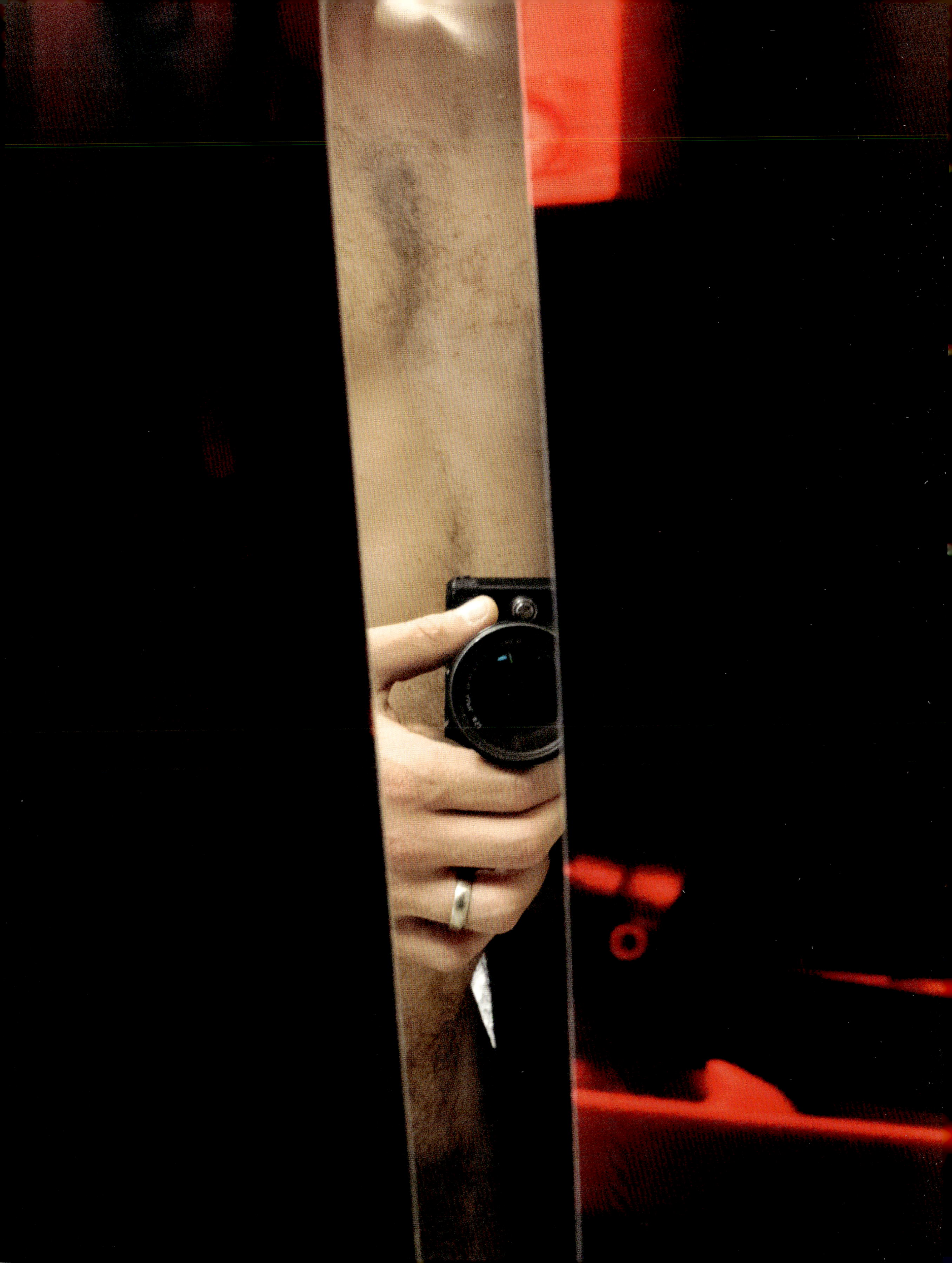

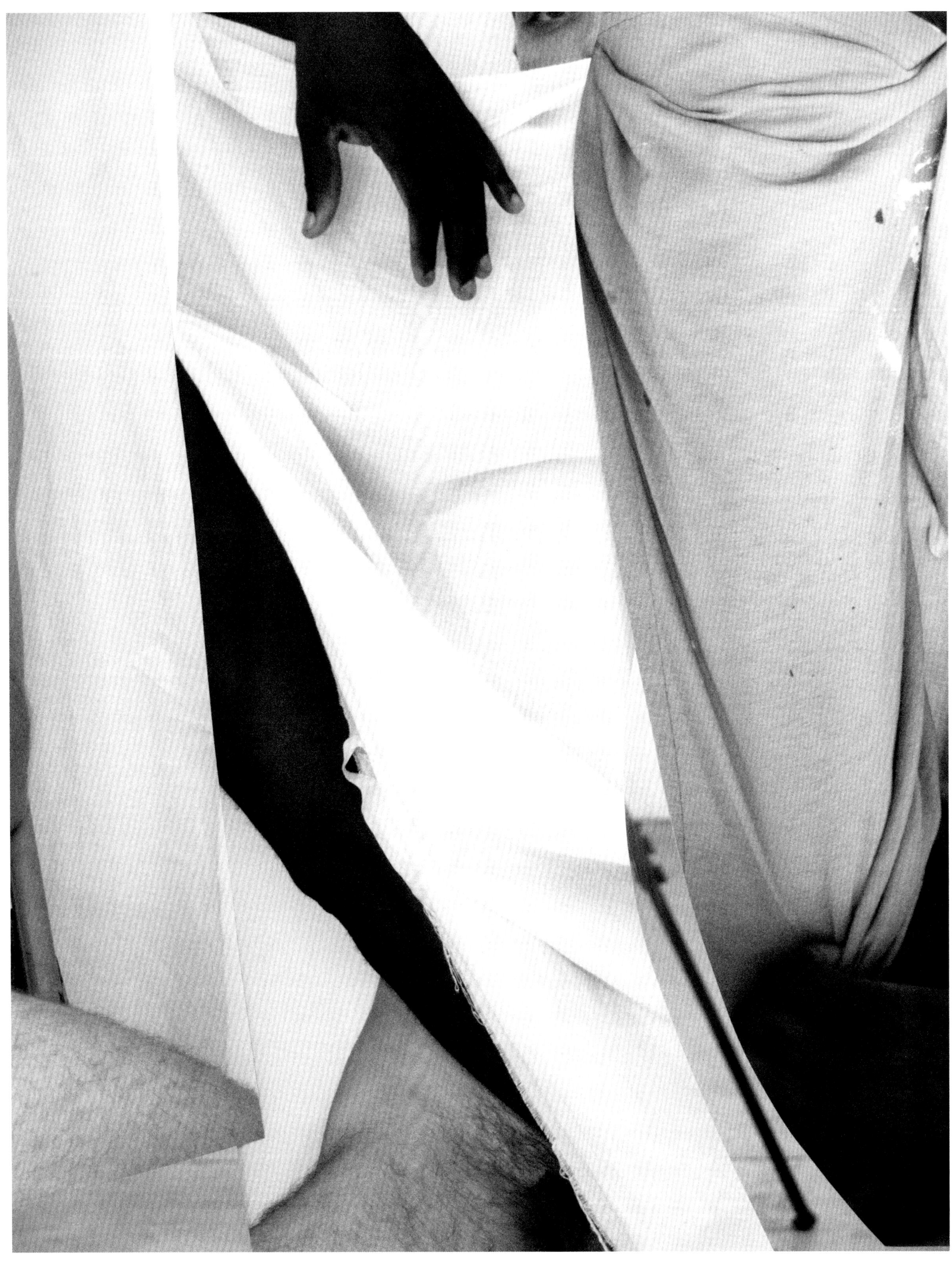

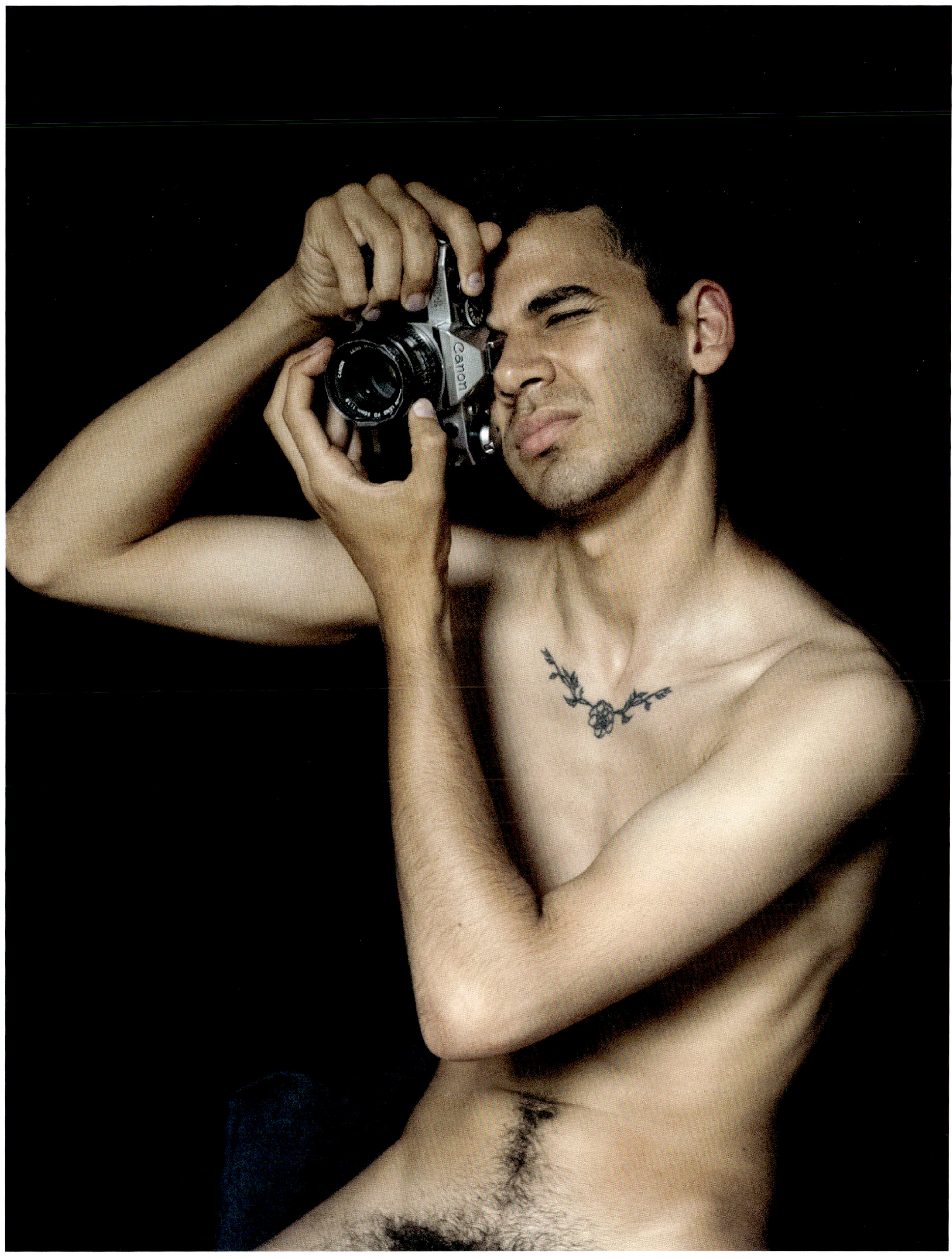
Canon

Carter Mull

Jonathan Griffin

Around five years ago, Carter Mull started taking photographs of fashionable club kids he met at underground parties near his downtown Los Angeles studio. At these events, he used his camera as a social lubricant, initiating conversations and developing relationships but rarely using the photographs themselves in his artwork. Instead, he invited certain individuals to pose in his studio, positioning them in juxtaposition with his art or asking them to physically interact with objects such as the prototype jackets he had made in collaboration with Guess Jeans. The deal was that his models could freely use Mull's images for self-promotion, just as he used them as components of his art.

Mull makes art across all media—from drawing and video to collage and sculpture—reflecting critically on today's hyperabundance of images by establishing idiosyncratic, speculative archives within his own prodigious output. Almost always, he incorporates photographs into these works, some of which he's appropriated and others that he's taken. A typical work by Mull will include drawings and photographs inset within a larger scheme, a montage of patterns (maybe a digitally manipulated paint effect or a repeated glyph), abstract incidents (perhaps from a crumpled sheet of printer's foil), and found images. While he makes paintings, they tend to consist of inkjet-printed organza or cotton stretched over or glued onto an aluminum panel. In recent years, he has rarely used paper, and never canvas. The motifs of cut flowers and clockfaces recur throughout Mull's oeuvre, *vanitas* signifiers that—as with the numbers one through twelve that he scatters across compositions—allude not only to the passing of time, but also to the instability of what we understand as contemporary. Mull's work feels self-consciously young and new, taking the very ideas of youth and newness as subjects to be isolated and picked apart.

"I'm interested in how subcultures create images, and how images create subcultures," Mull told me recently. He considers the museological art world to be as much a subculture as that of lowrider custom cars, for instance, or of the advanced pop styling of the social media influencers he photographs. The insularity of such worlds, he says, is "the tragedy of network culture."

Since 2015, everything Mull has made has landed within the stylistic paradigms of one of three fictitious corporate entities, conceptual and aesthetic categories that he likens to sections in a newspaper. Through these imaginary "companies," he emulates the kinds of corporations—photo agencies, news media outlets, fashion houses, film studios, advertising firms—that capitalize on the production of images. Mull's Eye Eye Productions is a fashion and lifestyle brand, the natural home for his photographs of millennial models. Nations Bank, by contrast, adopts a documentary aesthetic, predominantly in black and white, and refers to both postindustrial urban blight and 1960s Conceptual art. Finally, through the fictitious corporation Metropolitan & Co., Mull appropriates the language of global news media, colliding digital motifs such as computer keyboards with a parody of expressionist painting. While, from a distance, Mull's project emanates a sense of breadth and encyclopedic totality, it is actually an entirely subjective, self-constructed universe, with his studio at its geographical and theoretical center.

All works from the series *Not Yet Titled Form*, 2017–18
Courtesy the artist; Onestar Press, Paris; and Lundgren Gallery, Palma de Mallorca

Jonathan Griffin is a writer based in Los Angeles and a contributing editor of *frieze*.

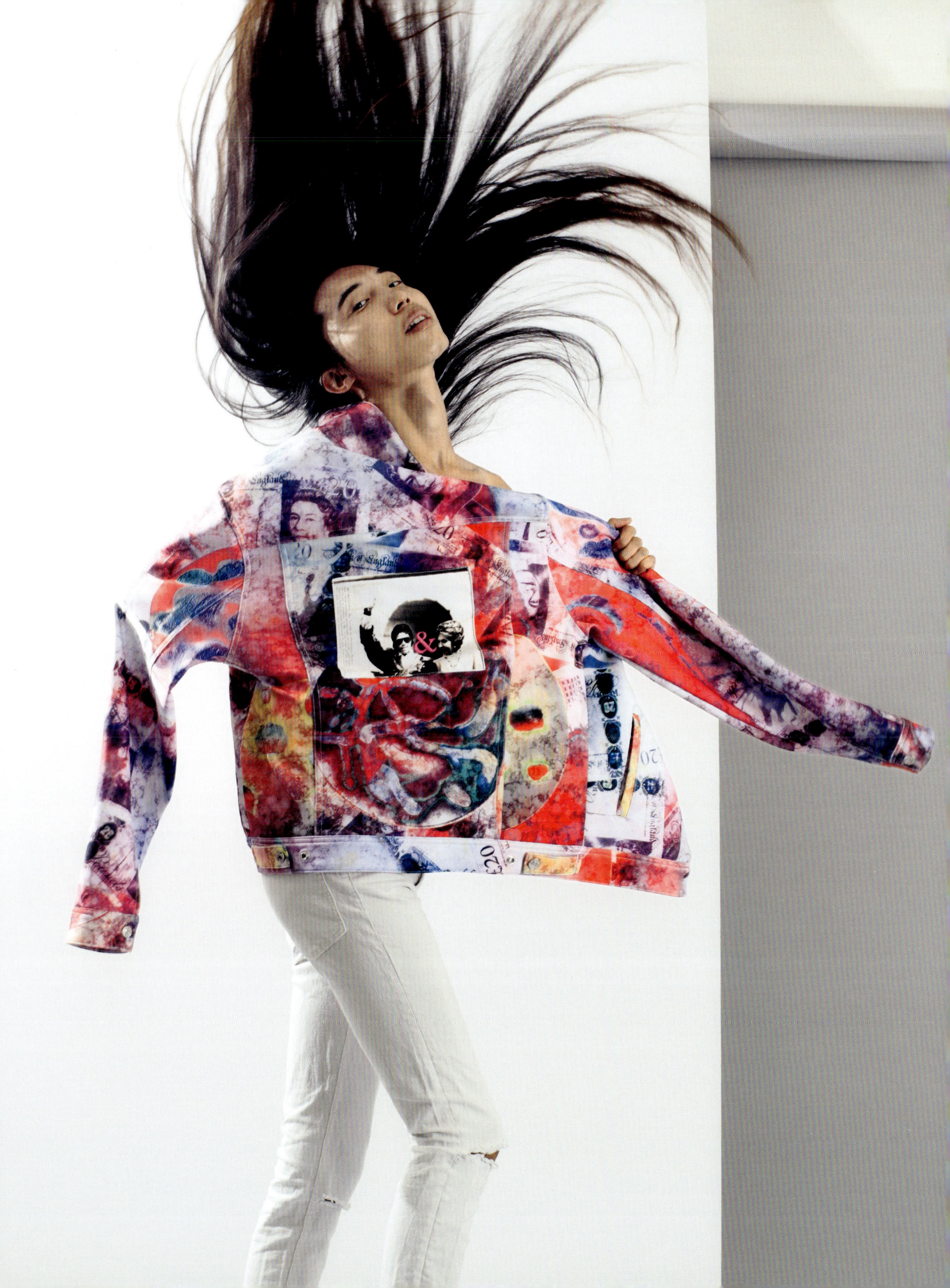

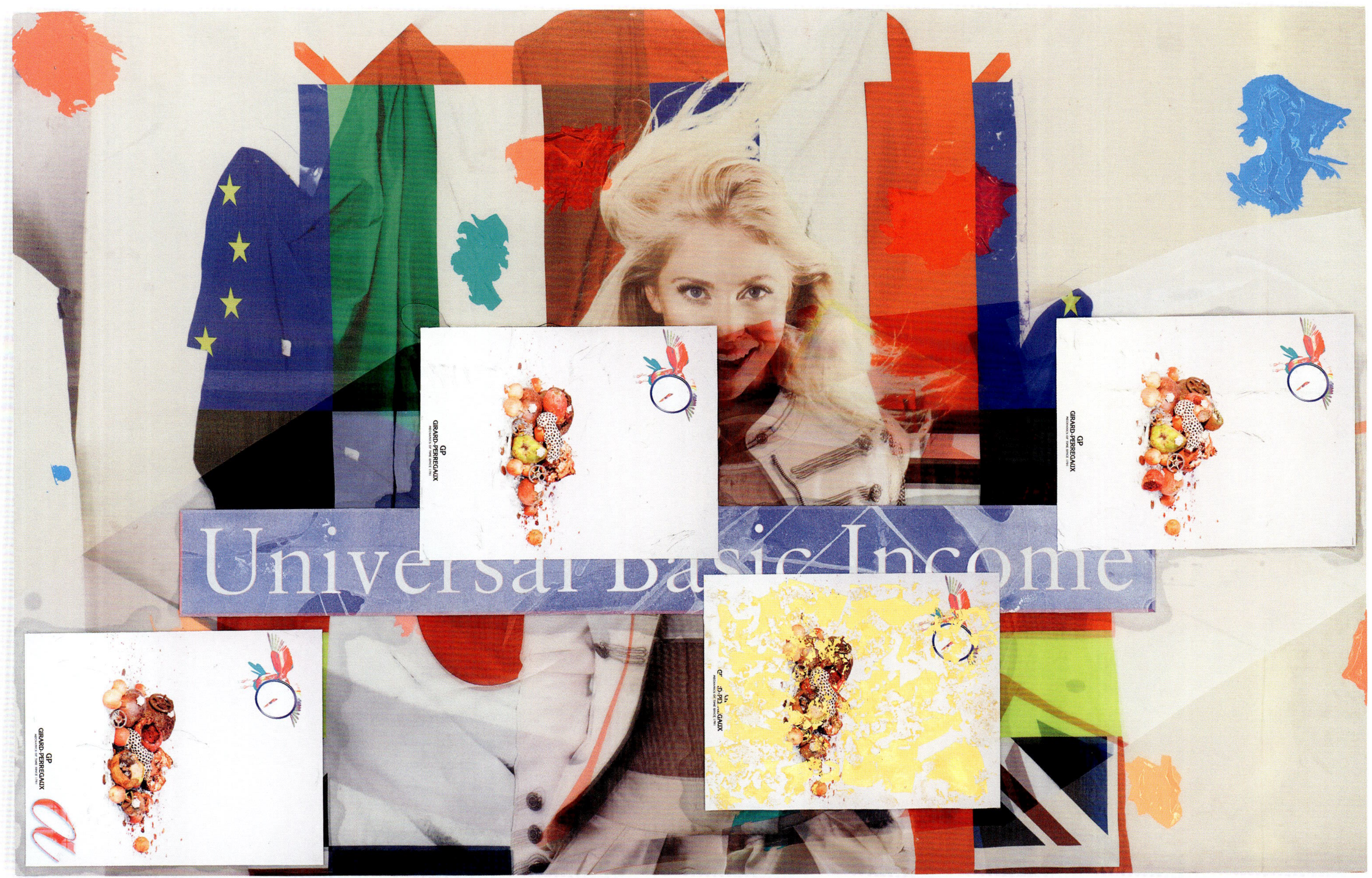
Universal Basic Income
GP
GIRARD-PERREGAUX

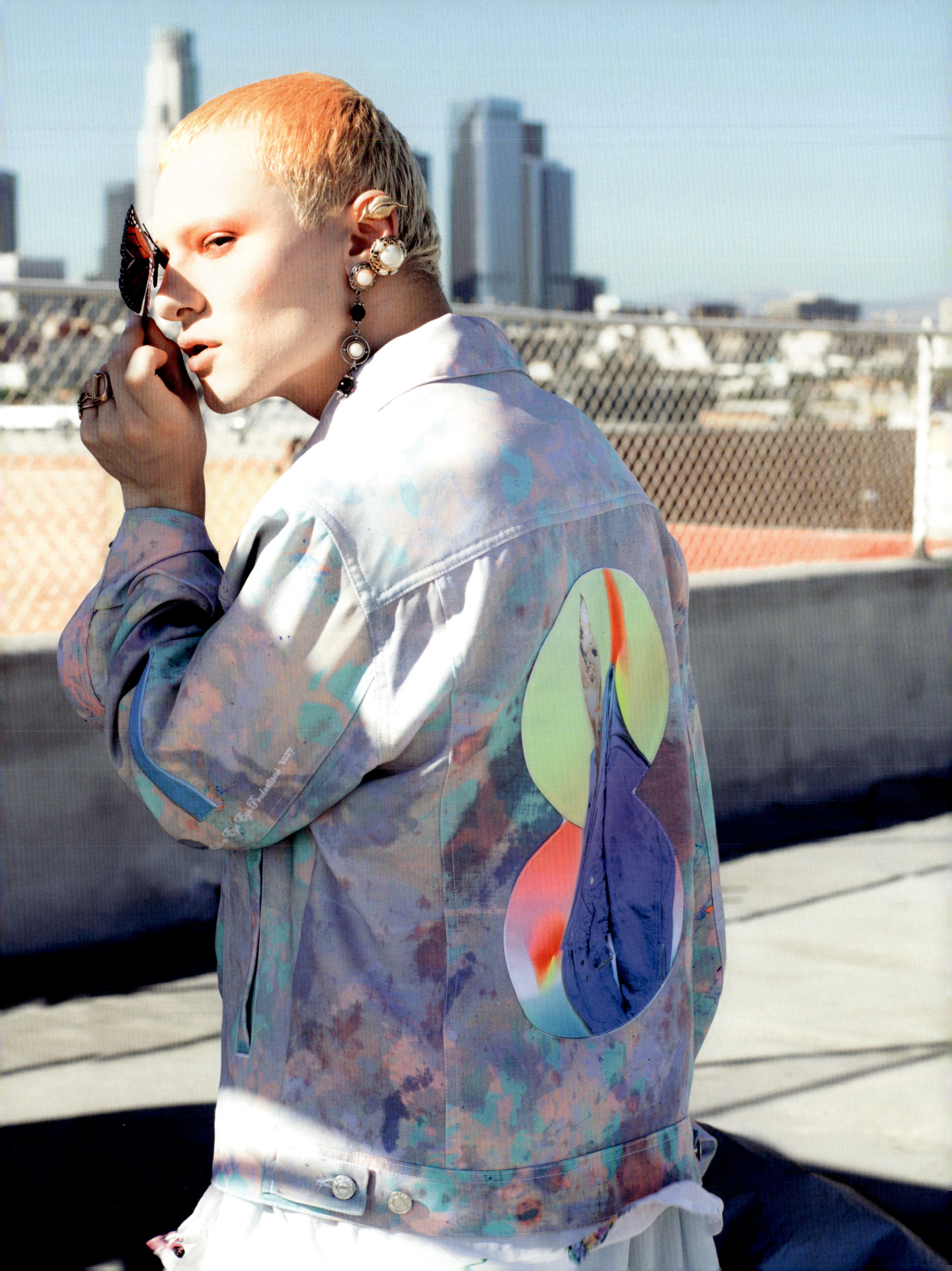

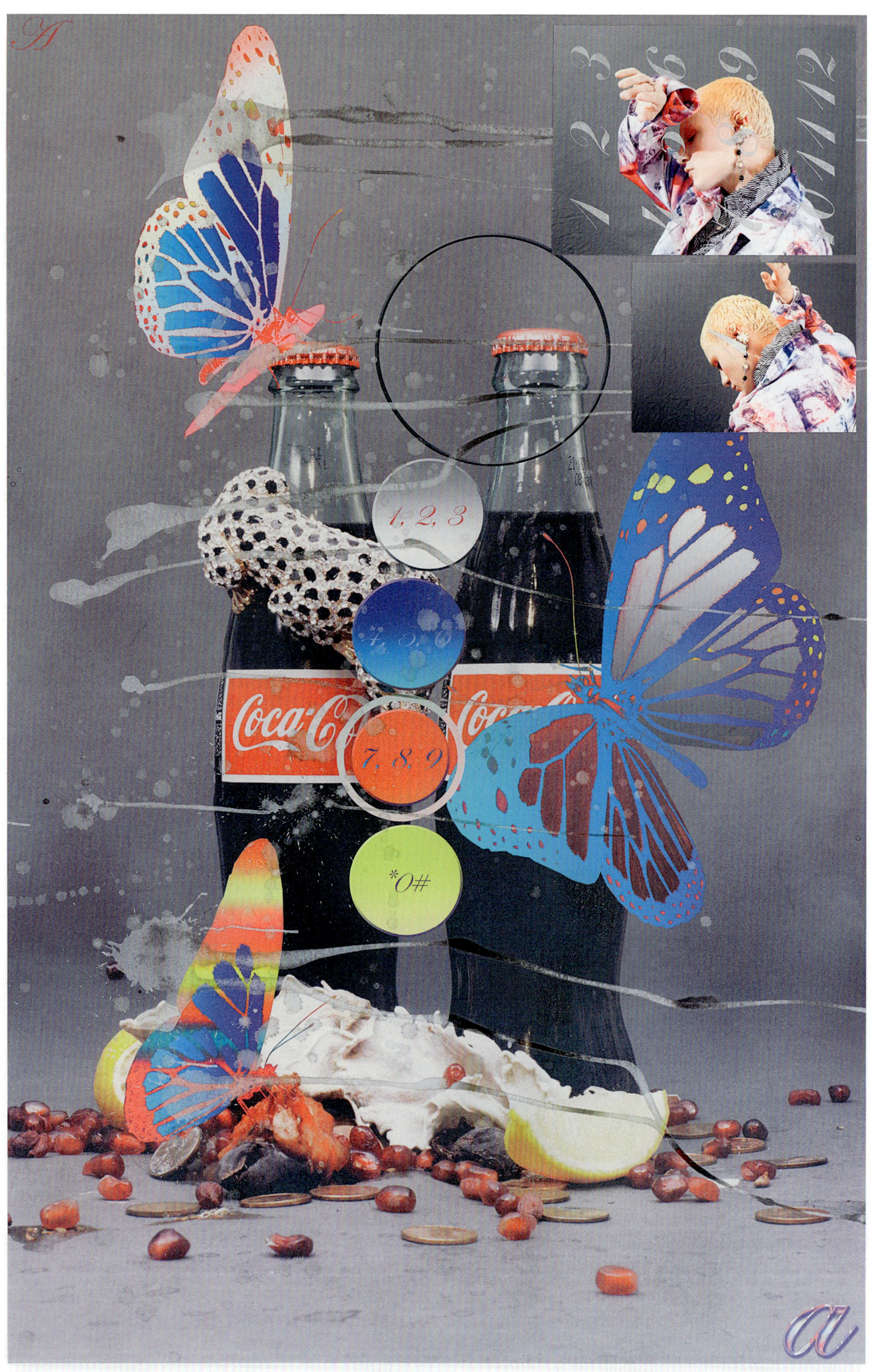
1, 2, 3
7, 8, 9
*0#

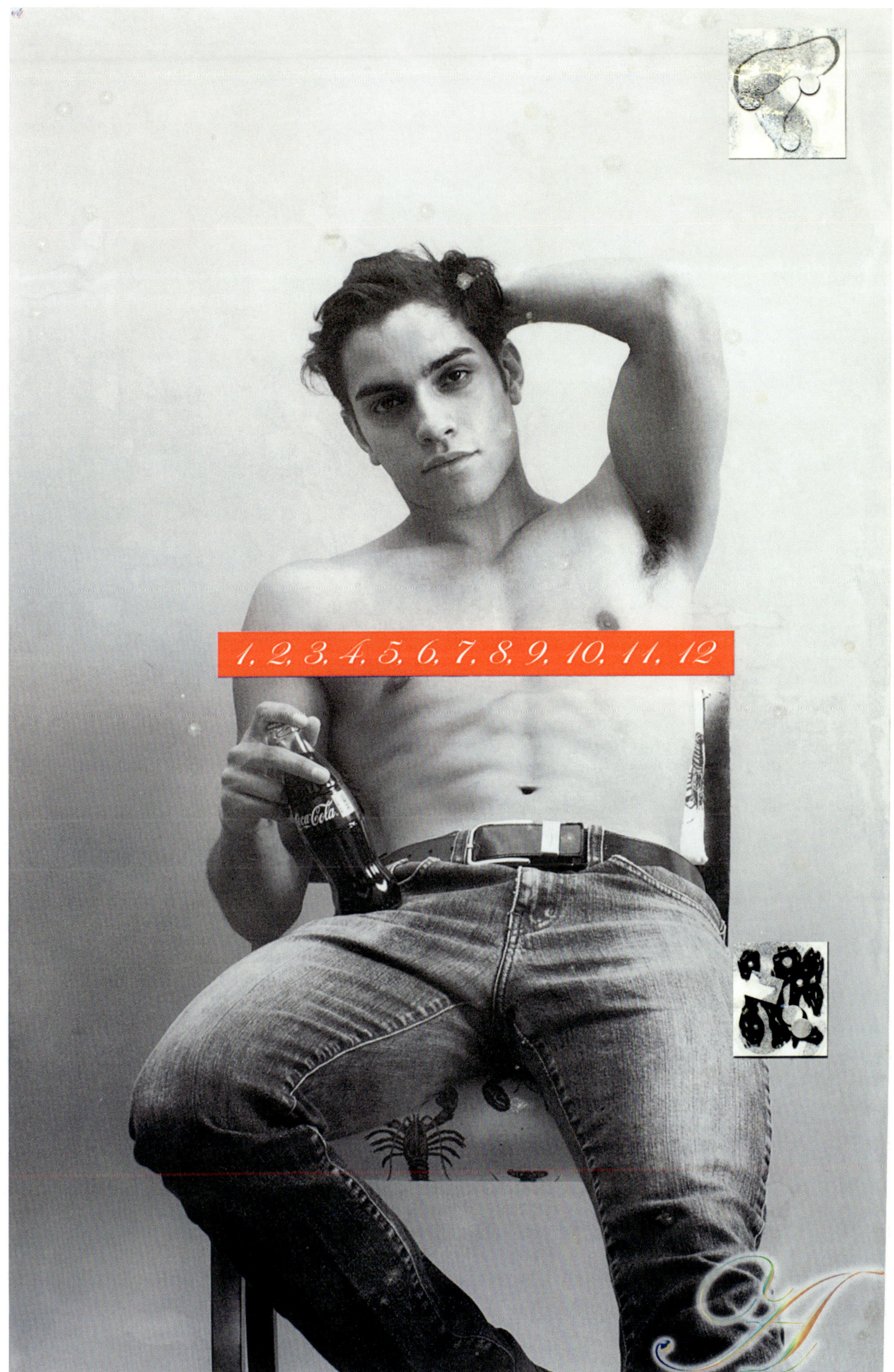
1, 2, 3, 4, 5, 6, 7, 8, 9, 10, 11, 12

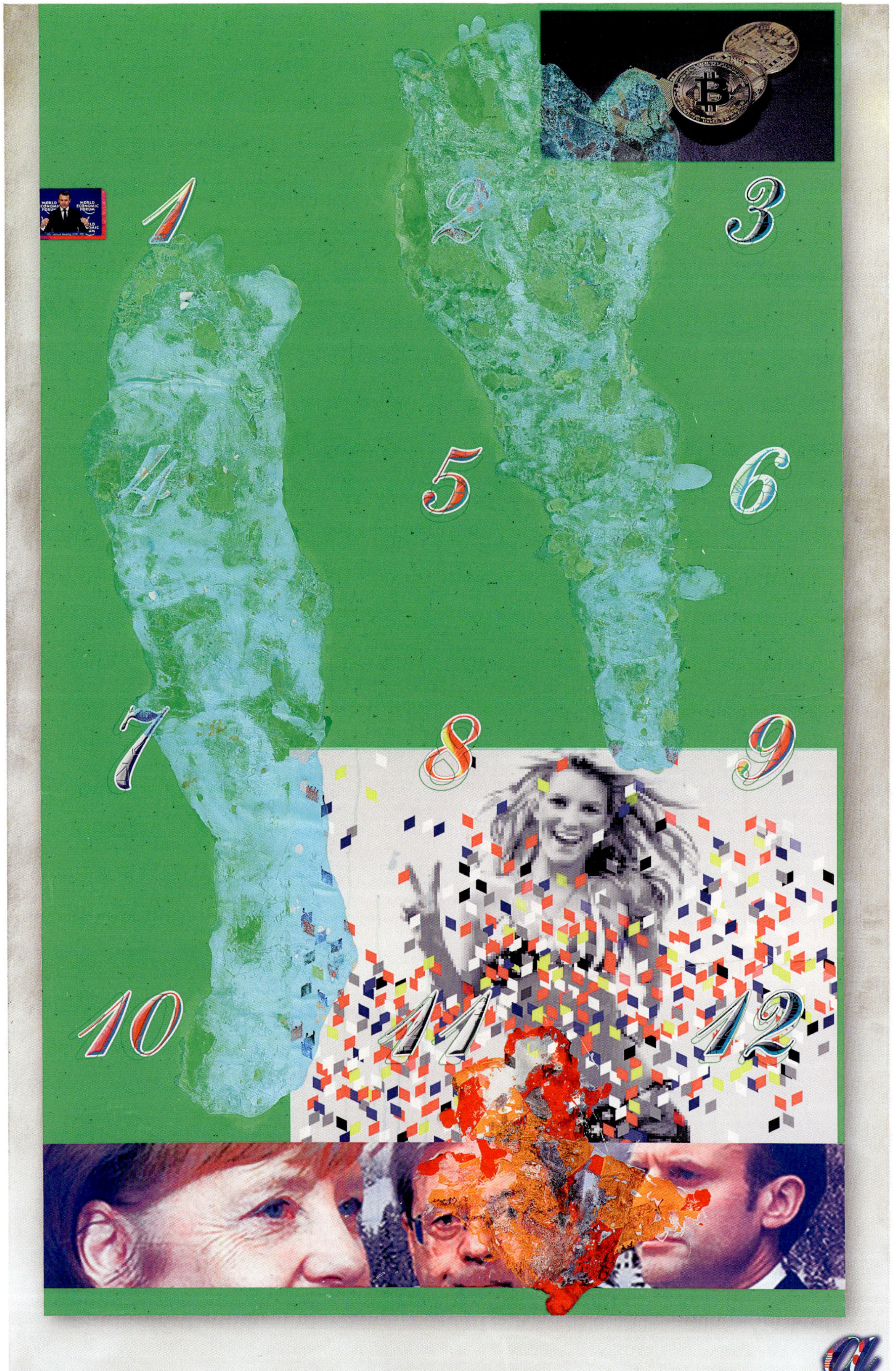
1
2
3
4
5
6
7
8
9
10
11
12

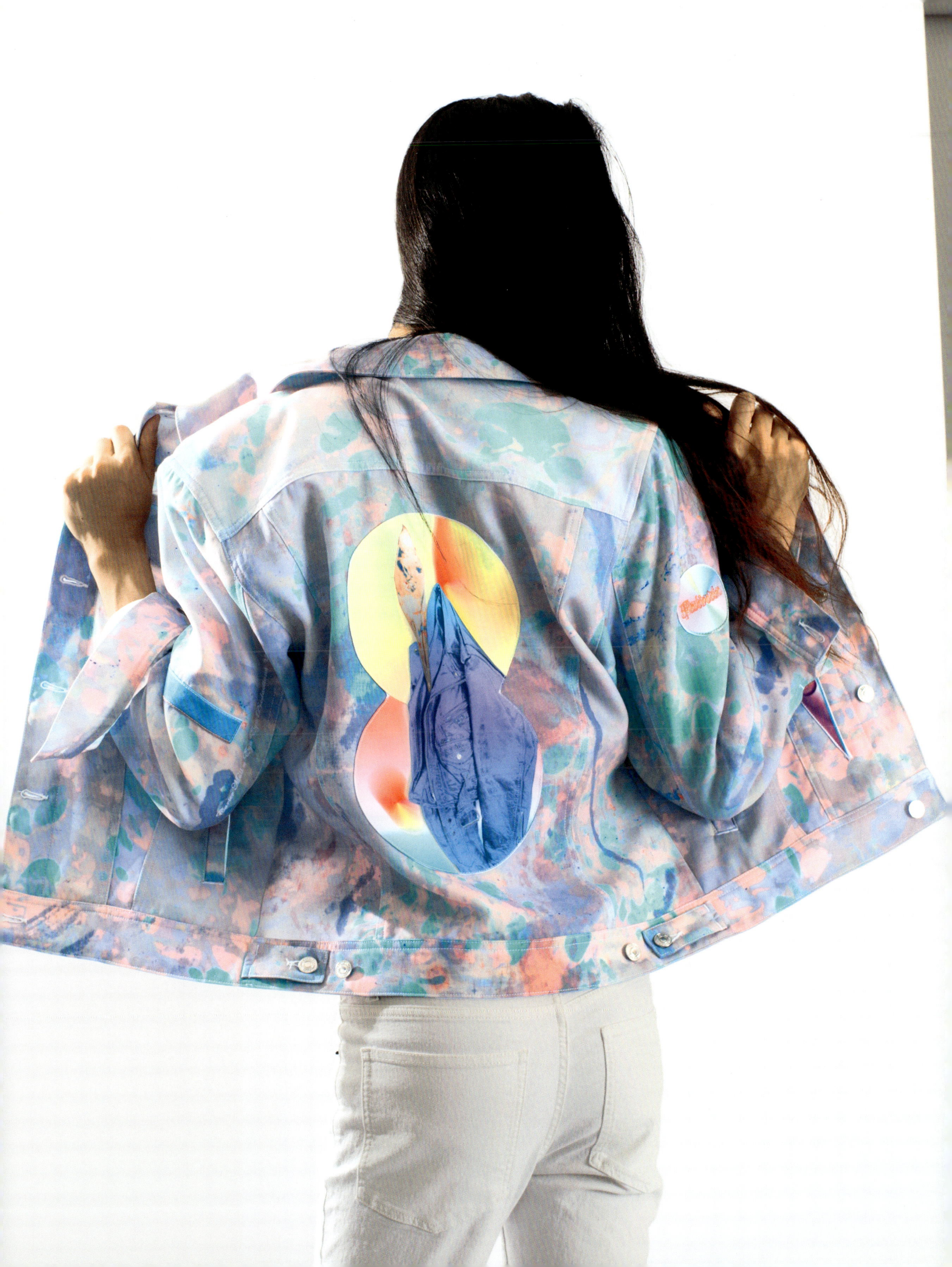

Rodrigo Valenzuela

Matthew Schum

In *General Song*, his solo exhibition at Klowden Mann Gallery in Culver City earlier this year—the title is a nod to Pablo Neruda—Rodrigo Valenzuela amplified the photographs in his series *Barricades* (2017) with a departure, a dramatic sculptural installation of a riot barricade. This new work productively harangued about the politics of exhibition and created a physical imposition, as all effective installation art does, that had been missing from Valenzuela's previous series. This sculptural turn took the primary subject of his primary medium, photography, and accentuated its rebellious energy.

Valenzuela is a fine arts professor of photography at the UCLA School of the Arts and Architecture, who replaced renowned postconceptualist James Welling. This impressive ascent began in 2005, when Valenzuela traveled from Chile and crossed, undocumented, into the United States. *Barricades* and his new series *Masks* (2018) trace a journey through the dictatorial shadow of Pinochet and take special inspiration from Neruda.

For *Masks*, Valenzuela re-created profiles of crafty protesters on the streets of Santiago who use plastic bottles and duct tape to make improvised tear gas masks. Using simple devices of dissent, the DIY respirators reframe the human body and its visage. In Valenzuela's images, each special design overwhelms the face (actually the artist incognito). His protesters are not only humans, they also resemble alien creatures, transformed by single-serving plastic containers. Insectile features radiate from a painted darkness Valenzuela designs in his studio down to the last pigment. As Valenzuela tells the story of these brave protesters in Chile, it is clear he envisions their actual struggle with empathy. These are not the dispossessed and disenfranchised masses found in newspapers, but architects of another world unsatisfied with this one.

Masks was inspired by *Canto General*, the collection of poems that established Neruda as an international literary figure. I can hear the internal monologue of both Valenzuela's protester and Neruda's protagonist in the fourth canto of "The Heights of Macchu Picchu" (1947), from *Canto General*, in these lines:

> Mighty death invited me many times:
> it was like the invisible salt in the waves,
> and what its invisible taste disseminated
> was like halves of sinking and rising
> or vast structures of wind and glacier.

Barricades presents Valenzuela's curious series of "portraits" of barricades. He assembles them in his studio and photographs them from a single vantage. These images show cinder blocks, sawhorses, folding chairs, jags of rebar and lumber, tires, corrugated metal, chains, and crates painted in whitewash. Because they are beautifully sad, they capture the paradox of being a politically minded studio artist today. Long hours of isolation producing art while our collective world explodes may lead to melancholy. A pall overwhelms these facsimiles of revolutionary zeal, as though Eugène Delacroix's famous 1830 barricade in *Liberty Leading the People* had been re-encoded in the digital dust of 2018. We are left with pulchritude masquerading as political potential.

The artist says that materials perform for the camera in *Barricades*. To take this anthropomorphism further, I wonder if the camera hasn't seen the artist performing his artistic labor on the stage set of his viewfinder. Rather than politics, Valenzuela pictures contemporary art itself as the uprooting of politics that speaks in protest while dissembling activism. He is not unique in this labor. The larger question is whether this work functions like *engagé* art might have in earlier times—as coherent inspiration—or if studio art hasn't often become a mirror in a mine shaft: a space where older notions of solidarity are dug out, even exploded, but ultimately fruitless due to the solitary demands of the studio.

Matthew Schum, PhD, is a writer based in Los Angeles. His current projects include curating the Desert X 2019 Biennial in the Coachella Valley.

Opposite:
Barricade No. 2, 2017

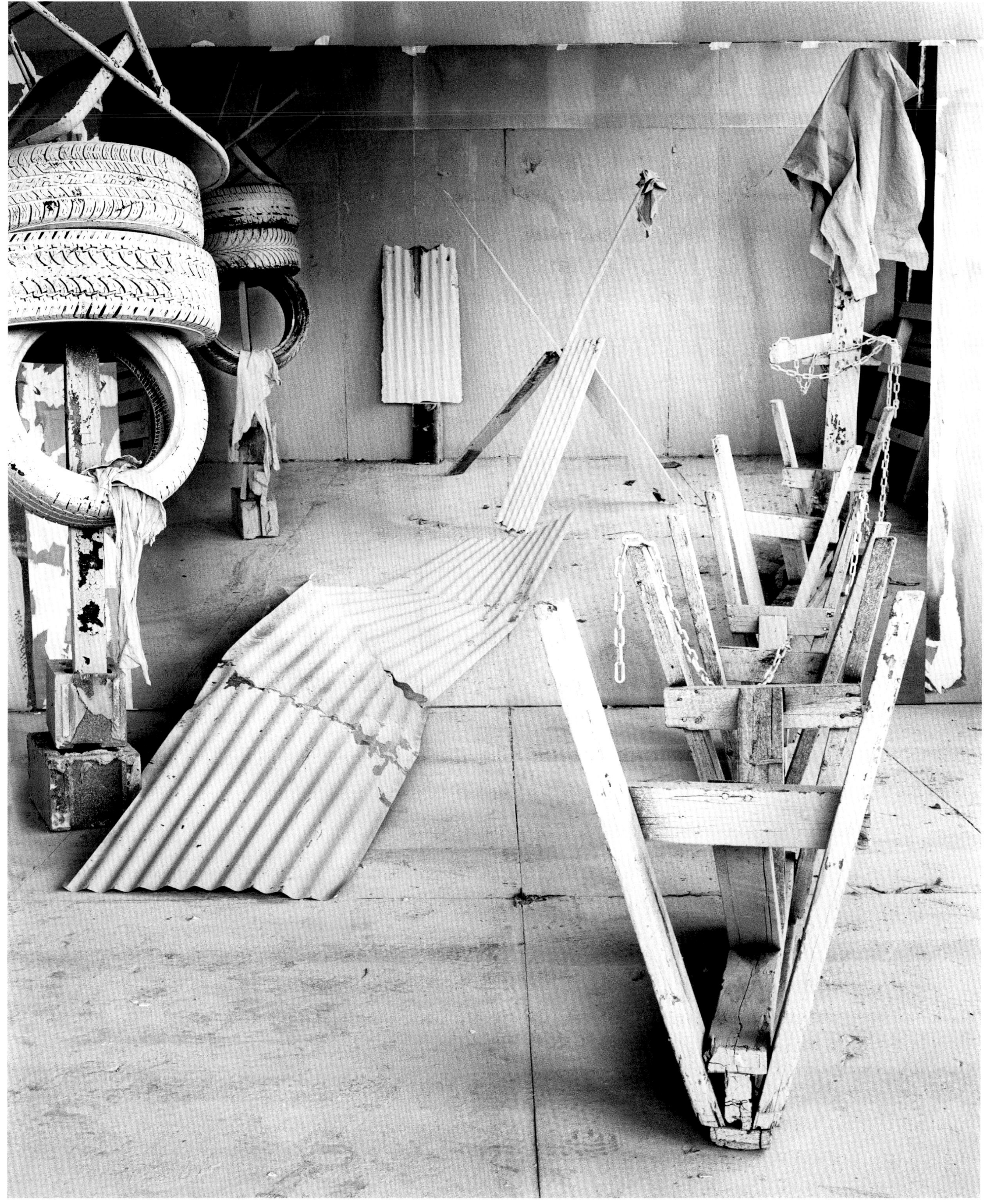

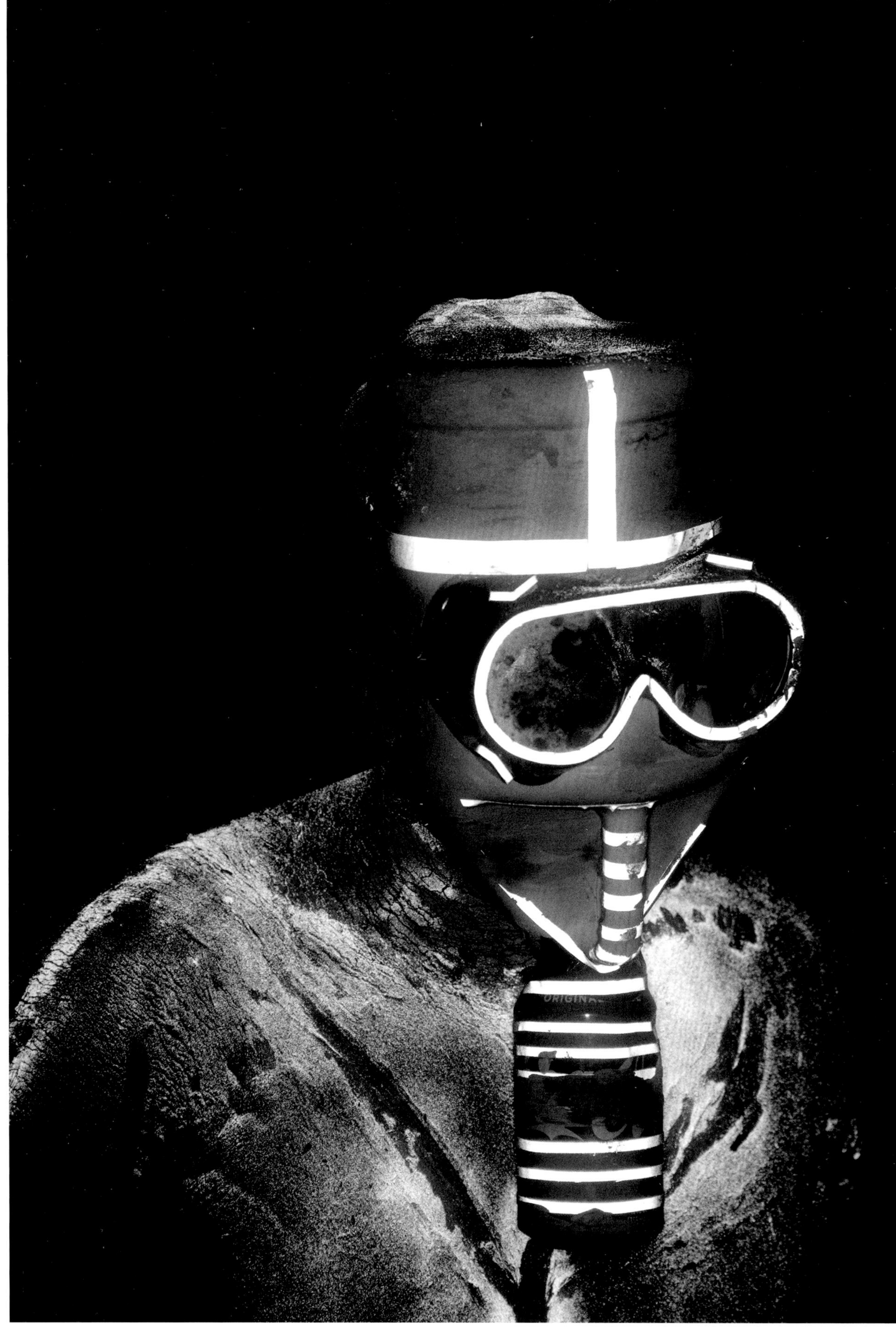

This page:
Mask #6, 2018

Opposite:
Barricade No. 3, 2017

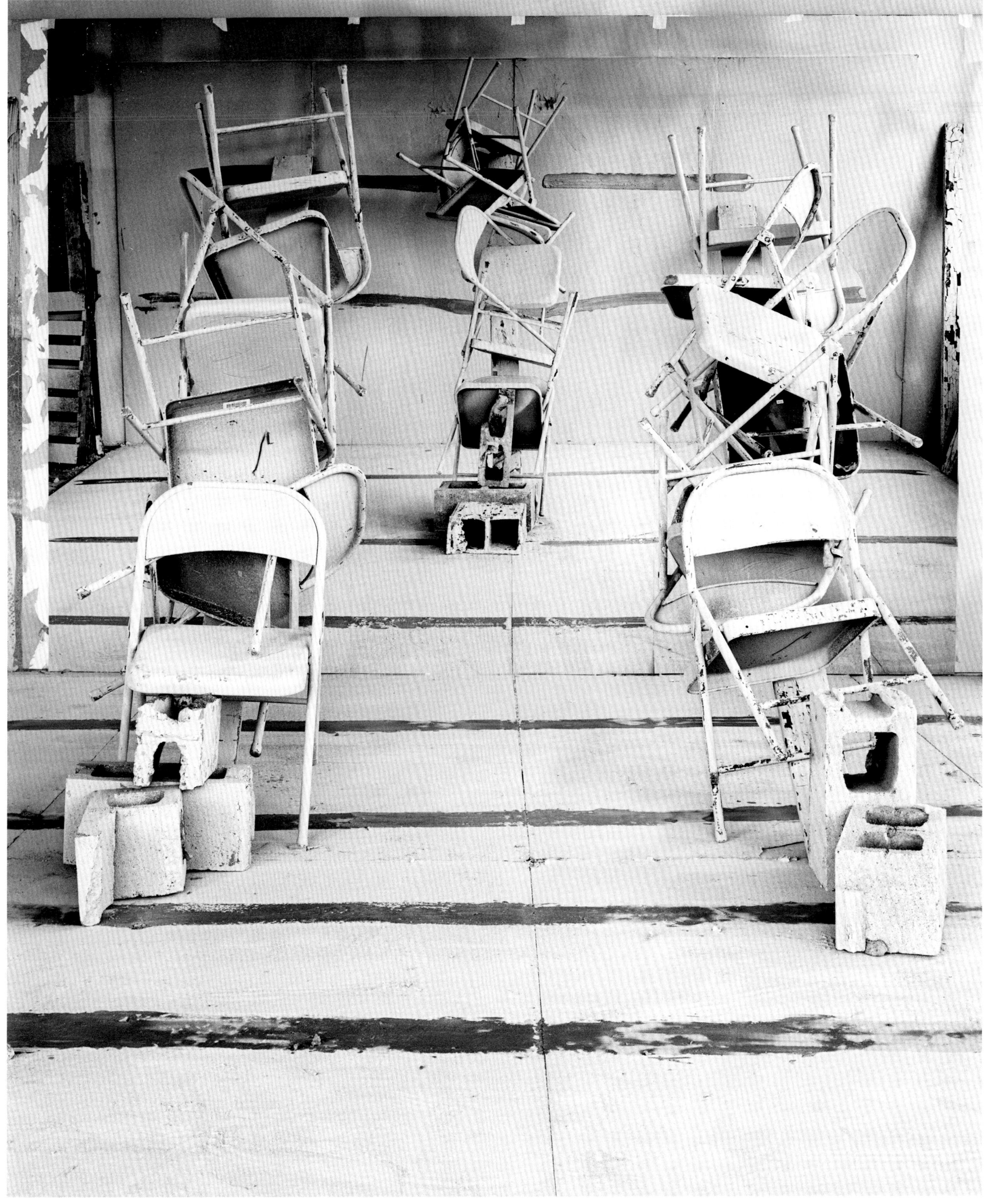

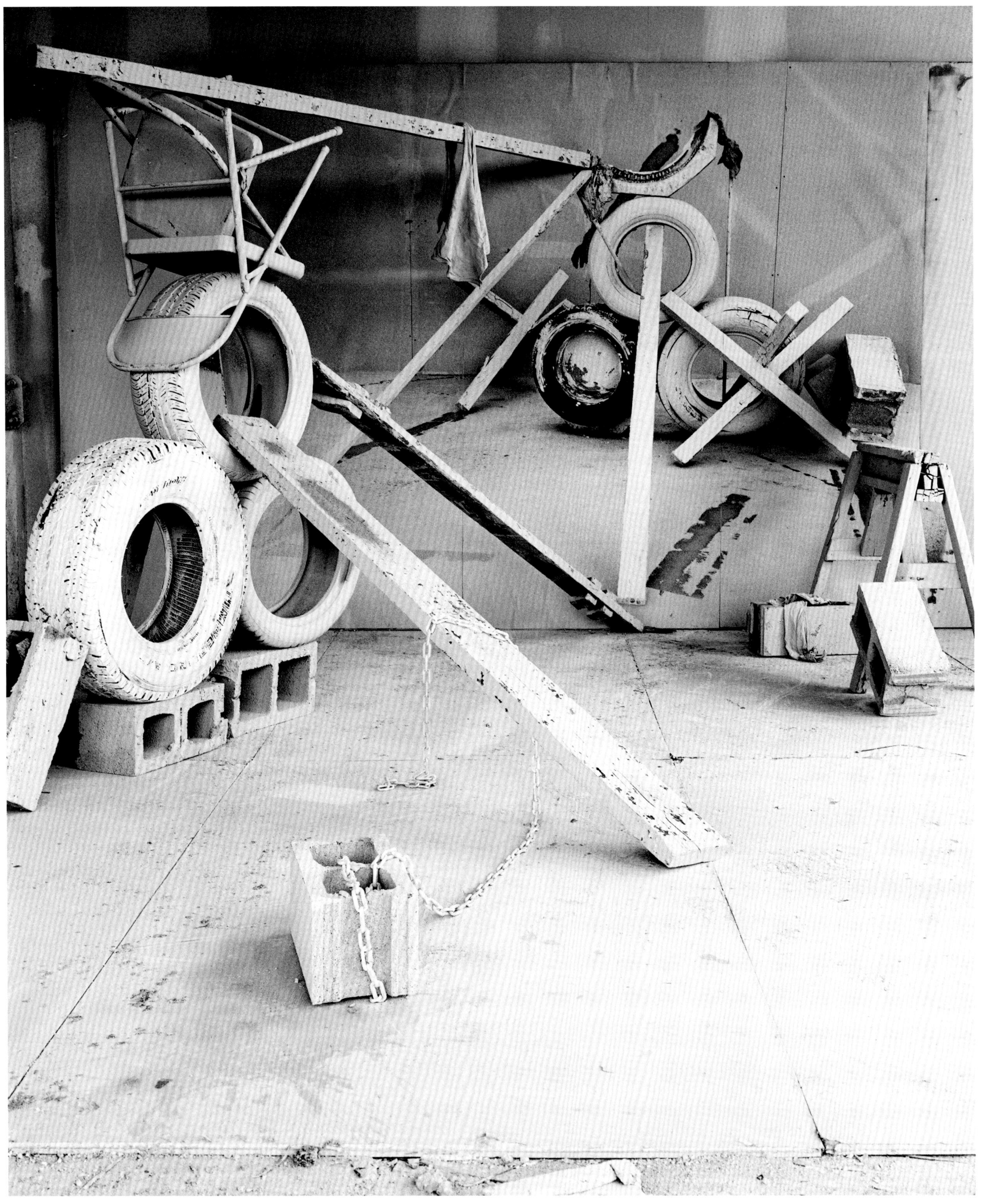

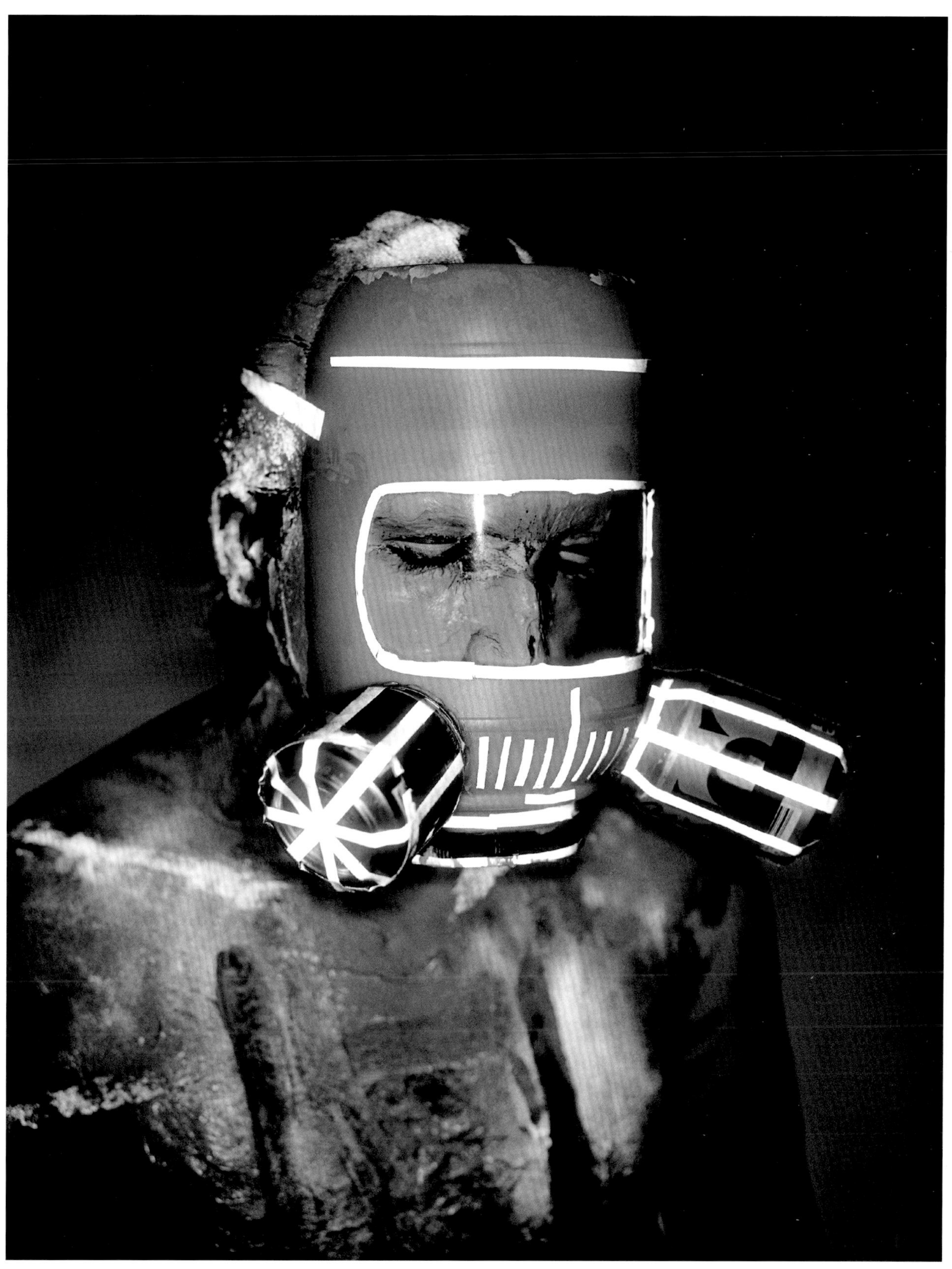

Opposite:
***Barricade No. 5*, 2017**

This page:
***Mask #2*, 2018**
All photographs courtesy the artist; Klowden Mann Gallery, Culver City; and UPFOR Gallery, Portland, Oregon

Boys will be boyz will be bois. Or so it seems. This play on masculinity—repetition with a difference—isn't lost on David Alekhuogie, who titled his 2017 solo show at Skibum MacArthur in Los Angeles, *Them Boys*. While the naming was a nod to the Wiz Khalifa tune "We Dem Boyz," the LA-born photographer also considered the exhibition as "a way of talking about how you see black men in the streets, and what the formal signifiers of that are." Despite the many tropes surrounding the spectacle of black masculinity, Alekhuogie insists on the salvo of rhetorical strategies: "It's not always the storytelling. Sometimes it's the accent, the cadence, the how: *how* a person is speaking, *how* they are telling the story." For Alekhuogie, this emphasis on stylistics extends to the form an image takes on when framing the signifiers of black masculinity.

In *Pull_Up* (2017), a photographic series shown in *Them Boys*, Alekhuogie fashions a picture of black masculinity that, for him, pervades our "collective cultural subconscious." Enter the image of the sagging pants, a style synonymous with African American men. Emerging in the late 1980s, sagging was soon theorized in Richard Majors and Janet Mancini Billson's 1992 book, *Cool Pose: The Dilemmas of Black Manhood in America*: this "cool" posing and posturing mitigated against everyday racism.

Homing in on the sagging aesthetic, *Pull_Up* finds Alekhuogie abstracting this racial surround to the point where we, the viewer, cannot easily categorize the figure. In *Pull_Up k/w/r* (2017), three swaths of fabric greet our gaze: a black ribbed shirt, white underpants, and a pair of orange jeans. Alekhuogie considers each as a "horizon," a form reminiscent of Color Field painting. In a way, nothing in *Pull_Up k/w/r* immediately hints at race, sex, gender, age. But does that even matter? "If this sagging can make my mother—who is from South Los Angeles—uncomfortable," Alekhuogie says, "then I want to explore this feeling in a purely abstract, formal way so I can start to get people to realize there are certain parts of a political discourse that are purely aesthetic, purely formal." Indeed, *Pull_Up* does not cohere easily around contemporary identity politics, which are now fraught with reductive and moralizing attitudes. The affective bent of Alekhuogie's musings underscores a shift, an avenue to build collectivity on tense topics rather than foster an antagonistic calculus in reading an aesthetic image.

Taken together, *Pull_Up* reckons with questionable ideas of black masculinity: by abstracting how we sense and apprehend sagging, Alekhuogie asks the viewer to question how they arrive at certain rhetorical biases that breed staunch, moralistic horizons. While the images appear genderless—that queer undulation of boys, boyz, bois—the infamy of such crotch shots in relation to black masculinity isn't new: Robert Mapplethorpe's photograph *Man in Polyester Suit* (1980) helped to ignite debates. Alekhuogie finds value in the "body as an arena" for contestation, rather than in the subject of his photographs as inured to fixed, denigrating ideas of masculinity. Alas, bodily sovereignty is never willingly granted to blackness.

Against this backdrop, Alekhuogie's hand-toned cyanotype series *Untitled (Nikes)* (2017) takes on an added resonance in how it "colors" classical Greek statuary, those idealized icons of athleticism. In these works, race is absent and omnipresent. The shadowy wash of colors over the statues' fragmented torsos subsumes the white marble surfaces as bearers of beauty and of good. How, then, can the blue-black of blackness achieve this Grecian corollary with goodness? For Alekhuogie, it rests in the rhetoric of it all.

David Alekhuogie

Ikechukwu Onyewuenyi

Ikechukwu Onyewuenyi is a curatorial assistant at the Hammer Museum, Los Angeles.

Opposite:
Pull_Up k/w/r
Overleaf:
Pull_Up w/o/r; Untitled (Nikes) c/c
Pages 124–25:
Untitled (Nikes) c/o; Pull_Up n/o/r
All photographs 2017.
Courtesy the artist

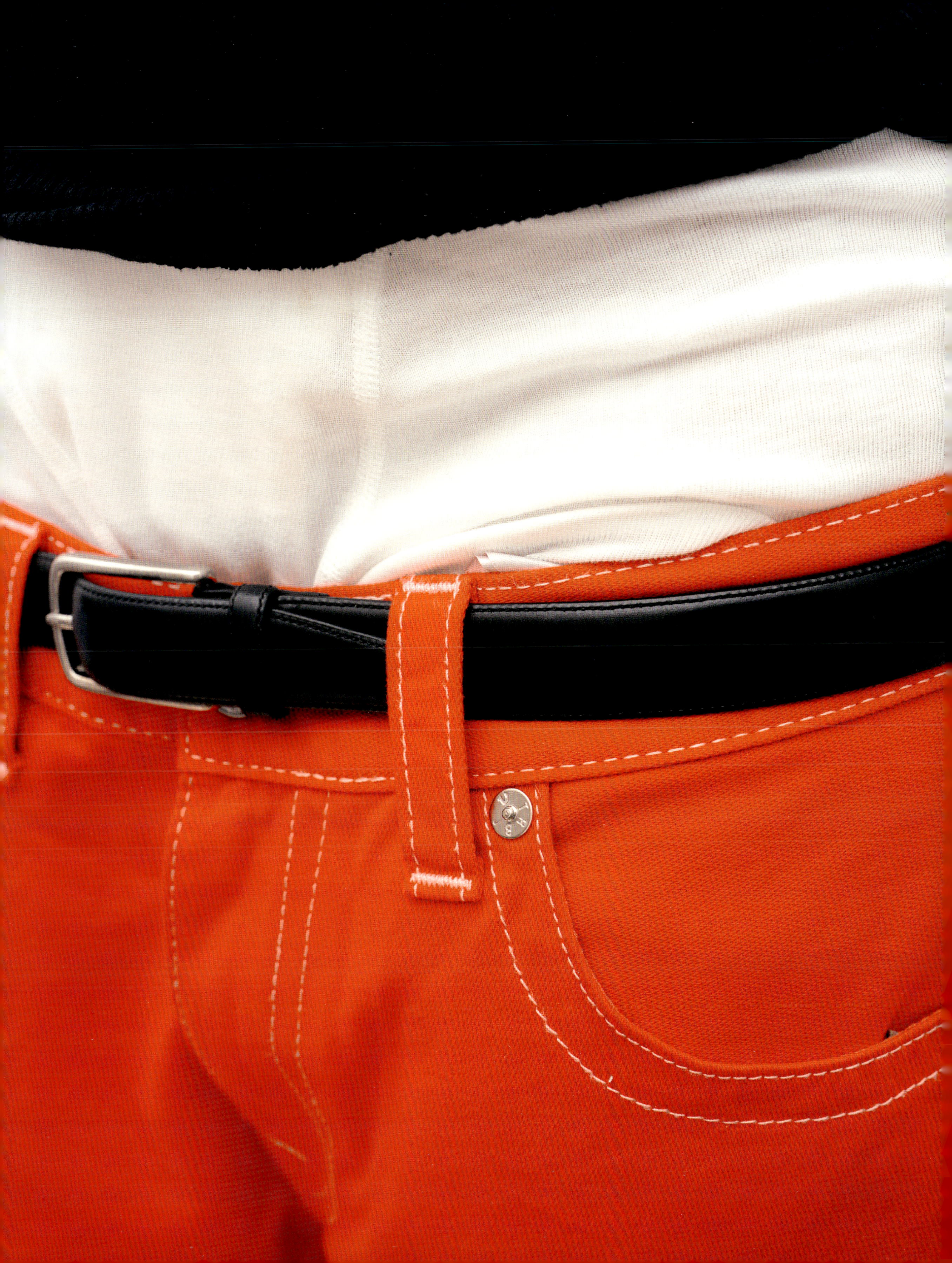

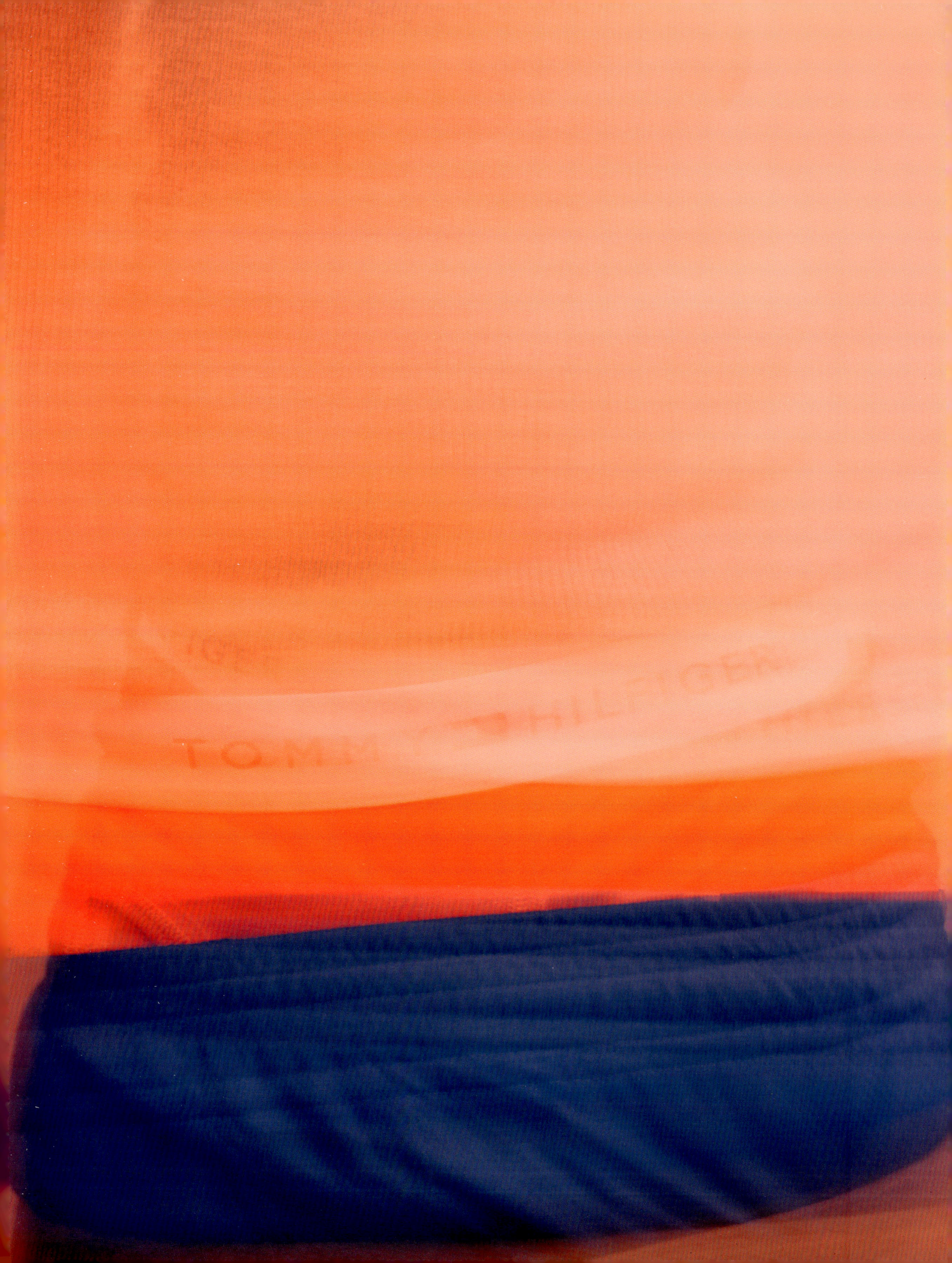
HILFIGER

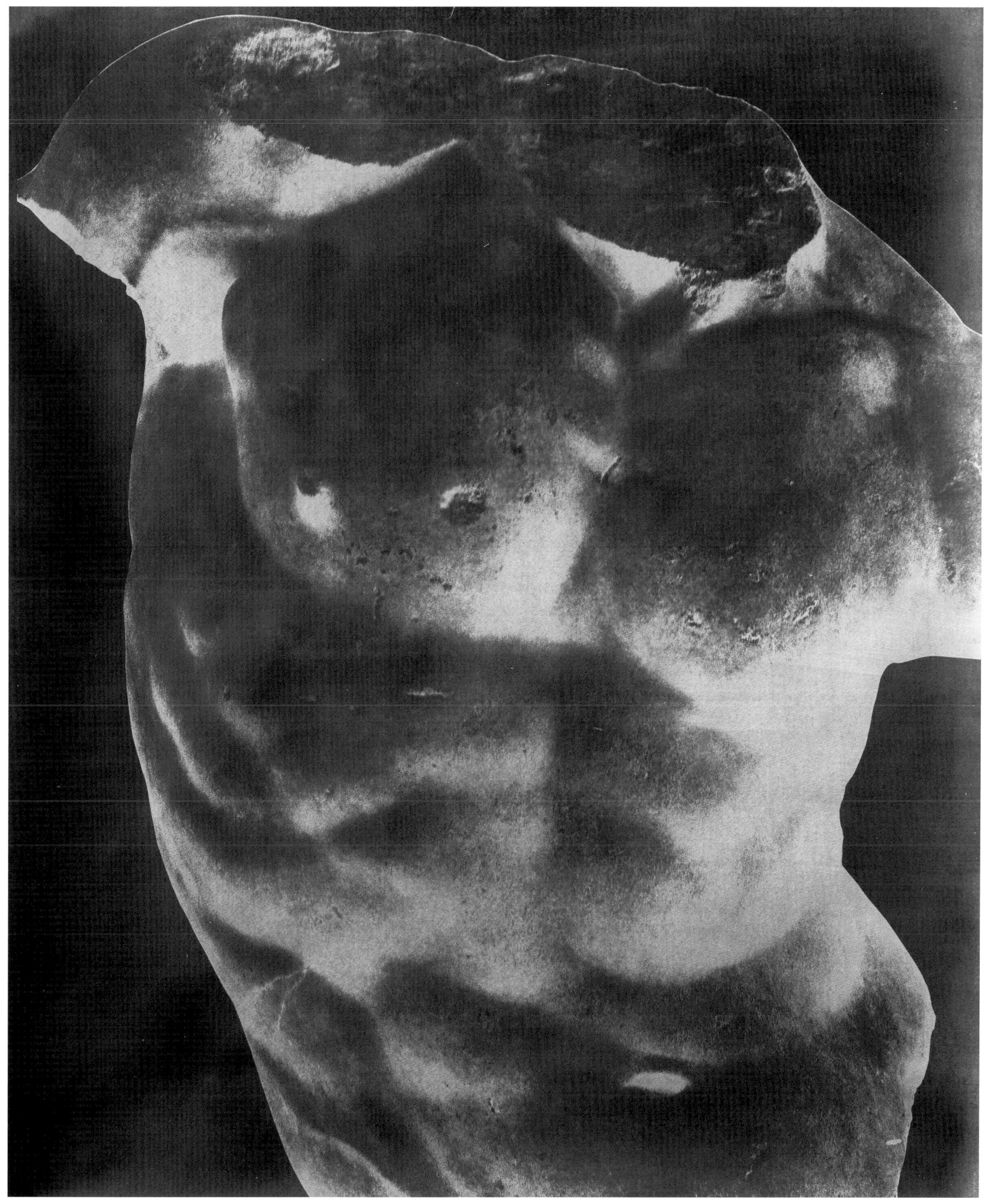

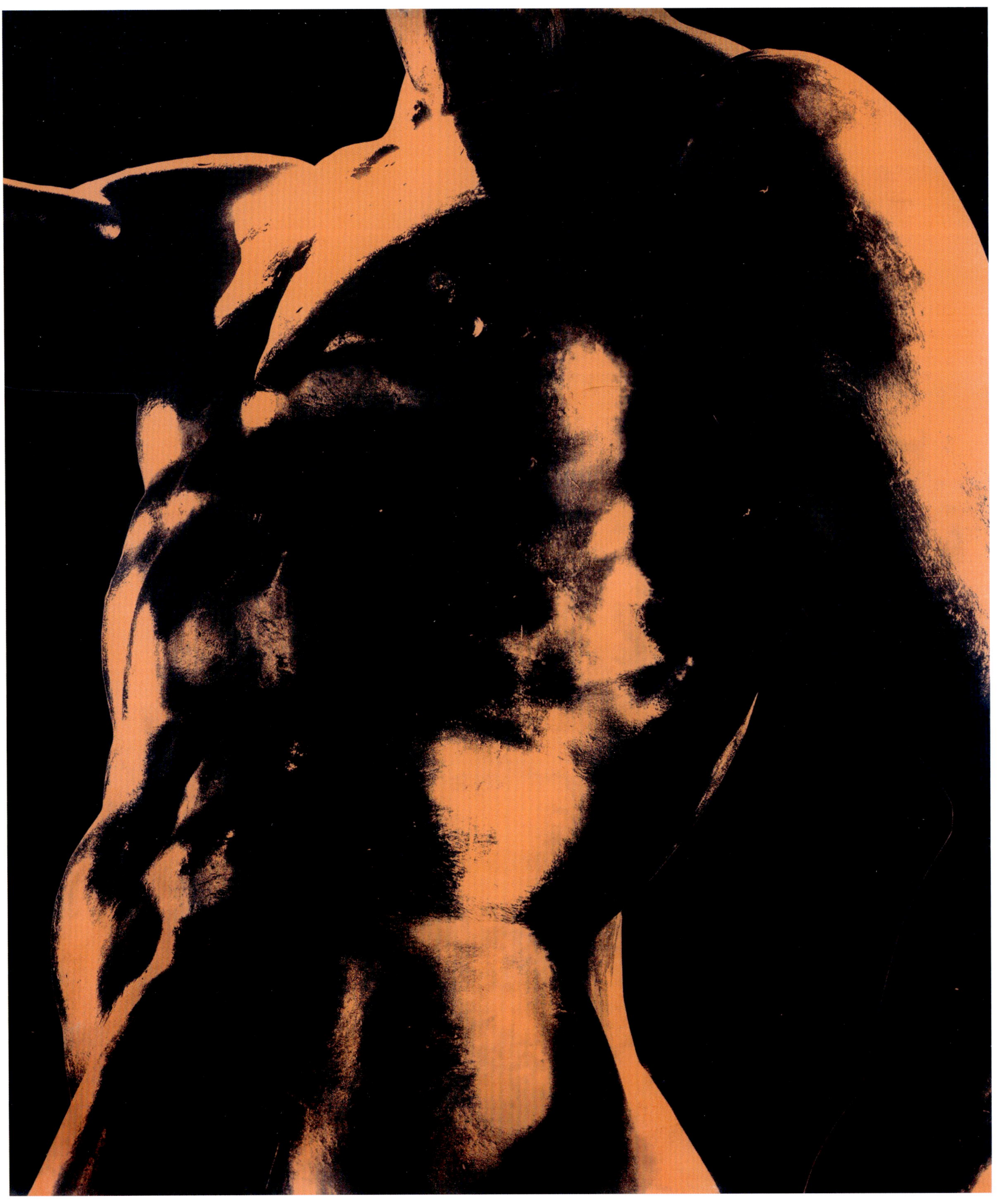

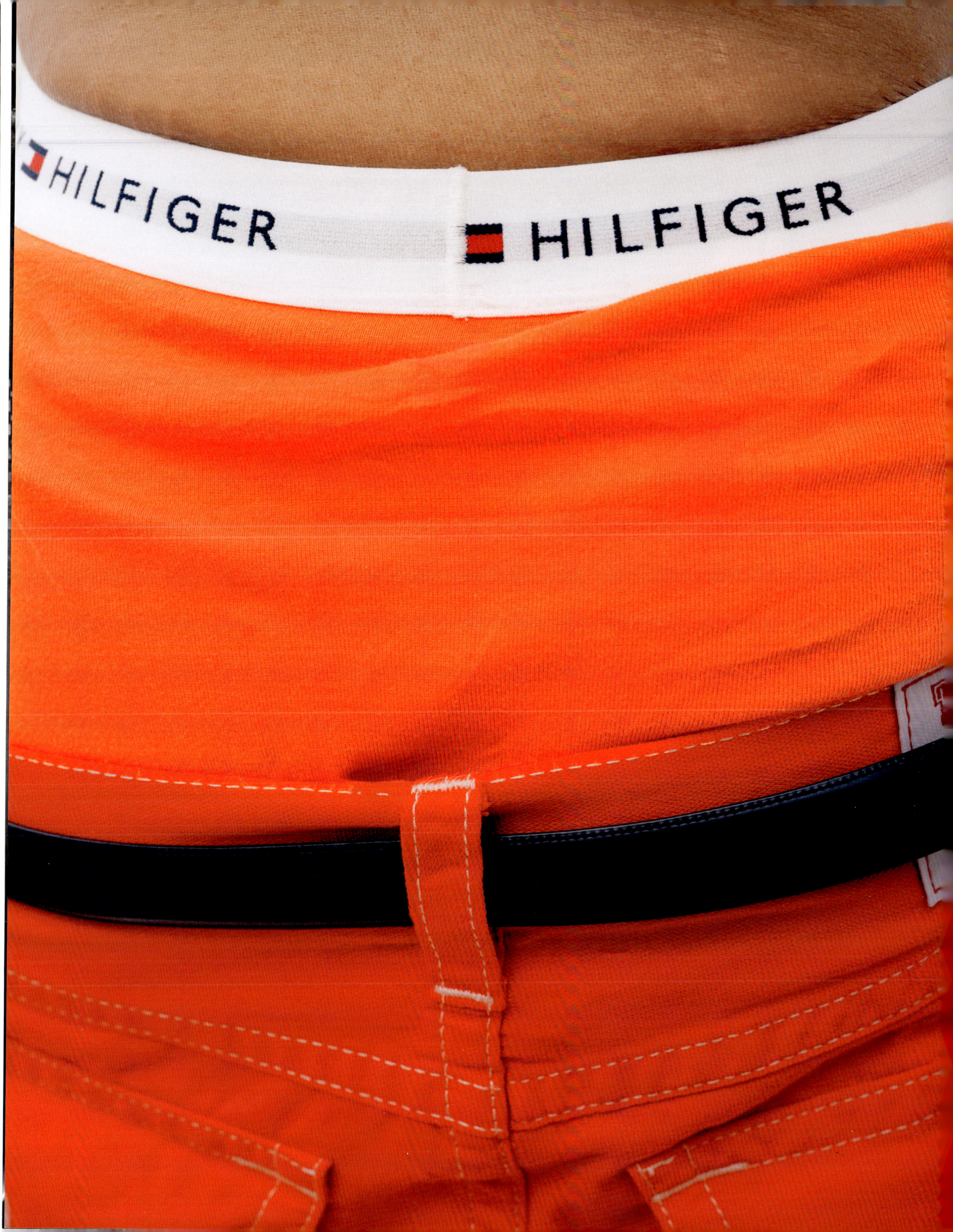

HILFIGER
HILFIGER

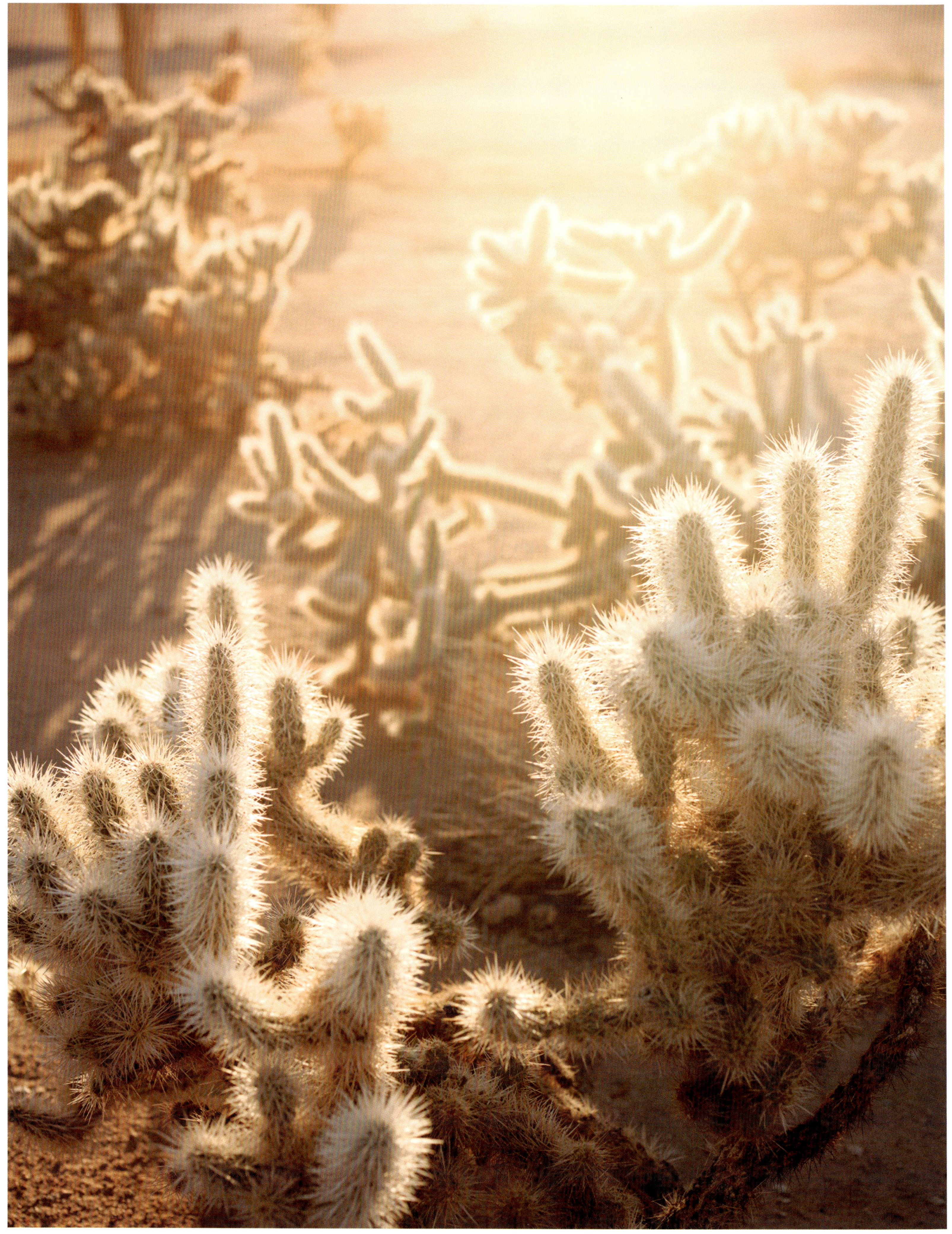

Previous spread:
AD 6705*, 2014, from the series *She Disappeared into Complete Silence*; *Schindler House #2*, 2018, from the series *Schindler House

This spread:
AD 6046*, 2014, from the series *She Disappeared into Complete Silence

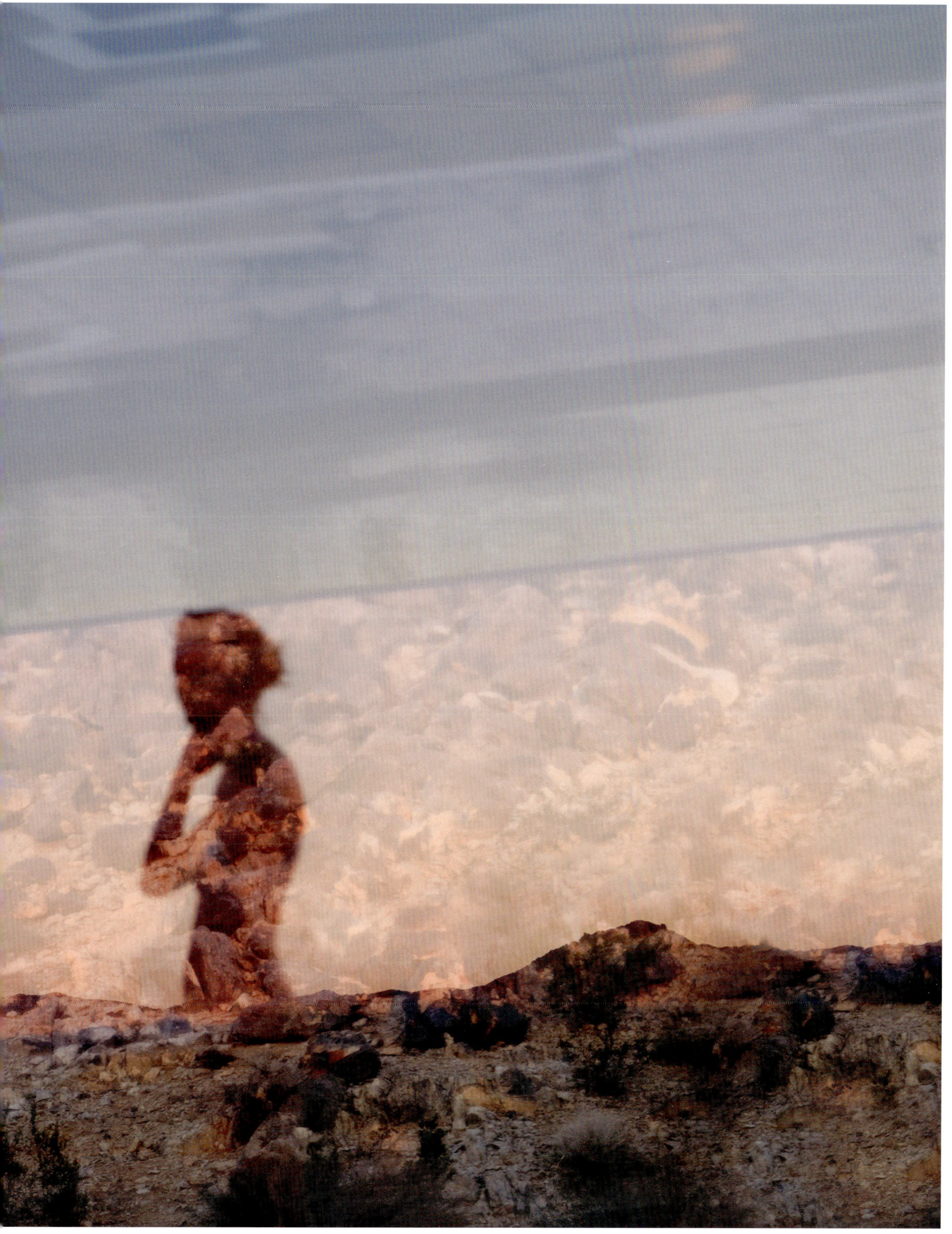

TORBJØRN RØDLAND

Travis Diehl

INTO THE LIGHT

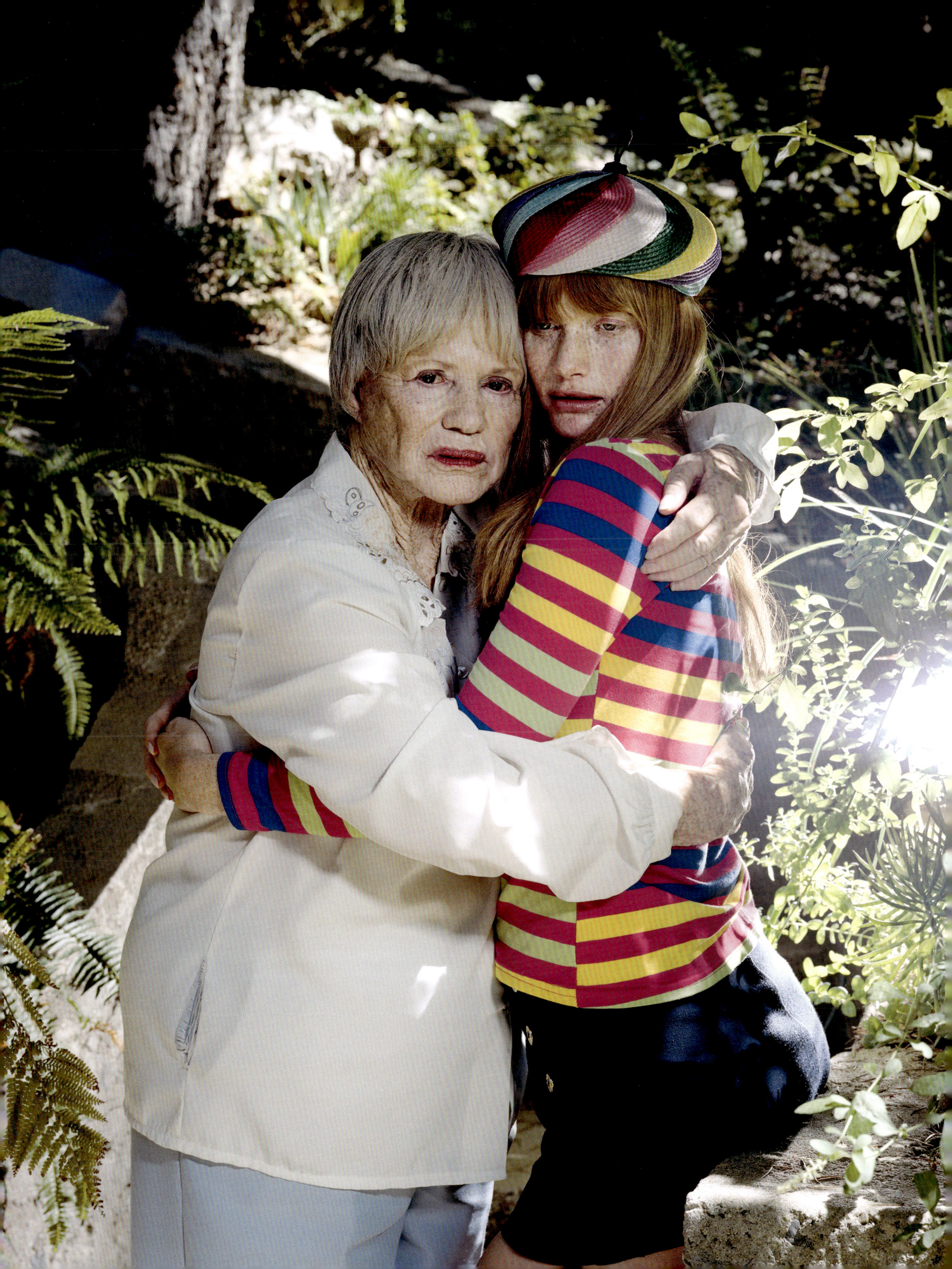

There are the situations we find ourselves in, and then there are the situations Torbjørn Rødland puts us in. The Norwegian, Los Angeles–based photographer describes his process as being "like casting and directing a movie. Different actors will give you a different reaction to the same piece of direction," he says, "and you do need them to give form and physicality to something vague and abstract." But in these photographs "the difference is—there's no script, no plot, no story." Here, in the pliable romanticism of LA's magic hour, under a blustering, set-flat version of Scandinavia's thin sun, his images captivate the beautiful people.

Rødland's recent work might be summed up as variations on "two things touching"—a young, red-haired woman and an old, gray-haired one hug among some ferns; two youthful men, on either side of a chain-link fence, hold hands, as if each is the other's reflection—prompting direct comparisons between model and model, and between model and prop. There is a separation of the image's content and its maker's comments on the medium, evinced in Rødland's work as much by the cold tension of his subjects as by the blown-out flashes and visible edges of backdrops. This is where Rødland departs from his influences, such as Stan Douglas's homages to cinema and expositions of its artifice, or Cindy Sherman's self-referential register. With Rødland's pictures, there is no neat choice between these two paths. There is an aberrant quality sometimes described as lecherous, perverted, or perverse. It would be too easy to say that Rødland's scenes of a little blond boy in a pet cage, for instance, or of a man's head squashed by a sneakered foot—or any of his many images of people forced into intimacy, both pinioned and connected at the same time—constitute a moral test.

In another recent photograph, *Sophie* (2017), an ambiguous model poses belly down on a hardwood floor in front of what appears to be an art-shipping crate. It's not the tripe-like top or gaudy floral skirt that's off here, but the stilettos—which are much too small and perched on the heels of the model's feet. The picture engages in some old-fashioned gender-bending, in a mode as dry as the dust on the gallery floor. Rødland's human subjects exude a deadness, a bagginess, even a clownishness that deflate any implied eroticism. "An object is like a person unconscious," he says. "If I cannot help partly objectifying people I photograph, then I also cannot help looking for life and interiority in objects." Indeed, in one backlit, exterior shot, two young men pose with a motorcycle; one with his hand on the other's shoulder, and the other with a hand on the handlebars. It's difficult to say if the models sigh over the bike, or if the bike wears the models. Whatever is uncannily joined in this setup follows from Rødland's craftsman-like insistence that all his effects be produced in camera. If his pictures are perfectly imperfect, it's because we are too.

Travis Diehl is a writer based in Los Angeles.

Previous page:
In the Garden, 2016–18

Opposite:
The Song of the Wind and the Trees, 2016–18

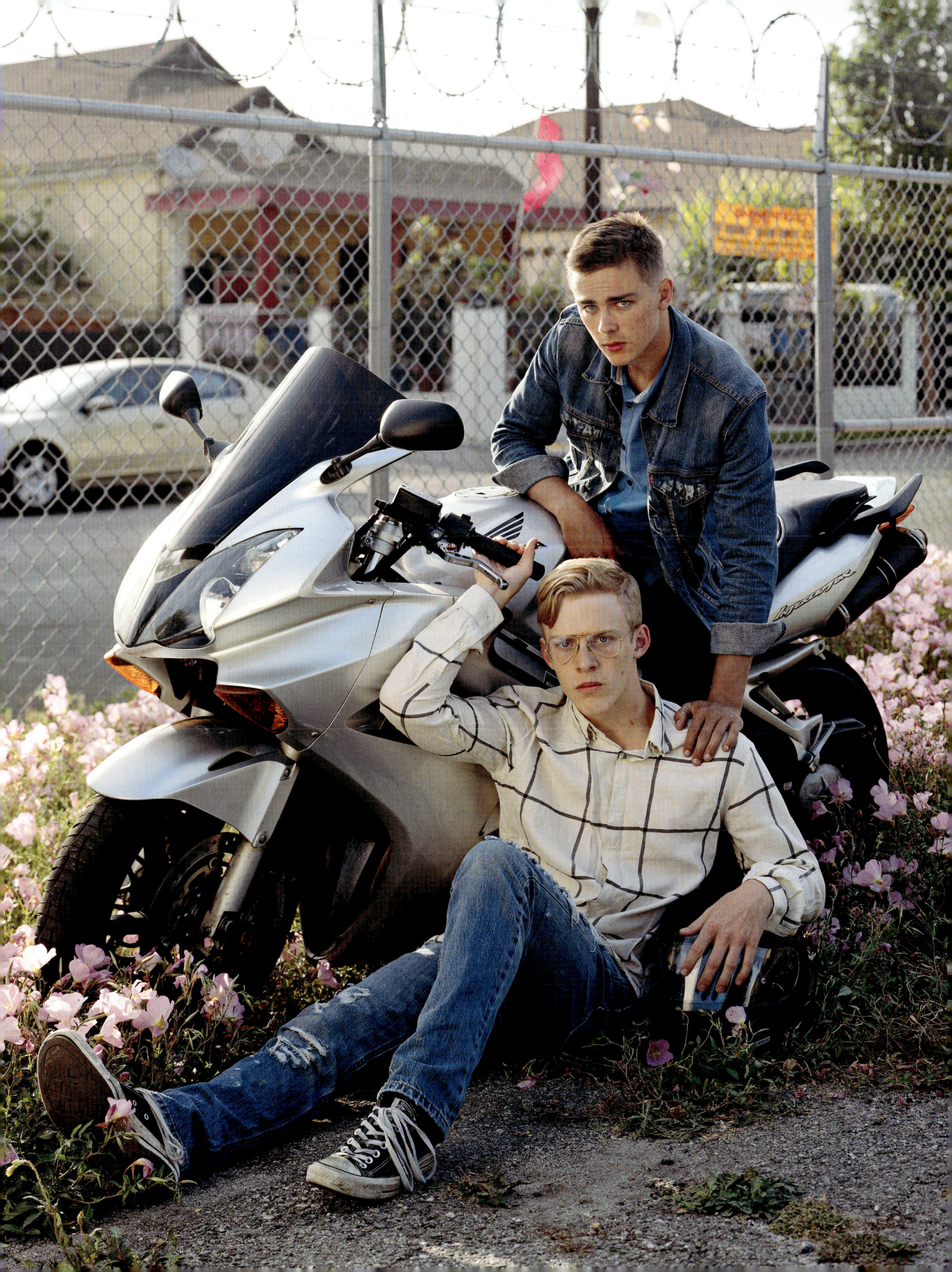

Sophie, 2017

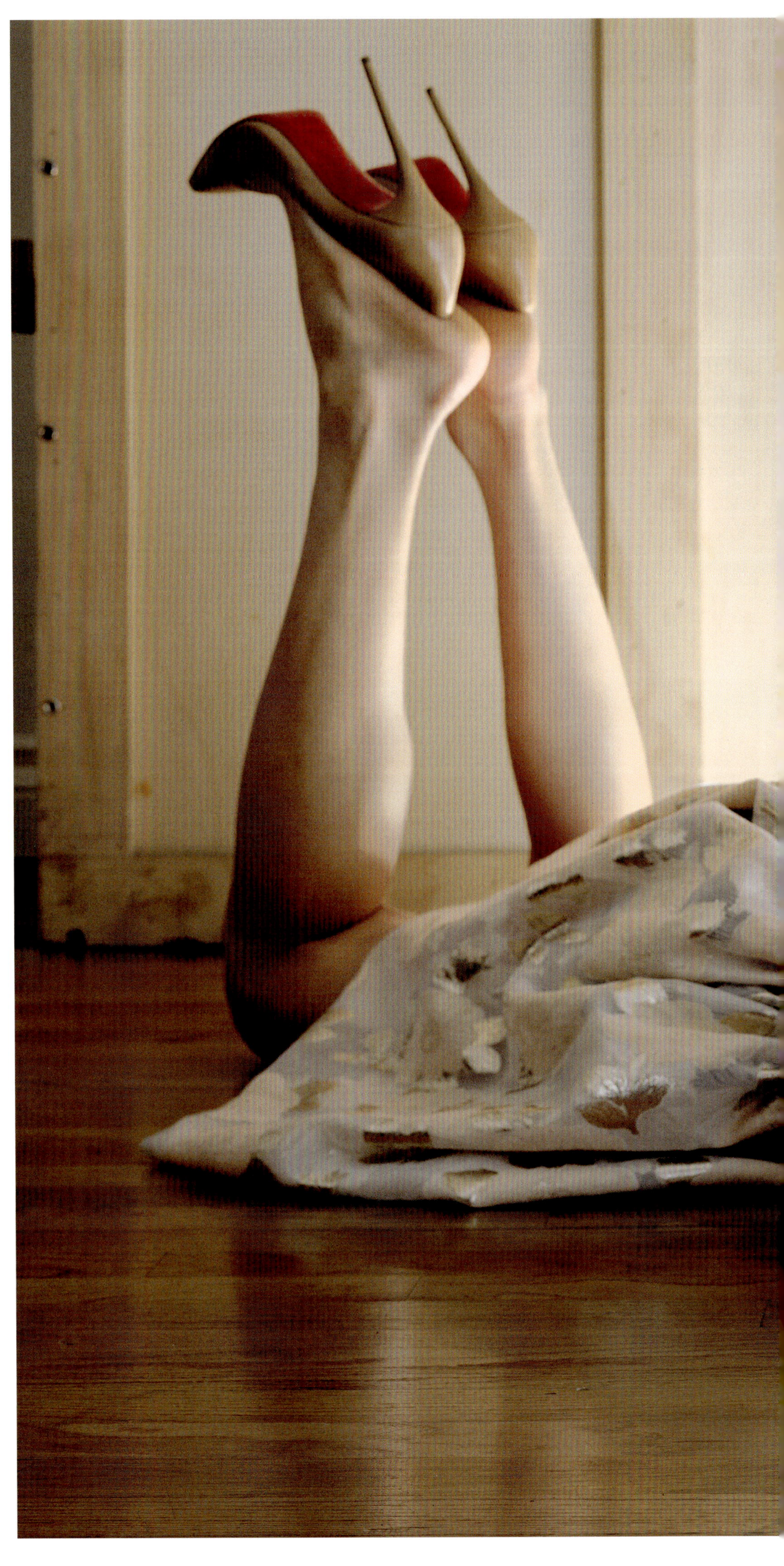

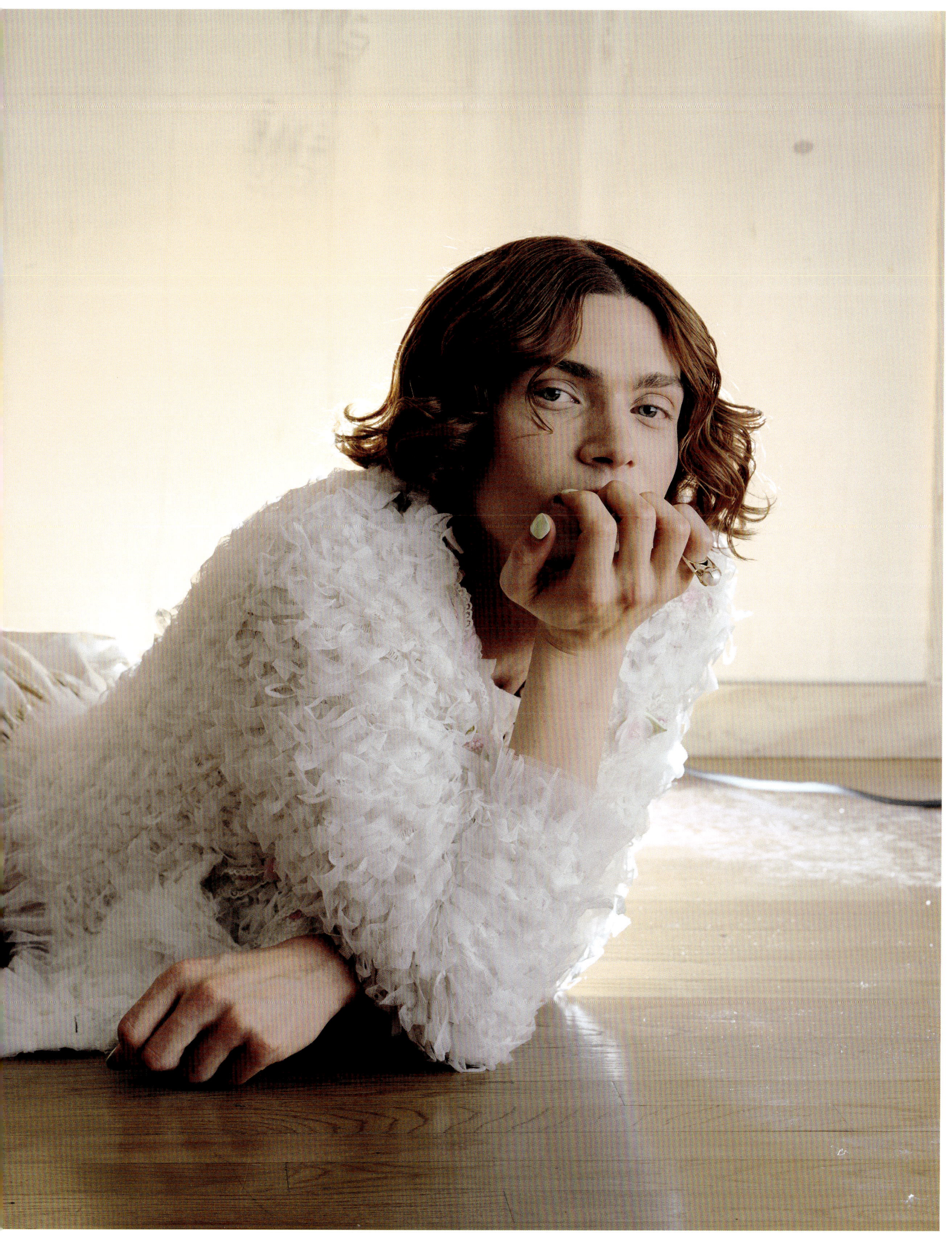

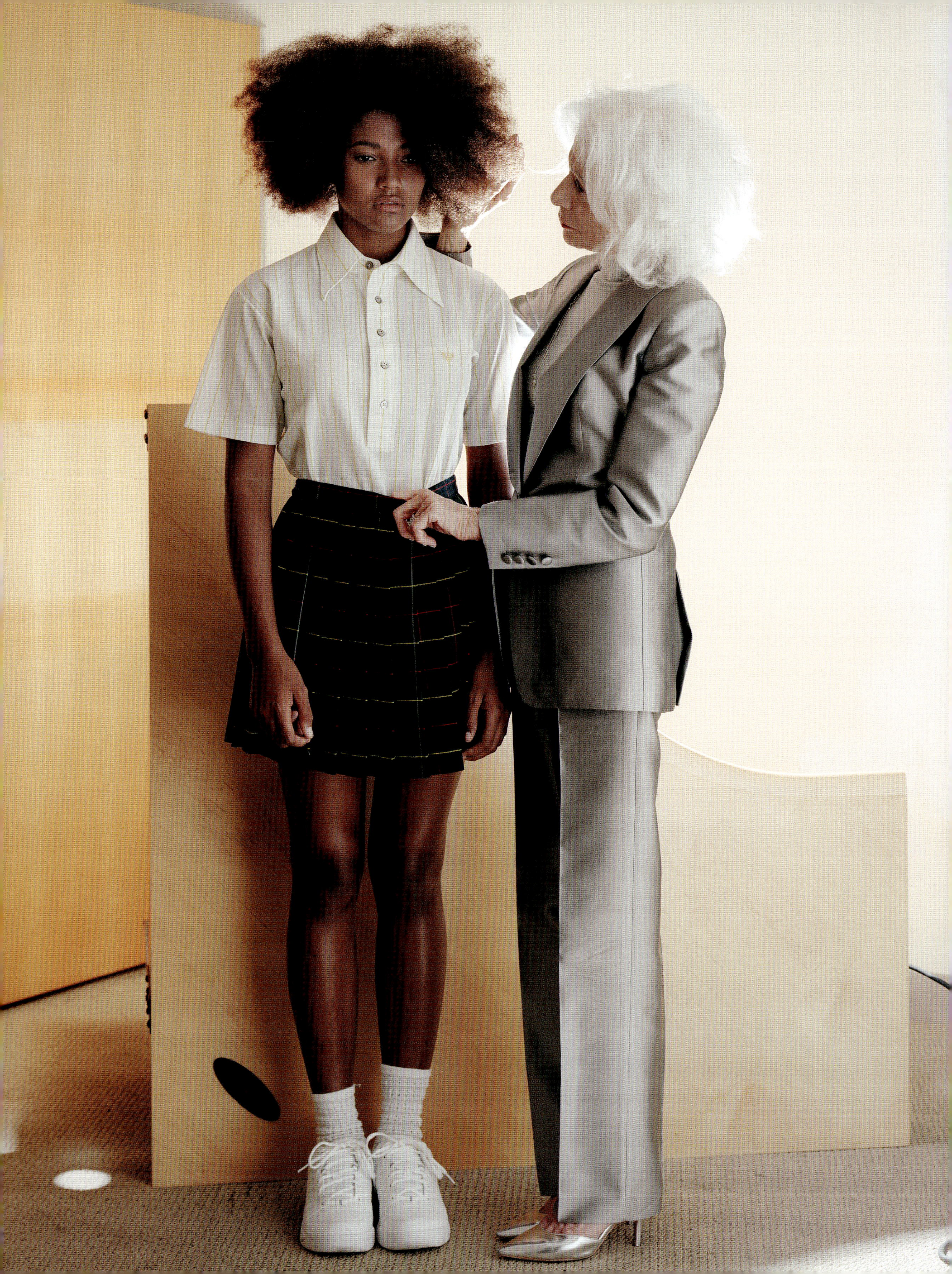

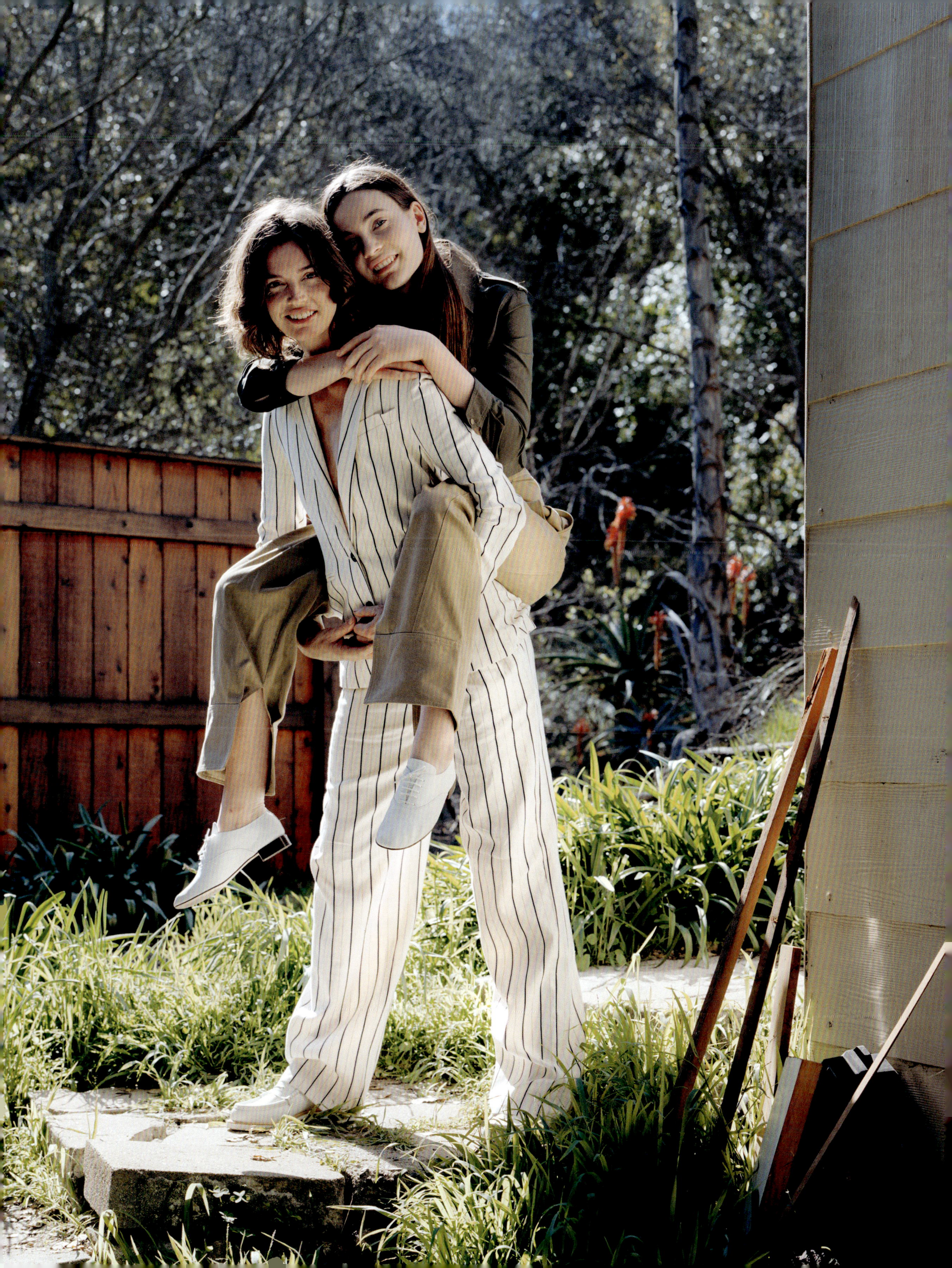

Page 146:
***Correction*, 2017**

Previous page:
***Piggyback*, 2017**

This page:
***Pitcher Down*, 2017**

Opposite:
***Greeting*, 2015**
All photographs courtesy the artist; Air de Paris; David Kordansky Gallery, Los Angeles; Nils Stærk, Copenhagen; STANDARD (OSLO); and Galerie Eva Presenhuber, Zurich

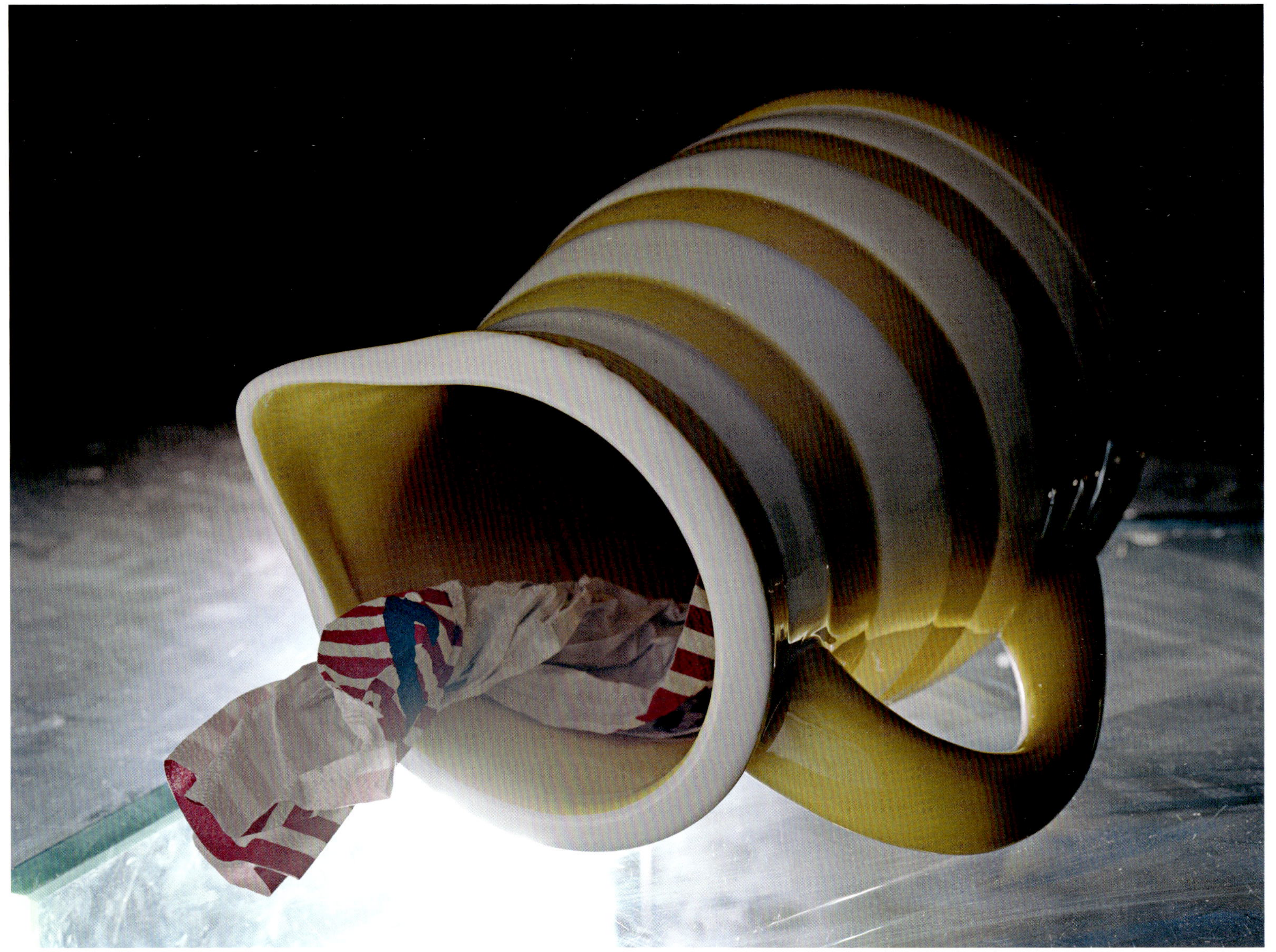

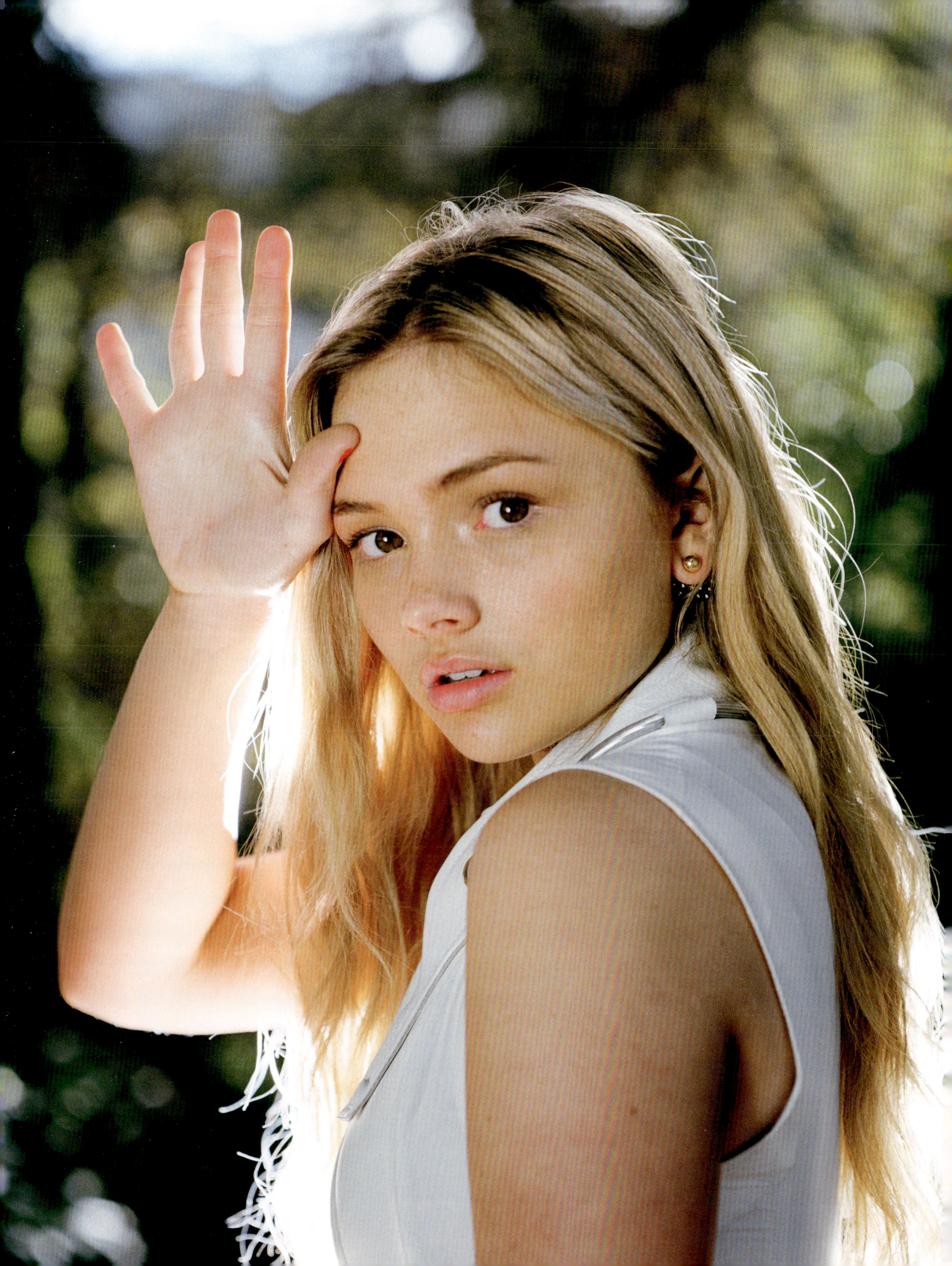

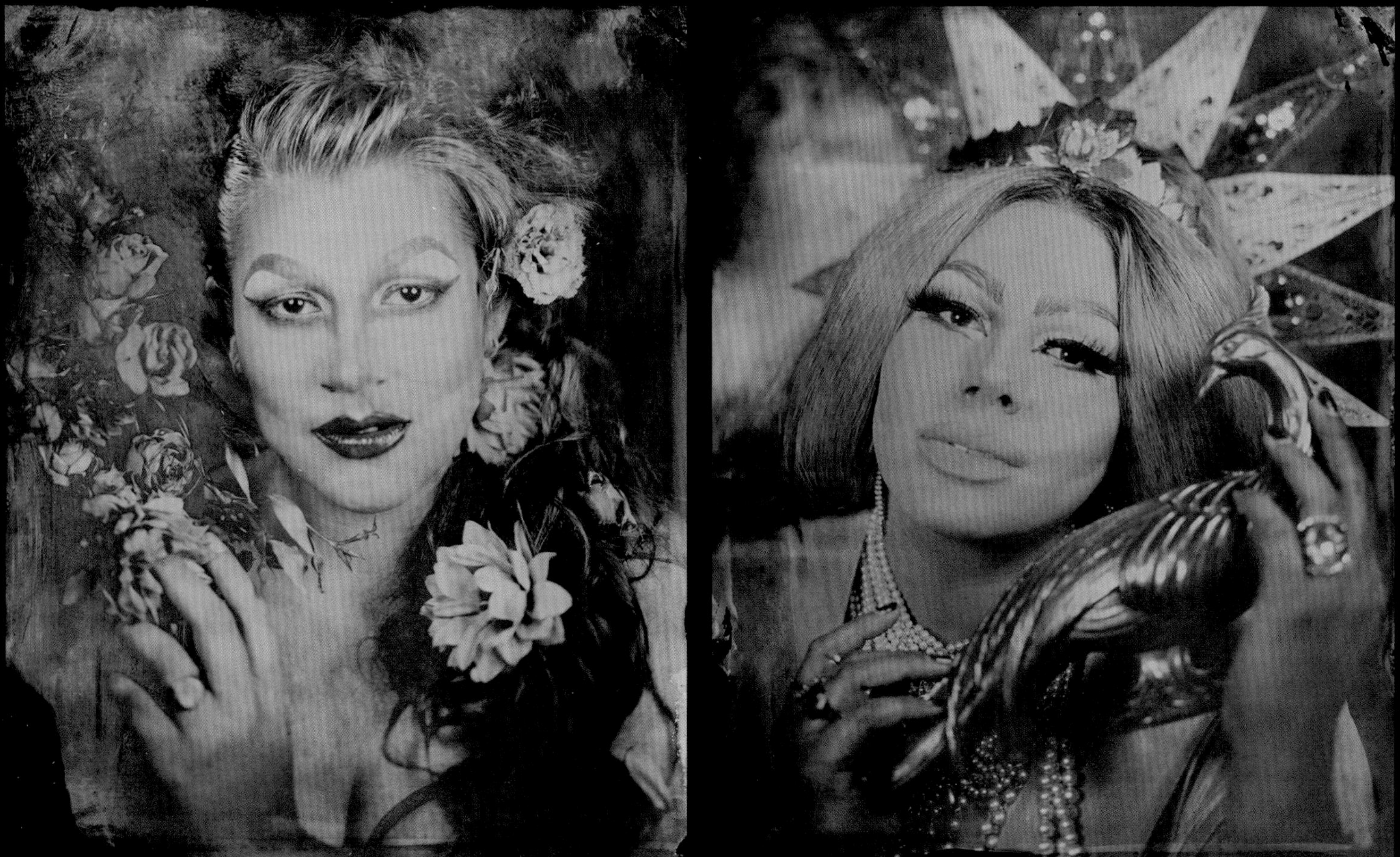

Object Lessons

Ed Ruscha's Production Notebooks, 1973–90

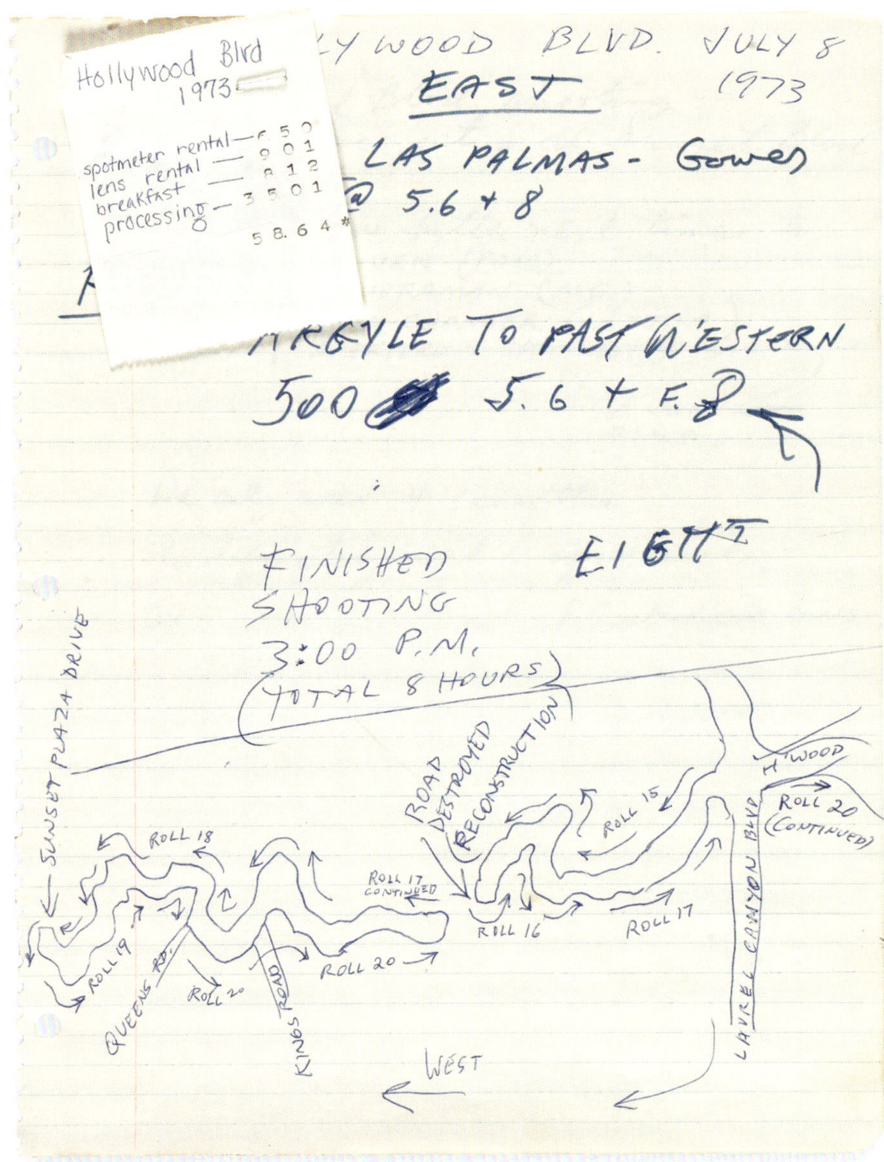

In 1956, when he was eighteen years old, Ed Ruscha moved from Oklahoma City to Los Angeles to attend art school. Along the way, he kept a notebook, writing down every stop for gas and how much he spent on meals. That signature balance of banality and precision—and an enduring fascination with American vernacular style—would find legendary outlets in Ruscha's early artist's books *Twentysix Gasoline Stations* (1963) and *Some Los Angeles Apartments* (1965). But the making of *Every Building on the Sunset Strip* (1966), a fifty-four-page, twenty-five-foot-long, accordion-folded book that documents more than two miles of Sunset Boulevard in two continuous views, was an enterprise unto itself.

"It's one of the most extraordinary records of an artist engaging with an urban form," says Andrew Perchuk, acting director of the Getty Research Institute, which holds Ruscha's Streets of Los Angeles Archives. Among the Getty's collection of more than one million images, contact sheets, and objects, including the original maquette for *Sunset Strip*, is a set of notebooks in which Ruscha methodically detailed every aspect of producing his panoramas of LA's major streets and boulevards—a project that continues to this day.

To make the images, Ruscha and his team would get up early in the morning, mount a motorized camera on a tripod to the back of a pickup truck, and begin driving. Ruscha noted the f-stop and the type of film used. He drew intricate maps of city blocks. He sketched pictures of clapper boards showing the exact time and address where a reel started. And he even listed the cost of breakfast. "Keeping notes complete with timing (dates, hours, et cetera) was a way to pinch myself and stay awake for some project I chose to address," Ruscha says. "It was always excessive but kept me in line."

Ruscha once described LA as "the ultimate card-board cut out town. It's full of illusions and allows its people to indulge in all these illusions." Even so, Ruscha's project on LA's streets, which precedes Google Street View by four decades, has become an indelible record of a changing city. —**The Editors**